Josh Brown

CHENG & TSUI
"Bringing Asia to the World"™

中文聽說讀寫

INTEGRATED CHINESE

Traditional Characters

1

Textbook

4th Edition

Yuehua Liu and Tao-chung Yao
Nyan-Ping Bi, Liangyan Ge, Yaohua Shi

Original Edition by Tao-chung Yao and Yuehua Liu
Liangyan Ge, Yea-fen Chen, Nyan-Ping Bi, Xiaojun Wang, Yaohua Shi

CHENG & TSUI

"Bringing Asia to the World"™

Fourth Edition 2017
Third Edition 2009
Second Edition 2005
First Edition 1997

20 19 18 17 16 1 2 3 4 5

ISBN 978-1-62291-132-5
[Fourth Edition, Traditional Characters, Hardcover]

ISBN 978-1-62291-134-9
[Fourth Edition, Traditional Characters, Paperback]

Library of Congress Cataloging-in-Publication Data [Third Edition]

Integrated Chinese = [Zhong wen ting shuo du xie]. Traditional character edition. Level 1, part 1/ Yuehua Liu . . . [et. al]. – 3rd. ed.

p. cm.

Chinese and English.

Includes indexes.

Parallel title in Chinese characters.

ISBN 978-0-88727-645-3 – ISBN 978-0-88727-639-2 (pbk.) – ISBN 978-0-88727-644-6 – ISBN 978-0-88727-638-5 (pbk.) 1. Chinese language–Textbooks for foreign speakers–English. I. Liu, Yuehua. II. Title: Zhong wen ting shuo du xie.

PL1129.E5I683 2008

495.1–dc22

Printed in Canada

The *Integrated Chinese* series includes textbooks, workbooks, character workbooks, teacher's resources, streaming audio, video, and more. Visit chengtsui.co for more information on the other components of *Integrated Chinese*.

Publisher
JILL CHENG

Editorial Manager
BEN SHRAGGE

Editors
LEI WANG with LIJIE QIN, MIKE YONG, RANDY TELFER, and SHUWEN ZHANG

Creative Director
CHRISTIAN SABOGAL

Illustrator/Designer
KATE PAPADAKI

Photographs
© Adobe Stock
© Cheng & Tsui

Cheng & Tsui Company, Inc.
Phone (617) 988-2400 / (800) 554-1963
Fax (617) 426-3669
25 West Street
Boston, MA 02111-1213 USA
chengtsui.co

This Fourth Edition of *Integrated Chinese* is dedicated to the memory of our dearest colleague and friend Professor Tao-chung (Ted) Yao.

Publisher's Note

When *Integrated Chinese* was first published in 1997, it set a new standard with its focus on the development and integration of the four language skills (listening, speaking, reading, and writing). Today, to further enrich the learning experience of the many users of *Integrated Chinese* worldwide, Cheng & Tsui is pleased to offer this revised and updated Fourth Edition of *Integrated Chinese*. We would like to thank the many teachers and students who, by offering their valuable insights and suggestions, have helped *Integrated Chinese* evolve and keep pace with the many positive changes in the field of Chinese language instruction. *Integrated Chinese* continues to offer comprehensive language instruction, with many new features, including a new and innovative web application, as detailed in the Preface.

The Cheng & Tsui Chinese Language Series is designed to publish and widely distribute quality language learning materials created by leading instructors from around the world. We welcome readers' comments and suggestions concerning the publications in this series. Please contact the following members of our Editorial Board, in care of our Editorial Department (e-mail: editor@cheng-tsui.com).

Contents

Preface

The *Integrated Chinese* (IC) series is an internationally acclaimed Mandarin Chinese language course that delivers a cohesive system of print and digital resources for highly effective teaching and learning. First published in 1997, it is now the leading series of Chinese language learning resources in the United States and beyond. Through its holistic focus on the language skills of listening, speaking, reading, and writing, IC teaches novice and intermediate students the skills they need to function in Chinese.

What's New

It has been eight years since the publication of the Third Edition of IC. We are deeply grateful for all the positive feedback, as well as constructive suggestions for improvement, from IC users. In the meantime, China and the world have seen significant transformations in electronic communications, commerce, and media. Additionally, the technology available to us is transforming the way teachers and students interact with content. The teaching of Chinese as a second language needs to keep pace with these exciting developments. Therefore, the time seems right to update IC across delivery formats.

In developing this latest edition of IC, we have consulted the American Council on the Teaching of Foreign Languages (ACTFL) *21st Century Skills Map for World Languages*. The national standards for foreign language learning in the 21st century focus on goals in five areas—communication, cultures, connections, comparisons, and communities. In addition to classifying the applicable **Language Practice** activities by communication mode (interpersonal, interpretive, and presentational), we have added a host of materials that address the 5 Cs. The delivery of IC via the new ChengTsui Web App elevates the teaching and learning experience by presenting multimedia and interactive content in a truly blended and integrated way.

New, visually rich supplementary modules that recur in each lesson have been introduced. These can be taught in any sequence to serve as prompts for classroom discussion and student reflection:

- **Get Real with Chinese** draws on realia to situate language learning in real-life contexts. Students are required to analyze, predict, and synthesize before coming to conclusions about embedded linguistic and cultural meaning. Photos and questions connect the classroom to authentic Chinese experiences.
- **Chinese Chat** provides opportunities for language practice in the digital environment. Realistic texting, microblogging, and social media scenarios show students how the younger generation has adapted Chinese to new communication technologies.
- **Characterize It!** encourages students to approach Chinese characters analytically. The exercises in the first five lessons introduce a major pattern to teach character structure; then a major radical to teach characters' meanings. The remaining lessons introduce two major radicals each to allow students to continue to expand their knowledge strategically. Additional activities are provided on the ChengTsui Web App.
- While not a new segment, **How About You?** has been revamped for the Fourth Edition. This module encourages students to personalize their study of vocabulary and learn words and phrases that relate to their own interests and background. Questions now appear in both Chinese and English, while visual cues, which typically correspond to possible answers, promote vocabulary expansion and retention. Vocabulary items corresponding to the visual cues are listed in a separate index.

Moreover, to promote students' awareness of cultural diversity in a world of rapid globalization, we have included **Compare & Contrast** activities in the **Cultural Literacy** (formerly Culture Highlights) section. This section as a whole has been given a lavishly illustrated, magazine-style treatment to better engage students. Users who subscribe to the ChengTsui Web App will have access to additional cultural content related to the lesson themes.

We have also updated the **Grammar** section to include exercises tailored to each grammar point, so students can immediately put into practice the language forms they have just learned. Additional practice exercises for each grammar point are accessible via the ChengTsui Web App.

The **Basics** (formerly Introduction) section has been completely redesigned to emphasize its foundational importance in the book. More information on its pedagogical function can be found on page 1. **Keeping It Casual** (formerly That's How the Chinese Say It!) remains a review of functional expressions after Lessons 5 and 10 that encourages students to build their own personalized list of useful expressions.

Finally, the new **Lesson Wrap-Up** section includes context-based tasks that prepare students to communicate with native Chinese speakers. Also in this section are **Make It Flow!** exercises, which help students develop and apply strategies to organize information coherently and cohesively in written and spoken discourse. We created this activity to address the common phenomenon of novice and intermediate students speaking in choppy, isolated sentences. The ultimate purpose of acquiring a language is communication, and a hallmark of effective communication is the ability to produce continuous discourse. The **Lesson Wrap-Up** activities are intended as assessment instruments for the **Can-Do Checklist**, which encourages students to measure their progress at the end of the lesson.

As previous users of IC will note, we have renamed the four-volume series. The new sequencing of Volumes 1 to 4 better reflects the flexibility of the materials and the diversity of our user groups and their instructional environments.

As with the Third Edition, the Fourth Edition of IC features both traditional and simplified character versions of the Volume 1 and 2 textbooks and workbooks, and a combination of traditional and simplified characters in the Volume 3 and 4 textbooks and workbooks. However, in response to user feedback, we have updated the traditional characters to ensure they match the standard set currently used in Taiwan. For reference, we have consulted the Taiwan Ministry of Education's *Revised Chinese Dictionary*.

The most significant change to the Fourth Edition is the incorporation of innovative educational technology. Users of the print edition have access to streaming audio (at chengtsui.co), while subscribers to the ChengTsui Web App have access to streaming audio plus additional, interactive content.

Users who choose to subscribe to the *Basic Edition* of the ChengTsui Web App will have access to:

- Audio (Textbook and Workbook)
- Video of the lesson texts
- Vocabulary flashcards
- Additional grammar exercises
- Additional character practice
- Additional cultural content

Users who choose to subscribe to the *Essential Edition* of the ChengTsui Web App will, in addition to the above, have access to the Workbook with auto-grading and the Character Workbook as a download.

In addition to the student editions, the ChengTsui Web App is available in an *Educator Edition*. The *Educator Edition* web-application overlay suggests teaching tips and strategies and conveniently makes connections between the Textbook and the additional resources provided in the Teacher's Resources, such as video activity sheets, quizzes, and answer keys.

A key feature of the ChengTsui Web App is coherence. The innovative instructional design provides an integrated user experience. Learners can move seamlessly between the transmission, practice, application, and evaluation stages, navigating the content to suit their particular learning needs and styles. For more information and a free trial, please visit chengtsui.co.

Both in its print and digital versions, the new IC features a contemporary layout that adds clarity and rigor to our instructional design. Rich new visuals complement the text's revised, user-friendly language and up-to-date cultural content. We hope that students and teachers find the many changes and new features timely and meaningful.

Organizational Principles

In the higher education setting, the IC series of four volumes often covers two years of instruction, with smooth transitions from one level to the next. The lessons first cover topics from everyday life, then gradually move to more abstract subject matter. The materials do not follow one pedagogical methodology, but instead blend several effective teaching approaches. Used in conjunction with the ChengTsui Web App, incorporating differentiated instruction, blended learning, and the flipped classroom is even easier. Here are some of the features of IC that distinguish it from other Chinese language resources:

Integrating Pedagogy and Authenticity

We believe that students should be taught authentic materials even in their first year of language instruction. Therefore, most of our pedagogical materials are simulated authentic materials. Authentic materials (produced by native Chinese speakers for native Chinese speakers) are also included in every lesson.

Integrating Traditional and Simplified Characters

We believe that students should learn both traditional and simplified Chinese characters. However, we also realize that teaching students both forms from day one could be overwhelming. Our solution is for students to focus on one form during their first year of study, and to acquire the other during their second. Therefore, the first two volumes of IC are available in separate traditional and simplified versions, with the alternative character forms of the texts included in the Appendix.

By their second year of study, we believe that all students should be exposed to both forms of written Chinese. Accordingly, the final two volumes of IC include both traditional and simplified characters. Students in second-year Chinese language classes come from different backgrounds, and should be allowed to write in their preferred form. However, it is important that the learner write in one form only, and not a hybrid of both.

Integrating Teaching Approaches

Because no single teaching method can adequately train a student in all language skills, we employ a variety of approaches in IC. In addition to the communicative approach, we also use traditional methods such as grammar-translation and the direct method.

Users of the ChengTsui Web App can employ additional teaching approaches, such as differentiated learning and blended learning. Students can self-pace their learning, which is a very powerful instructional intervention. The product also facilitates breaking down direct instruction into more engaging "bites" of learning, which improves student engagement. Moreover, the ChengTsui Web App allows students to interact with the content at home and practice and apply their learning in the classroom with corrective teacher feedback, which has the potential to improve student outcomes. Additionally, teachers and learners do not need to follow the instructional flow of the underlying book. They can navigate using multiple pathways in flexible and customized ways and at varying paces for true individualized learning.

Acknowledgments

We would like to thank users around the world for believing in IC. We owe much of the continued success of IC to their invaluable feedback. Likewise, we would be remiss if we did not acknowledge the University of Notre Dame for sponsoring and inviting us to a one-day workshop on IC on April 9, 2016. Leading Chinese language specialists from across the country shared their experiences with the IC authors. We are especially indebted to Professor Yongping Zhu, Chair of the Department of East Asian Languages and Cultures at Notre Dame, and his colleagues and staff for organizing the workshop.

Professors Fangpei Cai and Meng Li of the University of Chicago took time out from their busy teaching schedules to compile a detailed list of comments and suggestions. We are profoundly touched by their generosity. In completing this Fourth Edition, we have taken into consideration their and other users' recommendations for revision. Indeed, many of the changes are in response to user feedback. The authors are naturally responsible for any remaining shortcomings and oversights.

For two summers in a row, Professor Liangyan Ge's wife, Ms. Yongqing Pan, warmly invited the IC team to their home to complete the bulk of the work of revising the IC series. Words are inadequate to express our thanks to Ms. Pan for her warm hospitality and her superb cooking day in and day out.

We are deeply grateful to our publisher Cheng & Tsui Company and to Jill Cheng in particular for her unswerving support for IC over the years. We would also like to express our heartfelt appreciation to our editor Ben Shragge and his colleagues for their meticulous attention to every aspect of this new edition.

As we look back on the evolution of IC, one person is never far from our thoughts. Without Professor Tao-chung Yao's commitment from its inception, IC would not have been possible. Sadly, Professor Yao passed away in September 2015. Throughout that summer, Professor Yao remained in close contact with the rest of the team, going over each draft of IC 1 with an eagle eye, providing us with the benefit of his wisdom by phone and email. This Fourth Edition of IC is a living tribute to his vision and guidance.

Note: Prefaces to the previous editions of IC are available at chengtsui.co.

Series Structure

The IC series has been carefully conceptualized and developed to facilitate flexible delivery options that meet the needs of different instructional environments.

Component per Volume	Description	Print/Other Formats	ChengTsui Web App
Textbook	• Ten engaging lessons per volume, each with readings, grammar explanations, communicative exercises, and culture notes	• Paperback or Hardcover • Simplified or Traditional Characters (Volumes 1 and 2) • Simplified with Traditional Characters (Volumes 3 and 4)	• *Basic*, *Essential*, and *Educator Editions*
Workbook	• Wide range of integrated activities covering the three modes of communication (interpersonal, interpretive, and presentational)	• Paperback • Simplified or Traditional Characters (Volumes 1 and 2) • Simplified with Traditional Characters (Volumes 3 and 4)	• *Essential* and *Educator Editions*
Character Workbook	• Radical- and character-writing and stroke order practice	• Paperback • Simplified with Traditional Characters	• *Essential* and *Educator Editions*
Audio	• Audio for Textbook vocabulary, lesson texts, and pronunciation exercises, plus pronunciation and listening exercises from the Workbook • Normal and paused versions	• Streaming audio available to print users at chengtsui.co	• *Basic*, *Essential*, and *Educator Editions*
Video	• Volumes 1 and 2: acted dialogues and narratives presented in the Textbooks; also includes theme-related Culture Minutes sections in authentic settings • Volumes 3 and 4: documentary-style episodes correlating to the lesson themes in authentic settings	• One DVD per volume	• *Basic*, *Essential*, and *Educator Editions* • Streaming video
Teacher's Resources	• Comprehensive implementation support, teaching tips, syllabi, tests and quizzes, answer keys, and supplementary resources	• Downloadable resources that include core lesson guides along with ancillary materials previously on the companion website	• *Educator Edition*

Lesson Structure

All components of IC (Textbooks, Workbooks, and Teacher's Resources) are considered core and are designed to be used together to enhance teaching and learning. Recurrent lesson subsections are highlighted in the Textbook Elements column. Note that Supplementary Modules do not compose a separate section, but are rather discrete entities that appear throughout each lesson.

Section	Textbook Elements	Interactive Content	Workbooks	Teacher's Resources
Lesson Opener	• Learning Objectives state what students will be able to do by the end of the lesson • Relate & Get Ready helps students reflect on similarities and differences between Chinese culture and their own		• Opportunity for students to revisit learning objectives and self-assess	• Overview of language functions, vocabulary, grammar, pronunciation, and characters taught in the lesson • Sequencing recommendations and teaching aids
Lesson Text	• Two Chinese lesson texts demonstrate practical vocabulary and grammar usage • *Pinyin* versions of the lesson texts provide pronunciation support • Language Notes elaborate on important structures and phrases in the lesson texts	• Audio builds receptive skills • Video provides insight into non-verbal cues and communication plus context through authentic settings	• Listening comprehension and speaking exercises based on the lesson texts • Reading comprehension	• Strategies for teaching the lesson texts, plus question prompts • Pre- and post-video viewing activity worksheets and scripts
Vocabulary	• Vocabulary lists define and categorize new words from the lesson texts (proper nouns are listed last)	• Audio models proper pronunciation • Flashcards assist with vocabulary acquisition	• Handwriting and stroke order practice is provided in the Character Workbook • All exercises use lesson vocabulary to support acquisition	• Explanations, pronunciation tips, usage notes, and phrasal combinations • Vocabulary slideshows
Grammar	• Grammar points, which correspond to numbered references in the lesson texts, explain and model language forms • Exercises allow students to practice the grammar points immediately	• Additional exercises deepen knowledge of the language	• Writing and grammar exercises based on grammar introduced in the lesson	• Explanations, pattern practice, and additional grammar notes • Grammar slideshows
Language Practice	• Role-plays, pair activities, contextualized drills, and colorful cues prompt students to produce language • Pronunciation exercises in the first three lessons	• Audio accompanies pronunciation exercises in the first three lessons	• Exercises and activities spanning the three modes of communication (interpersonal, interpretive, and presentational), plus *pinyin* and tone practice, to build communication and performance skills	• Student presentations, integrative practice, and additional practice activities • Additional activities categorized by macro-skill

Section	Textbook Elements	Interactive Content	Workbooks	Teacher's Resources
Cultural Literacy	• Culture notes provide snapshots of contemporary and traditional Chinese-speaking cultures • Compare & Contrast draws connections between cultures	• Additional content further develops cultural literacy of the lesson theme	• Authentic materials to develop predictive skills	• Background notes expand on the section and offer additional realia
Lesson Wrap-Up	• Make It Flow! develops students' ability to produce smooth discourse • Projects encourage review and recycling of lesson materials through different text types • Can-Do Checklist allows students to assess their fulfillment of the learning objectives			• Teaching tips for implementing self-diagnostic activities, answer keys for Make it Flow!, and additional sample quizzes and tests • Slideshows that summarize content introduced in the lesson
Supplementary Modules	• How About You? encourages students to personalize their vocabulary • Get Real with Chinese teaches students to predict meaning from context • Characterize It! explores the structure of Chinese characters • Chinese Chat demonstrates how language is used in text messaging and social media	• Additional Characterize It! exercises and slideshows increase understanding of characters	• Pattern exercises to build radical and character recognition	• Teaching tips and strategies for fully exploiting and implementing these new elements

Scope and Sequence

Lesson	Learning Objectives	Grammar	Cultural Literacy
Basics	• Learn about Chinese and its dialects • Become familiar with syllabic structure, *pinyin*, and pronunciation • Gain an understanding of the writing system and basic grammatical features • Use common expressions in the classroom and daily life		
1 Greetings	• Exchange basic greetings • Ask for a person's family name and full name and provide your own • Determine whether someone is a teacher or a student • Ask where someone's from	1. The verb 姓 (*xìng*) 2. Questions ending with 呢 (*ne*) 3. The verb 叫 (*jiào*) 4. Subject + verb + object 5. The verb 是 (*shì*) (to be) 6. Questions ending with 嗎 (*ma*) 7. The negative adverb 不 (*bù*) (not, no) 8. The adverb 也 (*yě*) (too, also)	• Family names • Full names
2 Family	• Use basic kinship terms for family members • Describe a family photo • Ask about someone's profession • Name some common professions	1. The particle 的 (*de*) (I) 2. Measure words (I) 3. Question pronouns 4. Indicating possession using 有 (*yǒu*) 5. Indicating existence using 有 (*yǒu*) 6. Using 二 (*èr*) and 兩 (*liǎng*) 7. The adverb 都 (*dōu*) (both, all)	• Kinship terms • Family structure
3 Time and Date	• Discuss times and dates • Talk about ages and birthdays • Arrange a dinner date with someone	1. Numbers up to 100 2. Dates 3. Time 4. Pronouns as modifiers and the particle 的 (*de*) (II) 5. The sentence structure of 我請你吃飯 (*wǒ qǐng nǐ chī fàn*) 6. Alternative questions 7. Affirmative + negative (A-not-A) questions (I) 8. The adverb 還 (*hái*) (also, too, as well)	• Calendars • Age • Birthday traditions
4 Hobbies	• Name common hobbies • Ask about someone's hobbies • Make plans for the weekend with friends	1. Word order 2. Affirmative + negative (A-not-A) questions (II) 3. The conjunction 那（麼）(*nà [me]*) (then, in that case) 4. 去 (*qù*) (to go) + action 5. Questions with 好嗎 (*hǎo ma*) (OK?) 6. The modal verb 想 (*xiǎng*) (want to, would like to) 7. Verb + object as a detachable compound	• Mahjong • Chinese chess • Go • Feasting

Lesson	Learning Objectives	Grammar	Cultural Literacy
5 Visiting Friends	• Welcome a visitor • Introduce one person to another • Be a gracious guest • Ask for beverages as a guest • Offer beverages to a visitor • Briefly describe a visit to a friend's place	1. Moderating tone of voice: 一下 *(yí xià)* and (一) 點兒 *(|yì| diǎnr)* 2. Adjectives as predicates using 很 *(hěn)* 3. The preposition 在 *(zài)* (at, in, on) 4. The particle 吧 *(ba)* 5. The particle 了 *(le)* (I) 6. The adverb 才 *(cái)* (not until)	• Tea • Greetings • Etiquette
Keeping It Casual (L1–L5)	• Review functional expressions	1. 算了 *(suàn le)* (forget it, never mind) 2. 誰呀 *(shéi ya)* (who is it?) 3. 是嗎 *(shì ma)* (really, is that so?)	
6 Making Appointments	• Answer a phone call and initiate a phone conversation • Set up an appointment with a teacher on the phone • Ask a favor • Ask someone to return your call	1. The preposition 給 *(gěi)* (to, for) 2. The modal verb 要 *(yào)* (will, be going to) (I) 3. The adverb 別 *(bié)* (don't) 4. Time expressions 5. The modal verb 得 *(děi)* (must, have to) 6. Directional complements (I)	• Phone etiquette • Cell phones • Terms for Mandarin
7 Studying Chinese	• Discuss your exam performance • Comment on your character writing • Discuss your experience learning Chinese • Talk about your study habits • Describe typical classroom situations	1. Descriptive complements (I) 2. The adverbs 太 *(tài)* (too), 真 *(zhēn)* (really), and 很 *(hěn)* (very) 3. The adverb 就 *(jiù)* (I) 4. Double objects 5. Ordinal numbers 6. 有 (一) 點兒 *(yǒu|yì|diǎnr)* (somewhat, rather, a little bit) 7. Question pronoun: 怎麼 *(zěnme)* (how, how come) 8. The 的 *(de)* structure (I) 9. Connecting sentences in continuous discourse	• Simplified vs. traditional characters • Writing conventions • Four treasures of the study
8 School Life	• Describe a student's daily routine • Write a simple diary entry or blog post • Write a brief letter or formal email applying appropriate conventions • Update a friend on recent activities • Express hope that a friend will accept your invitation	1. The position of time-when expressions 2. The adverb 就 *(jiù)* (II) 3. Describing simultaneity using 一邊…一邊… *(yìbiān . . . yìbiān . . .)* 4. Series of verbs/verb phrases 5. The particle 了 *(le)* (II) 6. The particle 的 *(de)* (III) 7. The 正在 v structure *(zhèngzài)* (be doing. . .) 8. Indicating inclusiveness: 除了…以外，還/也… *(chúle . . . yǐwài, hái/yě . . .)* (in addition to, also) 9. Comparing 能 *(néng)* and 會 *(huì)* (I) 10. The conjunctions 要是 *(yàoshi)* and 因為 *(yīnwèi)* and the adverb 就 *(jiù)* (III)	• Semesters • Letter-writing conventions

Lesson	Learning Objectives	Grammar	Cultural Literacy
9 Shopping	• Describe the color, size, and price of a purchase • Recognize Chinese currency • Pay in cash or with a credit card • Determine the proper change you should receive • Ask for merchandise in a different size or color • Exchange merchandise	1. The modal verb 要 *(yào)* (want to do) (II) 2. Measure words (II) 3. The 的 *(de)* structure (II) 4. Using 多 *(duō)* interrogatively 5. Denominations of currency 6. Comparing using 跟/和…（不）一樣 *(gēn/hé . . . [bù] yíyàng)* ([not] the same as . . .) 7. The conjunctions 雖然…，可是/但是… *(suīrán . . . , kěshì/dànshì . . .)* (although . . . yet . . .)	• Traditional clothes • Prices • Forms of address
10 Transportation	• Discuss different means of transportation • Explain how to transfer from one subway or bus line to another • Navigate public transit • Express gratitude after receiving a favor • Offer New Year wishes	1. Topic-comment sentences 2. Indicating alternatives: 或者 *(huòzhě)* (or) and 還是 *(háishi)* (or) 3. Indicating sequence: 先…再… *(xiān . . . zài)* (first . . . , then . . .) 4. Pondering alternatives: 還是…（吧） *(háishi . . . [ba])* (had better) 5. Indicating totality: 每…都… *(měi . . . dōu)* (every) 6. Indicating imminence: 要…了 *(yào . . . le)* (soon)	• High-speed rail • Taxi drivers • New Year traffic
Keeping It Casual (L6–L10)	• Review functional expressions	1. 喂 *(wéi)* (hello [on the phone]) 2. 沒問題 *(méi wèntí)* (no problem) 3. Expressions of gratitude 4. 哪裡，哪裡 *(nǎli, nǎli)* (I'm flattered) or 是嗎？*(shì ma)* (is that so?) 5. 就是它吧 *(jiù shì tā ba)* (let's go with that) or 就是他/她了 *(jiù shì tā le)* (we'll go with him/her) 6. 祝 *(zhù)* (I wish . . .)	

Abbreviations of Grammatical Terms

adj	adjective	**pr**	pronoun
adv	adverb	**prefix**	prefix
conj	conjunction	**prep**	preposition
interj	interjection	**qp**	question particle
m	measure word	**qpr**	question pronoun
mv	modal verb	**t**	time word
n	noun	**v**	verb
nu	numeral	**vc**	verb plus complement
p	particle	**vo**	verb plus object
pn	proper noun		

Legend of Digital Icons

The icons listed below refer to interactive content. Streaming audio is available at chengtsui.co to readers who have purchased the print edition. All other digital content is available exclusively to ChengTsui Web App subscribers.

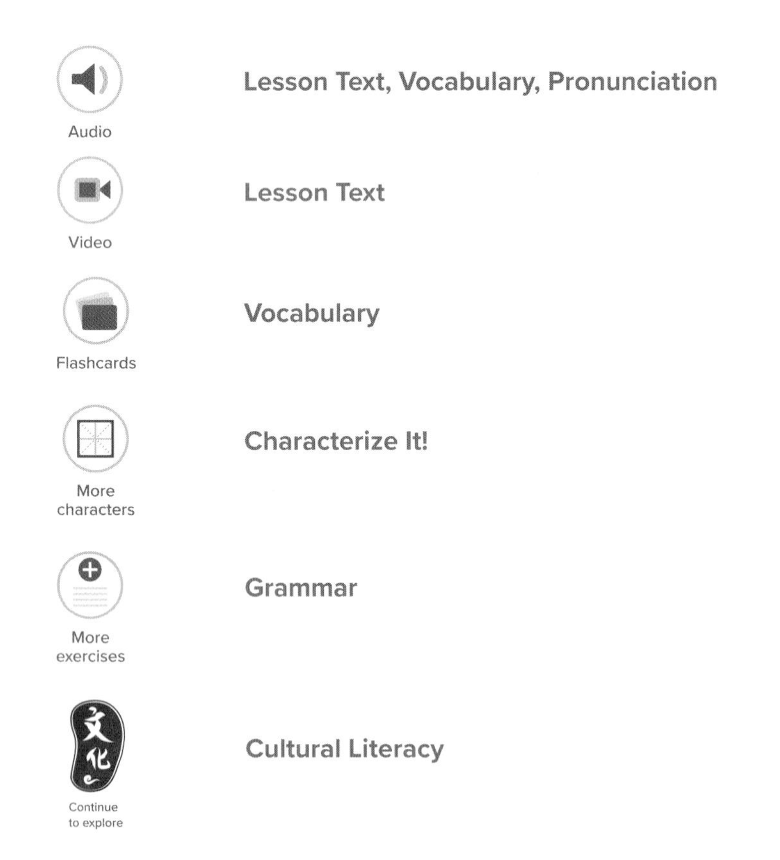

Cast of Characters

Wang Peng
王朋

A Chinese freshman from Beijing. He has quickly adapted to American college life and likes to play and watch sports.

Li You
李友

Amy Lee, an American student from New York State. She and Wang Peng meet each other on the first day of class and soon become good friends.

Gao Wenzhong
高文中

Winston Gore, an English student. His parents work in the United States. Winston enjoys singing, dancing, and Chinese cooking. He has a secret crush on Bai Ying'ai.

Gao Xiaoyin
高小音

Jenny Gore, Winston's older sister. She has already graduated from college, and is now a school librarian.

Bai Ying'ai
白英愛

Baek Yeung Ae, an outgoing Korean student from Seoul. She finds Wang Peng very "cool" and very "cute."

Chang Laoshi
常老師

Chang Xiaoliang, originally from China and in her forties. She has been teaching Chinese in the United States for ten years.

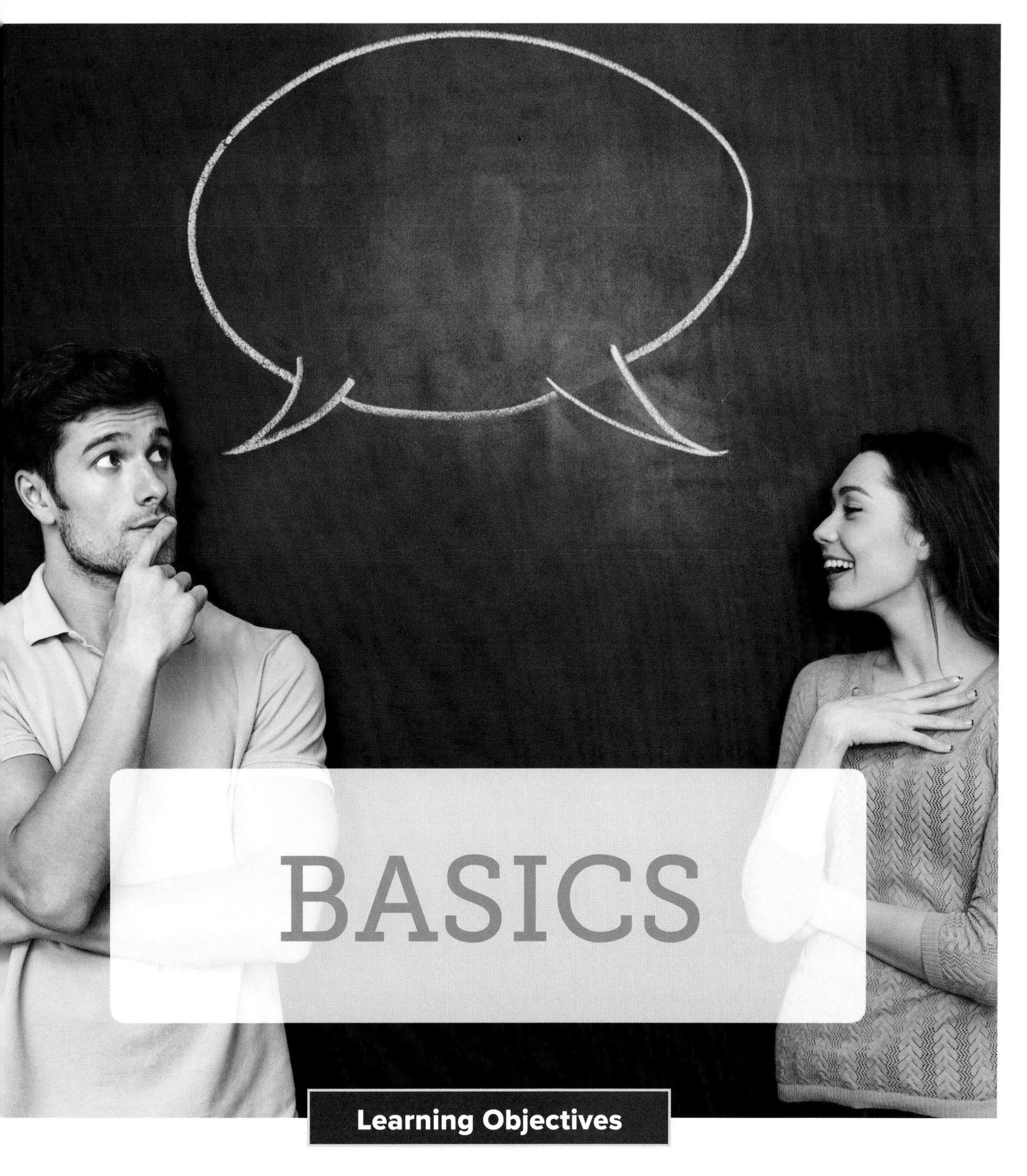

BASICS

Learning Objectives

This section gives students the fundamentals they need to begin studying Chinese. Background is provided on the language's syllabic structure, *pinyin*, and pronunciation; writing system; and important grammatical features. Practice exercises, along with accompanying audio recordings (indicated by 🔈), are provided to help students learn proper pronunciation. Lists of useful expressions are also included. Classes may devote three or four sessions to this core material before starting Lesson 1.

Mandarin and Dialects

China is roughly the same size as the United States. There are numerous regional dialects of Chinese. These dialects, most of which are mutually unintelligible, are often divided into eight groups: Mandarin, Wu, Hakka, Southern Min, Northern Min, Cantonese, Xiang, and Gan.

Conventional terms for Modern Standard Chinese include *Putonghua* ("common language") in Mainland China; *Guoyu* ("national language") in Taiwan; and *Huayu* ("language spoken by ethnic Chinese people") in other Chinese-speaking communities, such as those in Singapore and Malaysia. It is the *lingua franca* of intra-ethnic (among different Chinese dialect speakers) as well as inter-ethnic (among Han Chinese and non-Han minority groups) communication in China. Its grammar is codified from the modern Chinese literary canon, while its pronunciation is based on the Beijing dialect. Modern Standard Chinese is usually referred to as Mandarin in English.

China officially recognizes fifty-six ethnic groups. The Han, the largest group, accounts for over 90% of China's population. Many of the other fifty-five ethnic groups speak their own distinct languages.

Syllabic Structure, Pinyin, and Pronunciation

A Modern Standard Chinese syllable typically has three parts: an initial consonant, a final consisting of a vowel or a vowel and the ending consonant *-n* or *-ng*, and a tone. The tone is superimposed on the entire syllable. A syllable may also have no initial consonant.

syllable = (initial) + final/tone

syllable
(initial) *nà* tone / final

In this book, Chinese sounds are represented by *Hanyu Pinyin,* or *pinyin* for short. The *pinyin* system uses twenty-five of the twenty-six letters of the English alphabet. Although *pinyin* symbols are thus the same as English letters, the actual sounds they represent can vary widely from their English counterparts. This section is designed to raise your awareness of these distinctions. Over time, you will acquire a more nuanced understanding of Chinese pronunciation and improve your skills through listening and practice.

A Simple Finals

Audio

There are six simple finals in *pinyin*: *a, o, e, i, u, ü*

a is a central vowel when pronounced by itself. Keep your tongue in a relaxed position to pronounce it. *a* sounds similar to the "a" in "fa la la."

o is a rounded semi-high back vowel. Round your lips when pronouncing it. *o* seldom appears as a syllable by itself. Usually it compounds with the initials *b, p, m,* and *f,* and should be practiced with them. Because of the bilabial or labiodental nature of *b, p, m,* and *f, o* sounds almost like a diphthong or the double vowel *uo.* It glides from a brief *u* to *o.*

e is an unrounded semi-high back vowel. To pronounce it, first position your tongue as if you are about to pronounce *o*, then unround your mouth. At the same time, spread your lips apart as if you were smiling. This vowel is different from "e" in English, which is pronounced with the tongue raised slightly forward.

i is an unrounded high front vowel. To pronounce it, smile tightly and pull the corners of your mouth straight back. It is similar to the long vowel in "sheep." When pronouncing it, however, you raise your tongue higher.

u is a rounded high back vowel. Pucker up your lips when pronouncing it. *u* is similar to the long vowel in "coop," but, when pronouncing it, you raise your tongue higher and retract it more.

ü is a rounded high front vowel. To produce this vowel, first position your tongue as if you are about to pronounce *i*, then round your lips.

In the *pinyin* system, *i* represents two special vowels in addition to the high front vowel. One is a front apical vowel, the other a back apical vowel—that is to say, they are articulated with the front and back part of the tongue, respectively. Both of these vowels are homorganic with the very limited sets of initials with which they can co-occur (see *z*, *c*, *s* and *zh*, *ch*, *sh*, *r*). In other words, they are pronounced in the same area of the vocal tract as those consonants. You will learn how to pronounce *i* simply by prolonging the sounds of these two groups of consonants.

Initials

There are twenty-one initial consonants in *pinyin*. They are grouped as follows:

Audio

1. *b p m f*	4. *j q x*
2. *d t n l*	5. *z c s*
3. *g k h*	6. *zh ch sh r*

B.1 *b, p, m, f*

b is different from its English counterpart. It is not voiced, as the vocal cords do not vibrate upon its pronunciation, and sounds more like the "p" in "speak."

p is aspirated. In other words, there is a strong puff of breath when this consonant is pronounced. It is also voiceless, and sounds like the "p" in "pork."

m is produced in the same manner as the English "m." It is voiced.

Pronounce *f* as you would in English.

Only the simple finals *a*, *o*, *i*, and *u* and compound finals that start with *a*, *o*, *i*, or *u* can be combined with *b*, *p*, and *m*; only the simple finals *a*, *o*, and *u* and compound finals that start with *a*, *o*, or *u* can be combined with *f*. When these initials are combined with *o*, there is actually a short *u* sound in between. For instance, the syllable *bo* actually includes a very short *u* sound between *b* and *o*: it is pronounced *b(u)o*.

Practice your pronunciation with the audio exercises below:

Audio

B.1.a	(Initial-Final Combinations)		
ba	*bi*	*bu*	*bo*
pa	*pi*	*pu*	*po*
ma	*mi*	*mu*	*mo*
fa	*fu*	*fo*	

B.1.b	*b* vs. *p*		
ba	*pa*	*bu*	*pu*
po	*bo*	*pi*	*bi*

B.1.c	*m* vs. *f*		
ma	*fa*	*mu*	*fu*

B.1.d	*b, p, m, f*		
bo	*po*	*mo*	*fo*
fu	*mu*	*pu*	*bu*

B.2 *d, t, n, l*

When pronouncing *d*, *t*, and *n*, touch your upper gum with the tip of your tongue. The tongue is raised more to the back than it would be to pronounce their English counterparts. *d* and *t* are voiceless. Roughly, *d* sounds like the "t" in "stand," and *t* sounds like the "t" in "tea." When pronouncing *l*, touch your palate with the tip of your tongue. *n* is nasal.

Only the simple finals *a*, *i*, *e*, and *u* and compound finals that start with *a*, *i*, *e*, or *u* can be combined with *d*, *t*, *n*, and *l*; *n* and *l* can also be combined with *ü* and the compound finals that start with *ü*.

Practice your pronunciation with the audio exercises below:

Audio

B.2.a	(Initial-Final Combinations)			
da	*di*	*du*	*de*	
ta	*ti*	*tu*	*te*	
na	*ni*	*nu*	*ne*	*nü*
la	*li*	*lu*	*le*	*lü*

B.2.b	*d* vs. *t*		
da	*ta*	*di*	*ti*
du	*tu*	*de*	*te*

B.2.c	*l* vs. *n*		
lu	*lü*	*nu*	*nü*
lu	*nu*	*lü*	*nü*

B.2.d	*d, t, n, l*		
le	*ne*	*te*	*de*
du	*tu*	*lu*	*nu*

B.3 *g, k, h*

g is unaspirated and voiceless, whereas *k* is aspirated and voiceless. When pronouncing *g* and *k*, raise the back of your tongue against your soft palate. Roughly, *g* sounds like the "k" in "sky," and *k* sounds like the "k" in "kite."

h is voiceless. When pronouncing *h*, raise the back of your tongue towards your soft palate. Unlike the pronunciation of its English counterpart, the friction is noticeable.

Only the simple finals *a*, *e*, and *u* and the compound finals that start with *a*, *e*, or *u* can be combined with *g*, *k*, and *h*.

Practice your pronunciation with the audio exercises below:

Audio

B.3.a	(Initial-Final Combinations)	
gu	*ge*	*ga*
ku	*ke*	*ka*
hu	*he*	*ha*

B.3.b	*g* vs. *k*		
gu	*ku*	*ge*	*ke*

B.3.c	*g* vs. *h*		
gu	*hu*	*ge*	*he*

B.3.d	*k* vs. *h*		
ke	*he*	*ku*	*hu*

B.3.e	*g, k, h*	
gu	*ku*	*hu*
he	*ke*	*ge*

B.4 *j, q, x*

To make the *j* sound, first raise the flat center of your tongue to the roof of your mouth and position the tip of your tongue against the back of your bottom teeth; then loosen your tongue and let the air squeeze out through the channel you've made. It is unaspirated and the vocal cords do not vibrate. The *pinyin j* is similar to the "j" in "jeep," but it is unvoiced and articulated with the tip of the tongue resting behind the lower incisors. You also need to pull the corners of your mouth straight back to pronounce it.

q is pronounced in the same manner as *j*, but it is aspirated. The *pinyin q* is similar to the "ch" in "cheese," except that it is articulated with the tip of the tongue resting behind the lower incisors. When pronouncing *q*, don't forget to pull the corners of your mouth straight back.

To make the *x* sound, first raise the flat center of your tongue toward (but not touching) the hard palate and then let the air squeeze out. The vocal cords do not vibrate. *x*, like *j* and *q*, is articulated with the tip of the tongue resting behind the lower incisors. To pronounce *x* correctly, you also need to pull the corners of your mouth straight back, as if making a tight smile.

The finals that can be combined with *j*, *q*, and *x* are limited to *i* and *ü* and compound finals that start with *i* or *ü*. When *j*, *q*, and *x* are combined with *ü* or a compound final starting with *ü*, the umlaut is omitted and the *ü* appears as *u*.

Practice your pronunciation with the audio exercises below:

Audio

B.4.a	(Initial-Final Combinations)
ji	*ju*
qi	*qu*
xi	*xu*

B.4.b	*j* vs. *q*		
ji	*qi*	*ju*	*qu*

B.4.c	*q* vs. *x*		
qi	*xi*	*qu*	*xu*

B.4.d	*j* vs. *x*		
ji	*xi*	*ju*	*xu*

B.4.e	*j, q, x*	
ji	*qi*	*xi*
ju	*qu*	*xu*

B.5 *z, c, s*

z is similar to the English "ds" sound, as in "lids."

c is similar to the English "ts" sound, as in "students." It is aspirated.

s is similar to the English "s" sound.

To pronounce these sounds, touch the back of your upper teeth with your tongue.

The simple finals that can be combined with *z*, *c*, and *s* are *a*, *e*, *u*, and the front apical vowel *i* (not the regular palatal high front vowel *i*).

When pronouncing the syllables *zi*, *ci*, and *si*, hold your tongue in the same position; relax it slightly as the articulation moves from the voiceless initial consonant to the voiced vowel.

Practice your pronunciation with the audio exercises below:

Audio

B.5.a	(Initial-Final Combinations)		
za	*zu*	*ze*	*zi*
ca	*cu*	*ce*	*ci*
sa	*su*	*se*	*si*

B.5.b	*s* vs. *z*		
sa	*za*	*su*	*zu*
se	*ze*	*si*	*zi*

B.5.c	*z* vs. *c*		
za	*ca*	*zi*	*ci*
ze	*ce*	*zu*	*cu*

B.5.d	*s* vs. *c*		
sa	*ca*	*si*	*ci*
su	*cu*	*se*	*ce*

B.5.e	*z, c, s*	
sa	*za*	*ca*
su	*zu*	*cu*
se	*ze*	*ce*
si	*zi*	*ci*
za	*cu*	*se*
ci	*sa*	*zu*
su	*zi*	*ce*

B.6 *zh, ch, sh, r*

To make the *zh* sound, first curl up the tip of your tongue against your hard palate, then loosen it and let the air squeeze out through the channel you've made. It is unaspirated and the vocal cords do not vibrate. *zh* sounds rather like the first sound in "jerk," but it is unvoiced.

ch is pronounced like *zh*, but *ch* is aspirated. *ch* sounds rather like the "ch" in "chirp."

To make the *sh* sound, turn the tip of your tongue up toward (but not touching) the hard palate and then let the air squeeze out. The vocal cords do not vibrate. *sh* sounds rather like the "sh" in "shirt" and "Shirley."

r is pronounced in the same manner as *sh*, but it is voiced; therefore, the vocal cords vibrate. Pronounce it simply by prolonging *sh*, making sure your lips are not rounded.

The finals that can be combined with *zh, ch, sh,* and *r* are *a, e, u,* and the back apical vowel *i*, as well as compound finals that start with *a, e,* or *u*. When pronouncing the syllables *zhi, chi, shi,* and *ri*, hold your tongue in the same position; relax it slightly as the articulation moves from the initial consonant to the vowel.

Practice your pronunciation with the audio exercises below:

Audio

B.6.a	(Initial-Final Combinations)		
zha	*zhu*	*zhe*	*zhi*
cha	*chu*	*che*	*chi*
sha	*shu*	*she*	*shi*
ru	*re*	*ri*	

B.6.b	*zh* vs. *sh*		
sha	*zha*	*shu*	*zhu*

B.6.c	*zh* vs. *ch*		
zha	*cha*	*zhu*	*chu*

B.6.d	*ch* vs. *sh*		
chu	*shu*	*sha*	*cha*

B.6.e	*zh, ch, sh*		
shi	*zhi*	*chi*	*shi*
she	*zhe*	*che*	*she*

B.6.f	*sh* vs. *r*		
shu	*ru*	*shi*	*ri*

B.6.g	*r* vs. *l*		
lu	*ru*	*li*	*ri*

B.6.h	*sh, r, l*		
she	*re*	*le*	*re*

B.6.i	*zh, ch, r*		
zhe	*re*	*che*	*re*

B.6.j	*zh, ch, sh, r*		
sha	*cha*	*zha*	
shu	*zhu*	*chu*	*ru*
zhi	*chi*	*shi*	*ri*
che	*zhe*	*she*	*re*

Reference Chart for Initials

Manner of Articulation / Place of Articulation	Stop		Affricative		Fricative	Nasal	Lateral	Approximant
	Unaspirated	Aspirated	Unaspirated	Aspirated				
Bilabial	*b*	*p*				*m*		
Labiodentals					*f*			
Apical-toothback			*z*	*c*	*s*			
Apical-alveolar	*d*	*t*				*n*	*l*	
Apical-postalveolar			*zh*	*ch*	*sh*			*r*
Alveolo-palatal			*j*	*q*	*x*			
Velar	*g*	*k*			*h*			

C

Compound Finals

Consonant finals in *pinyin* are grouped as follows:

Audio

1. *ai ei ao ou*
2. *an en ang eng ong*
3. *ia iao ie iu* ian in iang ing iong*
4. *ua uo uai ui** uan un*** uang ueng*
5. *üe üan ün*
6. *er*

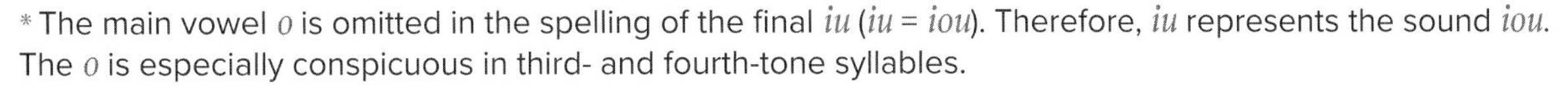

* The main vowel *o* is omitted in the spelling of the final *iu* (*iu* = *iou*). Therefore, *iu* represents the sound *iou*. The *o* is especially conspicuous in third- and fourth-tone syllables.

** The main vowel *e* is omitted in the final *ui* (*ui* = *uei*). Like *iu* above, it is quite conspicuous in third- and fourth- tone syllables.

*** The main vowel *e* is omitted in *un* (*un* = *uen*).

In *pinyin*, compound finals are composed of a main vowel and one or two secondary vowels, or a main vowel and one secondary vowel followed by the nasal ending *-n* or *-ng*. When the initial vowels are *a*, *e*, or *o*, they are stressed. The vowels following are soft and brief. When the initial vowels are *i*, *u*, or *ü*, the main vowels come after them. *i*, *u*, and *ü* are transitional sounds. If there are vowels or nasal consonants after the main vowels, they should be unstressed as well. In a compound final, the main vowel can be affected by the phonemes before and after it. For instance, the *a* in *ian* is pronounced with a lower degree of aperture and a higher position of the tongue than the *a* in *ma*; and to pronounce the *a* in *ang*, the tongue has to be positioned more to the back of the mouth than is usually the case with *a*.

When pronouncing the *e* in *ei*, the tongue must be positioned a bit toward the front and a bit higher than it would be if pronouncing the simple vowel *e* alone. The *e* in *ie* is pronounced with a lower position of the tongue than the *e* in *ei*. When pronouncing the *e* in *en* and the *e* in a neutral tone like the second syllable of *gēge*, you should position your tongue in the center of your mouth, as with the pronunciation of the "e" in "the."

As noted above, in *pinyin* orthography some vowels are omitted for the sake of economy, e.g., *i(o)u*, *u(e)i*. However, when pronouncing such sounds, these vowels must not be omitted.

Pinyin spelling rules are as follows:

1. If there is no initial consonant before *i*, *i* is written as a semi-vowel, *y*. Thus *ia*, *ie*, *iao*, *iu*, *ian*, and *iang* become *ya*, *ye*, *yao*, *you* (note that the *o* cannot be omitted here), *yan*, and *yang*. Before *in* and *ing*, add *y*, e.g., *yin* and *ying*.
2. If there is no initial consonant before *ü*, add a *y* and drop the umlaut: *yu*, *yuan*, *yue*, *yun*.
3. *u* becomes *w* if it is not preceded by an initial, e.g., *wa*, *wai*, *wan*, *wang*, *wei*, *wen*, *weng*, *wo*. *u* by itself becomes *wu*.
4. *ueng* is written as *ong* if preceded by an initial, e.g., *tong*, *dong*, *nong*, *long*. Without an initial, it is *weng*.
5. To avoid confusion, an apostrophe is used to separate two syllables with connecting vowels, e.g., *nǚ'ér* (daughter) and the city *Xī'ān* (*nǚ* and *ér*, *Xī* and *ān* are separate syllables). Sometimes an apostrophe is also needed even if the two syllables are not connected by vowels, e.g., *fáng'ài* (to hinder) and *fāng'àn* (plan, scheme).

Practice your pronunciation with the audio exercises below:

Audio

C.1 *ai ei ao ou*

pai	*lei*	*dao*	*gou*
cai	*mei*	*sao*	*shou*

C.2 *an en ang eng ong*

C.2.a	*an* vs. *ang*		
tan	*tang*	*chan*	*chang*
zan	*zhang*	*gan*	*gang*

C.2.b	*en* vs. *eng*		
sen	*seng*	*shen*	*sheng*
zhen	*zheng*	*fen*	*feng*

C.2.c	*eng* vs. *ong*		
cheng	*chong*	*deng*	*dong*
zheng	*zhong*	*keng*	*kong*

C.3 *ia iao ie iu ian in iang ing iong*

C.3.a	*ia* vs. *ie*		
jia	*jie*	*qia*	*qie*
xia	*xie*	*ya*	*ye*

C.3.b	*ian* vs. *iang*		
xian	*xiang*	*qian*	*qiang*
jian	*jiang*	*yan*	*yang*

C.3.c	*in* vs. *ing*		
bin	*bing*	*pin*	*ping*
jin	*jing*	*yin*	*ying*

C.3.d	*iu* vs. *iong*		
xiu	*xiong*	*you*	*yong*

C.3.e	*ao* vs. *iao*		
zhao	*jiao*	*shao*	*xiao*
chao	*qiao*	*ao*	*yao*

C.3.f	*an* vs. *ian*		
chan	*qian*	*shan*	*xian*
zhan	*jian*	*an*	*yan*

C.3.g	*ang* vs. *iang*		
zhang	*jiang*	*shang*	*xiang*
chang	*qiang*	*ang*	*yang*

C.4 *ua uo uai ui uan un uang*

C.4.a	*ua* vs. *uai*		
shua	*shuai*	*wa*	*wai*

C.4.b	*uan* vs. *uang*		
shuan	*shuang*	*chuan*	*chuang*
zhuan	*zhuang*	*wan*	*wang*

C.4.c	*un* vs. *uan*		
dun	*duan*	*kun*	*kuan*
zhun	*zhuan*	*wen*	*wan*

C.4.d	*uo* vs. *ou*		
duo	*dou*	*zhuo*	*zhou*
suo	*sou*	*wo*	*ou*

C.4.e	*ui* vs. *un*		
tui	*tun*	*zhui*	*zhun*
dui	*dun*	*wei*	*wen*

C.5 *üe üan ün*

C.5.a	*ün* vs. *un*		
jun	*zhun*	*yun*	*wen*

C.5.b	*üan* vs. *uan*		
xuan	*shuan*	*juan*	*zhuan*
quan	*chuan*	*yuan*	*wan*

C.5.c	*üe*	
yue	*que*	*jue*

C.6 *er*

ger (*er* with a first tone does not exist in Mandarin, but the word "*ger*" [*ge* with the *r* ending] contains the final *er* in first tone. See D.1 Practice III for more examples.)

D Tones

Every Chinese syllable has a tone.

D.1 Four Tones and Neutral Tone

There are four tones in Modern Standard Chinese.

The first tone is a high-level tone with a pitch value of 55 (see chart below); its tone mark is " ˉ ".

The second tone is a rising tone with a pitch value of 35; its tone mark is " ˊ ".

The citation form of the third tone has a pitch value of 214. However, in normal speech it almost always occurs as a "half third tone" with a pitch value of 21. Its tone mark is " ˇ ". Please see D.2. Tone Sandhi for a discussion of how to pronounce third-tone syllables in succession.

The fourth tone is a falling tone with a pitch value of 51; its tone mark is " ˋ ".

In addition to the four tones, there is also a neutral tone in Modern Standard Chinese. Neutral tone words include those that do not have fundamental tones (e.g., the question particle *ma*), and those which do have tones when pronounced individually, but are not stressed in certain compounds (e.g., the second *ba* in *bàba*, "father"). There are no tone marks for neutral tone syllables. A neutral tone syllable is pronounced briefly and softly, and its pitch value is determined by the stressed syllable immediately before it. A neutral tone following a first-tone syllable, as in *māma* (mother), carries a pitch tone of 2. When it follows a second-tone syllable, a third-tone syllable, or a fourth-tone syllable, its pitch tone will be 3, 4, and 1 respectively.

Tones are crucial in Chinese. The same initial-final combination with different tones may have different meanings. For instance, *mā* is "mother," *má* is "hemp," *mǎ* is "horse," *mà* is "to scold," and *ma* is an interrogative particle. The four tones can be diagrammed as follows:

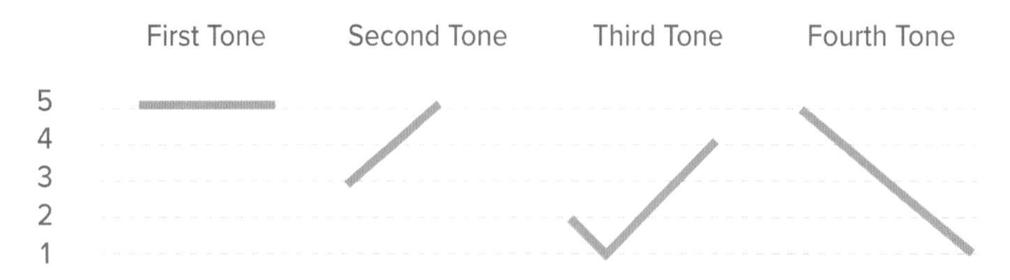

Tone marks are written above the main vowel of a syllable. The main vowel can be identified according to the following sequence: *a-o-e-i-u-ü*. For instance, in *ao* the main vowel is *a*. In *ei* the main vowel is *e*. There is one exception: when *i* and *u* are combined into a syllable, the tone mark is written on the second vowel: *iù*, *uì*.

D.1 Practice I: Monosyllabic Words

Audio

1.a	Four Tones		
bī	bí	bǐ	bì
pū	pú	pǔ	pù
dà	dǎ	dá	dā
shè	shě	shé	shē
tí	tī	tǐ	tì
kè	kě	kē	ké
jǐ	jí	jì	jī
gú	gù	gū	gǔ

1.b	1st vs. 2nd		
zā	zá	hē	hé
chū	chú	shī	shí

1.c	1st vs. 3rd		
tū	tǔ	xī	xǐ
mō	mǒ	shā	shǎ

1.d	1st vs. 4th		
fā	fà	qū	qù
dī	dì	kē	kè

1.e	2nd vs. 1st		
hú	hū	zhé	zhē
xí	xī	pó	pō

1.f	2nd vs. 3rd		
gé	gě	jú	jǔ
tí	tǐ	rú	rǔ

1.g	2nd vs. 4th		
lú	lù	cí	cì
mó	mò	zhé	zhè

1.h	3rd vs. 1st		
tǎ	tā	gǔ	gū
mǐ	mī	chě	chē

1.i	3rd vs. 2nd		
chǔ	chú	xǐ	xí
kě	ké	qǔ	qú

1.j	3rd vs. 4th		
bǒ	bò	chǔ	chù
nǐ	nì	rě	rè

1.k	4th vs. 1st		
jì	jī	sù	sū
là	lā	hè	hē

1.l	4th vs. 2nd		
nà	ná	jù	jú
zè	zé	lǜ	lǘ

1.m	4th vs. 3rd		
sà	sǎ	kù	kǔ
zì	zǐ	zhè	zhě

D.1

Practice II: Bisyllabic Words

Audio

	Tones	Examples		
2.a	1st+1st:	*chūzū*	*tūchū*	*chūfā*
2.b	1st+2nd:	*chātú*	*xīqí*	*chūxí*
2.c	1st+3rd:	*shēchǐ*	*gēqǔ*	*chūbǎn*
2.d	1st+4th:	*chūsè*	*hūshì*	*jīlǜ*
2.e	2nd+1st:	*shíshī*	*qíjī*	*shíchā*
2.f	2nd+2nd:	*jíhé*	*shépí*	*pígé*
2.g	2nd+3rd:	*jítǐ*	*bóqǔ*	*zhélǐ*
2.h	2nd+4th:	*qítè*	*fúlì*	*chíxù*
2.i	3rd+1st:	*zǔzhī*	*zhǔjī*	*lǐkē*
2.j	3rd+2nd:	*pǔjí*	*zhǔxí*	*chǔfá*
2.k	3rd+4th:	*lǚkè*	*gǔlì*	*tǐzhì*
2.l	4th+1st:	*zìsī*	*qìchē*	*lǜshī*
2.m	4th+2nd:	*fùzá*	*dìtú*	*shìshí*
2.n	4th+3rd:	*zìjǐ*	*bìhǔ*	*dìzhǐ*
2.o	4th+4th:	*mùdì*	*xùmù*	*dàdì*

D.1

Practice III: Words with "*er*" sound

Audio

3.a	*érzi*	*érqiě*
3.b	*ěrduo*	*mù'ěr*
3.c	*shí'èr*	*èrshí*

D.2

Tone Sandhi

If two third-tone syllables are spoken in succession, the first third tone becomes second tone (a tone change that linguists call tone sandhi), e.g.:

Audio

xǐlǐ	➡	*xílǐ*	(baptism)
chǐrǔ	➡	*chírǔ*	(shame)
qǔshě	➡	*qúshě*	(accept or reject)

Note: Following standard *pinyin* practice, we do not change the tone marks from third to second tone. Initially, the student has to consciously remember to pronounce the first syllable in the second tone; but through practice and imitation, it will soon become habit.

Practice your pronunciation with the audio exercises below:

Audio

chǔlǐ	→	*chúlǐ*	*jǔzhǐ*	→	*júzhǐ*
gǔpǔ	→	*gúpǔ*	*zǐnǚ*	→	*zínǚ*
bǐnǐ	→	*bínǐ*	*zhǐshǐ*	→	*zhíshǐ*

D.3 Neutral Tone

Audio

The neutral tone occurs in unstressed syllables, typically following a syllable with one of the four tones. It is unmarked, e.g.:

chēzi (car), *māma* (mom), *chúzi* (cook), *shūshu* (uncle), *lǐzi* (plum), *shìzi* (persimmon)

Practice your pronunciation with the audio exercises below:

Audio

1st+neutral	*māma*	*gēge*	*shīfu*	*chūqu*
2nd+neutral	*dízi*	*bóbo*	*bízi*	*chúle*
3rd+neutral	*lǐzi*	*qǐzi*	*dǐzi*	*fǔshang*
4th+neutral	*bàba*	*dìdi*	*kèqi*	*kùzi*

E Combination Exercises

Audio

1.

shān	*xiān*	*sān*
cháng	*qiáng*	*cáng*
zhǐ	*jǐ*	*zǐ*
lüè	*nüè*	*yuè*
kè	*lè*	*rè*

2.

Zhōngguó	*xīngqī*	*lìshǐ*	*zhàopiàn*
zàijiàn	*tóngxué*	*xǐhuan*	*diànshì*
yīnyuè	*kělè*	*yǎnlèi*	*shàngwǔ*
cèsuǒ	*chūntiān*	*xiàwǔ*	*bànyè*
gōngkè	*kāishǐ*	*rìjì*	*cāntīng*
zuìjìn	*xīwàng*	*yīsheng*	*chūzū*
zhōumò	*guānxi*	*dòufu*	*jiéhūn*
liúxué	*nǚ'ér*	*shénme*	*suīrán*
wǎngqiú	*xǐzǎo*	*niánjí*	*yóuyǒng*

Writing System

A

Formation of Characters

Unlike English, Chinese is written in characters, each of which represents a syllable. Two sets of Chinese characters are in use: simplified characters and traditional characters. Simplified characters typically have fewer strokes than their traditional counterparts, though many characters are shared between the two sets. Characters have historically been divided into the following six categories:

A.1 象形 (*xiàngxíng*) (pictographs, pictographic characters), e.g.:

人 (*rén*) person　山 (*shān*) mountain　日 (*rì*) sun　月 (*yuè*) moon　木 (*mù*) tree

A.2 指事 (*zhǐshì*) (simple ideograms), e.g.:

上 (*shàng*) above　下 (*xià*) below

A.3 會意 (*huìyì*) (compound ideograms), e.g.:

明 (*míng*) bright　休 (*xiū*) rest

A.4 形聲 (*xíngshēng*) (pictophonetic characters [with one element indicating meaning and the other sound]), e.g.:

江，河，飯，姑

A.5 轉注 (*zhuǎnzhù*) (mutually explanatory characters), e.g.:

老，考

A.6 假借 (*jiǎjiè*) (phonetic loan characters), e.g.:

來，我

A popular myth is that Chinese writing is pictographic, and that each Chinese character represents a picture. In fact, only a small proportion of Chinese characters evolved from pictures. The vast majority are pictophonetic characters consisting of a radical and a phonetic element. The radical often suggests the meaning of a character, and the phonetic element indicates its original pronunciation, which may or may not represent its modern pronunciation.

Basic Radicals

Although there are more than fifty thousand Chinese characters, you only need to know two or three thousand to be considered literate. Mastering two or three thousand characters is, of course, still a rather formidable task. However, the learning process is easier if you grasp the basic components of Chinese characters. Traditionally, Chinese characters are grouped according to their common components, known as radicals, 部首 (*bùshǒu*). The 214 Kangxi radicals have been the standard set of radicals since the publication of the great *Kangxi Dictionary* (《康熙字典》) (《*Kāngxī Zìdiǎn*》) in 1716; although some contemporary dictionaries, which treat simplified characters as primary forms, have reduced that number to 189. If you know the radicals and other basic components well, you will find recognizing, remembering, and reproducing characters much easier. Knowing the radicals is also a must when using dictionaries that arrange characters according to their radicals. The following is a selection of forty radicals that everybody starting to learn characters should know. As you review the chart, identify where the radicals appear in the examples.

No.	Radical	Pinyin	English	Examples
1.	人(亻)	*rén*	person	今，他
2.	刀(刂)	*dāo*	knife	分，到
3.	力	*lì*	power	加，助
4.	又	*yòu*	right hand, again	友，取
5.	口	*kǒu*	mouth	叫，可
6.	囗*	*wéi*	enclose	回，因
7.	土	*tǔ*	earth	在，坐
8.	夕	*xī*	sunset	外，多
9.	大	*dà*	big	天，太
10.	女	*nǚ*	woman	婆，好
11.	子	*zǐ*	child	字，孩
12.	寸	*cùn*	inch	寺，封
13.	小	*xiǎo*	small	少，尖
14.	工	*gōng*	labor, work	左，差
15.	幺	*yāo*	tiny, small	幻，幼
16.	弓	*gōng*	bow	引，弟
17.	心(忄)	*xīn*	heart	想，忙
18.	戈	*gē*	dagger-axe	我，或
19.	手(扌)	*shǒu*	hand	拿，打
20.	日	*rì*	sun	早，明

No.	Radical	Pinyin	English	Examples
21.	月	*yuè*	moon	期，朗
22.	木	*mù*	wood	李，杯
23.	水（氵）	*shuǐ*	water	汞，洗
24.	火（灬）	*huǒ*	fire	燒，熱
25.	田	*tián*	field	男，留
26.	目	*mù*	eye	看，睡
27.	示（礻）	*shì*	show	票，社
28.	糸（糹）	*mì*	fine silk	素，紅
29.	耳	*ěr*	ear	聾，聊
30.	衣（衤）	*yī*	clothing	袋，衫
31.	言	*yán*	speech	說，話
32.	貝	*bèi*	cowrie shell	貴，財
33.	走	*zǒu*	walk	趣，起
34.	𧾷	*zú*	foot	跳，跑
35.	金	*jīn*	gold	錢，銀
36.	門	*mén*	door	間，開
37.	隹	*zhuī*	short-tailed bird	雖，集
38.	雨	*yǔ*	rain	雪，雲
39.	食（飠）	*shí*	eat	餐，飯
40.	馬	*mǎ*	horse	騎，驚

* Used as a radical only, not as a character by itself.

弓	弓字旁
子	子字旁
女	女字旁
糹	絞絲旁

馬	馬字旁
扌	提手旁
艹	草字頭
大	大字頭

Two Chinese radical charts.

Basic Character Structures

To help you learn Chinese characters, we present the major structures for Chinese characters below. However, this list is not intended to be exhaustive. Less common structures are not covered here, and some of the components can be further divided into subcomponents. For example, by our classification, 照 is in the Top-Bottom structure, but its top component can be seen as a combination of 日 on the left and 召 on the right. Teachers are encouraged to explain the structures of individual characters whenever appropriate, and to emphasize that it is much easier to memorize a character by component than by individual stroke.

No.	Pattern	Examples
1.	Unitary	上 水 人 女 山 長 東
2.	Left-Right	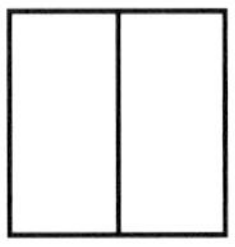 忙 唱 便 漢 都 找 湯
3.	Top-Bottom	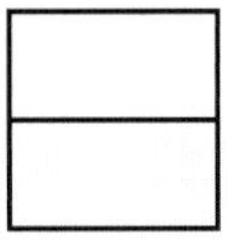 李 字 念 想 筆 花 緊
4.	Semi-Enclosing	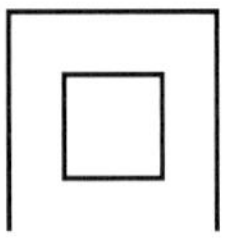 同 周 問 間 風
5.	Enclosing	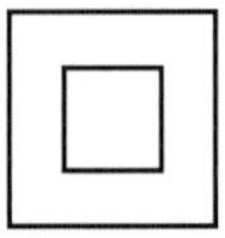 回 因 國 圖 圓
6.	Horizontal Trisection	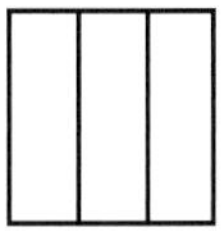 班 街 掰 粥
7.	Vertical Trisection	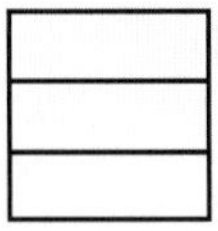 鼻 幕 曼
8.	Left-Bottom Enclosing	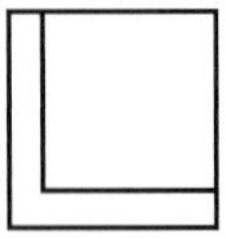 這 起 過 道 適 題
9.	Left-Top Enclosing	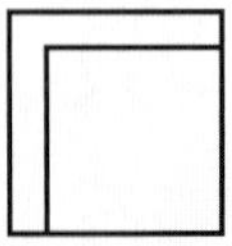 床 麻 病 歷 屋

D

Basic Strokes

As you review the chart, identify where the strokes appear in the examples.

Basic Stroke	Chinese	Pinyin	English	Examples
㇔	點	*diǎn*	dot	小，六
㇐	橫	*héng*	horizontal	一，六
㇑	豎	*shù*	vertical	十，中
㇒	撇	*piě*	downward left	人，大
㇏	捺	*nà*	downward right	八，人
㇀	提	*tí*	upward	我，江
㇖	橫鈎	*hénggōu*	horizontal hook	你，字
㇚	豎鈎	*shùgōu*	vertical hook	小，你
㇂	斜鈎	*xiégōu*	slanted hook	戈，我
㇕	橫折	*héngzhé*	horizontal bend	五，口
㇗	豎折	*shùzhé*	vertical bend	七，亡

Note: With the exception of the "*tí*" stroke (which moves upward to the right) and the "*piě*" stroke (which moves downward to the left), all Chinese strokes move from top to bottom, left to right.

Do you know the names of the strokes below? Can you write them properly?

E

Stroke Order

Following these stroke order rules will make it easier for you to accurately count the number of strokes in a character. Knowing the exact number of strokes in a character will help you find the character in a radical-based dictionary. Finally, your Chinese characters will look better if you write them in the correct stroke order!

1. From left to right 川，人
2. From top to bottom 三
3. Horizontal before vertical 十
4. From outside to inside 月
5. Middle before two sides 小
6. Inside before closing 日，回

Note: Learn the correct stroke order of the characters introduced in this book by using the associated Character Workbook.

Important Grammatical Features

Chinese grammar is relatively simple, since Chinese contains virtually no significant inflectional changes. However, beginners of Chinese should frequently review some fundamental characteristics of the language, even though not all these characteristics are unique to Chinese.

1. The most basic sentence structure in Chinese is:

Subject + Verb + Object

王朋	喜歡	打球。
Wang Peng	*like*	*play ball*

Wang Peng likes to play ball.

2. In Chinese, modifiers of nouns go before the nouns.

姐姐	給	我	買	的	襯衫。
older sister	*for*	*me*	*buy*		*shirt*

The shirt that my older sister bought me.

3. In Chinese, adverbials, which modify verbs, go before verbs. Adverbials typically follow the subject or the topic of the sentence.

王朋	昨天	看	了	一個	中國	電影。
Wang Peng	*yesterday*	*see*		*one*	*China*	*movie*

Wang Peng watched a Chinese movie yesterday.

Unlike in English, adverbials in Chinese never appear at the end of the sentence.

4. In general, Chinese nouns do not directly follow numerals; there must be a measure word in between.

一	個	人
a		*person*

三	本	書
three		*books*

5. If a sentence has multiple clauses with the same subject, the subject in the ensuing clauses is typically omitted. If two consecutive sentences have the same subject, the subject of the second sentence is typically represented by a pronoun.

李友	在	商店	買	衣服。	她	買	了	一件	襯衫，
Li You	*at*	*store*	*buy*	*clothes*	*she*	*buy*		*one*	*shirt*

還	買	了	一條	褲子，	花	了	六十	塊	錢。
also	*buy*		*one*	*pants*	*spend*		*sixty*	*dollar*	*money*

Li You went shopping for clothes. She bought a shirt. She bought a pair of pants as well. She spent sixty dollars.

6. When the "recipient" of an action becomes known information to both interlocutors, the "recipient" of the action often appears at the beginning of the sentence as the "topic," and the rest of the sentence functions as a "comment." So the sentence structure becomes: Topic-Comment.

Dad bought me a cell phone yesterday, and I don't like it.

Useful Expressions

A Classroom Expressions

You will hear these expressions every day in Chinese class.

1.	*Nǐ hǎo!*	How are you? How do you do? Hello.
2.	*Lǎoshī hǎo!*	How are you, teacher?
3.	*Shàng kè.*	Let's begin the class.
4.	*Xià kè.*	The class is over.
5.	*Dǎ kāi shū.*	Open the book.
6.	*Wǒ shuō, nǐmen tīng.*	I'll speak, you listen.
7.	*Kàn hēibǎn/báibǎn.*	Look at the blackboard/whiteboard.
8.	*Duì bu duì?*	Is it right?
9.	*Duì!*	Right! Correct!
10.	*Hěn hǎo!*	Very good!
11.	*Qǐng gēn wǒ shuō.*	Please repeat after me.
12.	*Zài shuō yí biàn.*	Say it again.
13.	*Dǒng bu dǒng?*	Do you understand?
14.	*Dǒng le.*	Yes, I/we understand; I/we do.
15.	*Zàijiàn!*	Goodbye!

B

Survival Expressions

Audio

These expressions will help you survive in a Chinese language environment. A good language student constantly learns new words by asking questions. Learn the following expressions and start to acquire Chinese on your own.

1.	*Duìbuqǐ!*	Sorry!
2.	*Qǐng wèn . . .*	Excuse me . . . May I ask . . .
3.	*Xièxie!*	Thanks!
4.	*Zhè shì shénme?*	What is this?
5.	*Wǒ bù dǒng.*	I don't understand.
6.	*Qǐng zài shuō yí biàn.*	Please say it one more time.
7.	*" . . . " Zhōngwén zěnme shuō?*	How do you say " . . . " in Chinese?
8.	*" . . . " shì shénme yìsi?*	What does " . . . " mean?
9.	*Qǐng nǐ gěi wǒ . . .*	Please give me . . .
10.	*Qǐng nǐ gàosu wǒ . . .*	Please tell me . . .

C

Numerals

Knowing Chinese numerals will help you with basic tasks like shopping and asking for the time. You can get a head start by memorizing 0 to 10 now. After you've memorized them, try saying your telephone number in Chinese.

Audio

〇 (*líng*) zero　一 (*yī*) one　二 (*èr*) two　三 (*sān*) three　四 (*sì*) four　五 (*wǔ*) five

六 (*liù*) six　七 (*qī*) seven　八 (*bā*) eight　九 (*jiǔ*) nine　十 (*shí*) ten

Lesson 1

第一課

Dì yī kè

問好

Wèn hǎo

GREETINGS

Learning Objectives

In this lesson, you will learn to:

- Exchange basic greetings
- Ask for a person's family name and full name and provide your own
- Determine whether someone is a teacher or a student
- Ask where someone's from

Relate & Get Ready

In your own culture/community:

- How do people greet each other when meeting for the first time?
- Which do people say first, their given name or family name?
- How do acquaintances or close friends address each other?

Exchanging Greetings

Dialogue 1

At school, Wang Peng and Li You meet each other for the first time.

Audio

Video

 你好[a]！

 你好！

 請問[b]，你[c]貴姓？

 我姓[1]*李。你呢[2]？

 我姓王。李小姐[d]，你叫[3]什麼名字？

 我叫李友。王先生，你叫什麼名字？

 我叫王朋[4]。

Pinyin Dialogue

 *Nǐ hǎo*[a] *!*

 *Nǐ hǎo!*

 *Qǐng wèn*[b]*, nǐ*[c] *guì xìng?*

 *Wǒ xìng*[1] *Lǐ. Nǐ ne*[2]*?*

 *Wǒ xìng Wáng. Lǐ xiǎojiě*[d]*, nǐ jiào*[3] *shénme míngzi?*

 *Wǒ jiào Lǐ Yǒu. Wáng xiānsheng, nǐ jiào shénme míngzi?*

 *Wǒ jiào Wáng Péng*[4]*.*

* Here and throughout the book, the blue lesson text and numbers correspond to explanations in the **Grammar section.**

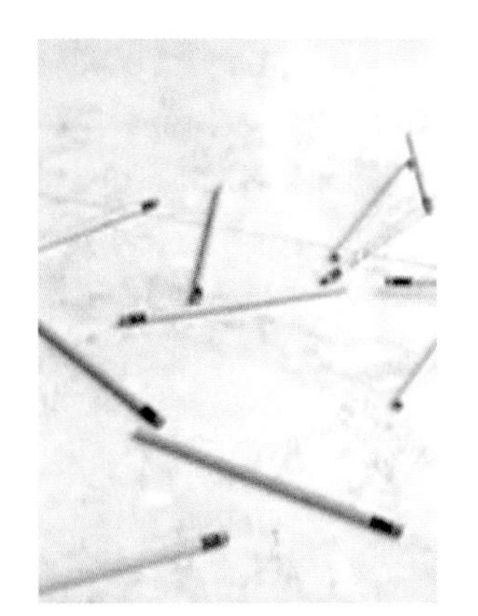

a 你好! *(Nǐ hǎo!)*

This common greeting is used to address strangers as well as old acquaintances. To respond, simply repeat the same greeting.

b 請問 *(qǐng wèn)*

This is a polite phrase used to get someone's attention before asking a question or making an inquiry, similar to "excuse me, may I ask" in English.

c 你 *(nǐ)* vs. 您 *(nín)*

To be more polite and respectful, replace 你 *(nǐ)* with its honorific form, 您 *(nín)*. [See Language Note A, Dialogue 1, Lesson 6.]

d 小姐 *(xiǎojiě)*

This is a word with two third-tone syllables. The tone sandhi rule applies, thus making the first third tone, 小 *(xiǎo)*, a second tone. The second syllable, 姐 *(jiě)*, can also be pronounced in the neutral tone.

Vocabulary

Audio

Flashcards

No.	Word	Pinyin	Part of Speech	Definition
1	你	*nǐ*	pr	you
2	好	*hǎo*	adj	fine, good, nice, OK, it's settled
3	請	*qǐng*	v	please (polite form of request), to treat or to invite (somebody)
4	問	*wèn*	v	to ask (a question)
5	貴	*guì*	adj	honorable, expensive
6	姓	*xìng*	v/n	(one's) family name is . . . ; family name [See Grammar 1.]
7	我	*wǒ*	pr	I, me
8	呢	*ne*	qp	(question particle) [See Grammar 2.]
9	小姐	*xiǎojiě*	n	Miss, young lady
10	叫	*jiào*	v	to be called, to call [See Grammar 3.]
11	什麼	*shénme*	qpr	what
12	名字	*míngzi*	n	name
13	先生	*xiānsheng*	n	Mr., husband, teacher
14	李友	*Lǐ Yǒu*	pn	(a personal name)
	李	*lǐ*	pn/n	(a family name); plum
15	王朋	*Wáng Péng*	pn	(a personal name)
	王	*wáng*	pn/n	(a family name); king

你叫什麼名字？

Nǐ jiào shénme míngzi?

What is your name?

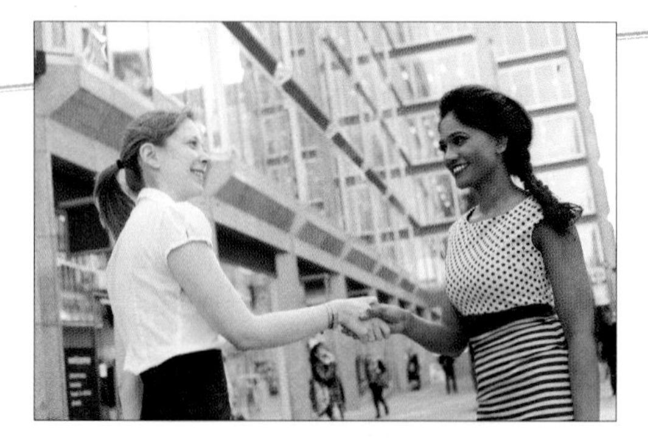

How About You?

我叫＿＿＿＿＿＿＿＿。

Wǒ jiào __________.

Grammar

1 The verb 姓 *(xìng)*

姓 *(xìng)* is both a noun and a verb. When it is used as a verb, it must be followed by an object.

A Q: 你姓什麼？
Nǐ xìng shénme?
What is your family name?

A: 我姓李。
Wǒ xìng Lǐ.
My family name is Li.

姓 *(xìng)* is usually negated with 不 *(bù)*. [See Grammar 7.]

B Q: 你姓李嗎？
Nǐ xìng Lǐ ma?
Is your family name Li?

A: 我不姓李。 [⊗ 我不姓。]
Wǒ bú xìng Lǐ.
My family name is not Li.

The polite way to ask for and give a family name is as follows.

C Q: 你貴姓？ [⊗ 你貴姓什麼？]
Nǐ guì xìng?
What is your family name?
(Lit. Your honorable family name is . . . ?)

Remember to drop the honorific 貴 *(guì)* when you reply.

A: 我姓王。 [⊗ 我貴姓王。]
Wǒ xìng Wáng.
My family name is Wang.

You can also respond to 你貴姓 *(nǐ guì xìng)* by saying 免貴姓王 *(miǎn guì xìng Wáng)*, 免貴姓李 *(miǎn guì xìng Lǐ)*. (Lit. Dispense with "honorable." [My] family name is Wang/Li.)

EXERCISES

Complete these exchanges with your own family name.

1 Q: 請問，你貴姓？ A: 我姓________。

2 Q: 你姓什麼？ A: 我姓________。

2 Questions ending with 呢 *(ne)*

呢 *(ne)* often follows a noun or pronoun to form a question when the content of the question is already clear from the context.

A Q: 請問，你貴姓？

Qǐng wèn, nǐ guì xìng?

What's your family name, please?

A: 我姓李，你呢？

Wǒ xìng Lǐ, nǐ ne?

My family name is Li. How about you?

B Q: 你叫什麼名字？

Nǐ jiào shénme míngzi?

What's your name?

A: 我叫王朋，你呢？

Wǒ jiào Wáng Péng, nǐ ne?

My name is Wang Peng. How about you?

When 呢 *(ne)* is used in this way, there must be some context. In each of the two examples above, the context is provided by the preceding sentence: 我姓李 *(wǒ xìng Lǐ)* in (A), and 我叫王朋 *(wǒ jiào Wáng Péng)* in (B).

EXERCISES

In pairs, ask and give your name and family name.

1 Q: 我姓________，你呢？ A: 我姓________。

2 Q: 我叫________，你呢？ A: 我叫________。

3 The verb 叫 *(jiào)*

While 叫 *(jiào)* has several meanings, it means "to be called" in this lesson. Like 姓 *(xìng)*, it must be followed by an object, which can be either a full name or a given name, but seldom a given name that consists only of one syllable.

A Q: 你叫什麼名字？ A: 我叫王小朋。

Nǐ jiào shénme míngzi? *Wǒ jiào Wáng Xiǎopéng.*

What is your name? My name is Wang Xiaopeng.

叫 *(jiào)* is usually negated with 不 *(bù)*. [See Grammar 7.]

B Q: 你叫李生嗎？ A: 我不叫李生。

Nǐ jiào Lǐ Shēng ma? *Wǒ bú jiào Lǐ Shēng.*

Is your name Li Sheng? My name is not Li Sheng.

EXERCISES

Take turns answering the questions below.

1 Q: 請問，你叫什麼名字？ A: 我叫________。

2 Q: 你叫李好嗎？ A: 我不叫________。

4 Subject + verb + object

From the examples in the previous Grammar Points, we can see that the basic word order in a Chinese sentence is subject + verb + object.

The word order remains the same in statements and questions. You don't place the question word at the beginning of a question as you do in English, unless that question word is the subject. [See also Grammar 3, Lesson 2, and Grammar 1, Lesson 4.]

Language Practice

A **Mix and mingle** INTERPERSONAL

Introduce yourself to your classmates using the outline below.

Student A 你好！

Nǐ hǎo!

Student B ________ 。

________.

Student A 請問，你貴姓？

Qǐng wèn, nǐ guì xìng?

Student B 我姓 ________ 。你呢？

Wǒ xìng ________. Nǐ ne?

Student A 我姓 ________ ，我叫 ________ 。你叫什麼名字？

Wǒ xìng ________, wǒ jiào ________. Nǐ jiào shénme míngzi?

Student B 我叫 ________ 。

Wǒ jiào ________.

Characterize it!

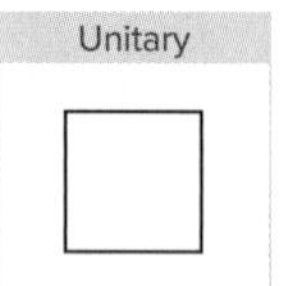

❶ 小 ❷ 請 ❸ 王 ❹ 生 ❺ 貴

Which of these characters are formed with the pattern on the left?

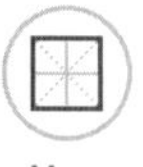

More characters

B Getting acquainted INTERPERSONAL

Complete the following exchange between two people who have never met before. Do a role-play based on the prompts.

Student A 你好！

Nǐ hǎo!

Student B ________。

________.

Student A 我姓 ________，請問，你貴姓？

Wǒ xìng ________, qǐng wèn, nǐ guì xìng?

Student B ________。

________.

Student A ________，你叫什麼名字？

________, nǐ jiào shénme míngzi?

Student B 我叫 ________。

Wǒ jiào ________.

Chinese Chat

You want to add Wang Peng and Li You to a group text message. From this contact list, which names would you select?

Where Are You From?

Dialogue 2

Wang Peng and Li You start chatting after bumping into each other on campus.

王先生，你是[5]老師嗎[6]？

我不[7][a]是老師，我是學生。李友，你呢？

我也[8]是學生。你是中國人嗎？

是[b]，我是北京人。你是美國人嗎？

是，我是紐約人。

Pinyin Dialogue

Wáng xiānsheng, nǐ shì[5] *lǎoshī ma*[6]*?*

Wǒ bú[7][a] *shì lǎoshī, wǒ shì xuésheng. Lǐ Yǒu, nǐ ne?*

Wǒ yě[8] *shì xuésheng. Nǐ shì Zhōngguó rén ma?*

Shì[b]*, wǒ shì Běijīng rén. Nǐ shì Měiguó rén ma?*

Shì, wǒ shì Niǔyuē rén.

China has the fastest growing air passenger market in the world. Based on his boarding pass, identify this traveler's flight plan.

GET Real WITH CHINESE

Language Notes

a 不

The original tone of 不 is the falling or fourth tone, "bù." However, when followed by another fourth tone syllable, 不 changes to second tone, as in 不是 *(bú shì)*.

b 是 *(shì)*/不是 *(bú shì)*

These are not universal equivalents of "yes" and "no." One does not always need to introduce an affirmative answer to a yes/no question with 是 *(shì)* or a negative answer with 不是 *(bú shì)*. For instance, to answer the question 你姓王嗎？*(Nǐ xìng Wáng ma?)* (Is your family name Wang?) affirmatively, one can reply, 對，我姓王 *(Duì, wǒ xìng Wáng)* (Yes, my family name is Wang) or simply, 我姓王 *(Wǒ xìng Wáng)*. To answer the question negatively, say 不，我不姓王 *(Bù, wǒ bú xìng Wáng)* (No, my family name is not Wang), or simply, 我不姓王 *(Wǒ bú xìng Wáng)*.

Vocabulary

Audio

Flashcards

No.	Word	Pinyin	Part of Speech	Definition
1	是	*shì*	v	to be [See Grammar 5.]
2	老師	*lǎoshī*	n	teacher
3	嗎	*ma*	qp	(question particle) [See Grammar 6.]
4	不	*bù*	adv	not, no [See Grammar 7.]
5	學生	*xuésheng*	n	student
6	也	*yě*	adv	too, also [See Grammar 8.]
7	人	*rén*	n	people, person
8	中國	*Zhōngguó*	pn	China
9	北京	*Běijīng*	pn	Beijing
10	美國	*Měiguó*	pn	America
11	紐約	*Niǔyuē*	pn	New York

Nǐ shì Měiguó rén ma?

Are you American?

How About You?

(不)是，我是＿＿＿＿＿＿人。

(Bú) shì, wǒ shì ＿＿＿＿＿＿ rén.

See index for corresponding vocabulary or research another term.

Grammar

5 The verb 是 *(shì)* (to be)

是 *(shì)* (to be) is a verb that can be used to link two things that are in some way equivalent. These two things can be nouns, pronouns, or noun phrases, e.g.:

A Q: 你是老師嗎？

Nǐ shì lǎoshī ma?

Are you a teacher?

A: 我是老師。

Wǒ shì lǎoshī.

I am a teacher.

B 李友是學生。

Lǐ Yǒu shì xuésheng.

Li You is a student.

是 *(shì)* is negated with 不 *(bù)*. [See also Grammar 7.]

C 王朋不是美國人。

Wáng Péng bú shì Měiguó rén.

Wang Peng is not American.

EXERCISES

Form questions and affirmative answers based on the information below. Use exercise 1 as an example.

1 王朋 學生

→ Q: 王朋是學生嗎？ A: 王朋是學生。

2 李友 美國人

3 王朋 北京人

More exercises

6 Questions ending with 嗎 *(ma)*

When 嗎 *(ma)* is added to the end of a declarative statement, that statement turns into a question. To answer the question in the affirmative, drop 嗎 *(ma)* from the end of the question. To answer the question in the negative, drop 嗎 *(ma)*, and insert a negative adverb—usually 不 *(bù)*—before the verb. [See Grammar 7.]

A

Q: 你是老師嗎？

Nǐ shì lǎoshī ma?

Are you a teacher?

A: 我是老師。

Wǒ shì lǎoshī.

I am a teacher. (affirmative)

A: 我不是老師。

Wǒ bú shì lǎoshī.

I am not a teacher. (negative)

B

Q: 你姓王嗎？

Nǐ xìng Wáng ma?

Is your family name Wang?

A: 我姓王。

Wǒ xìng Wáng.

My family name is Wang. (affirmative)

A: 我不姓王。

Wǒ bú xìng Wáng.

My family name is not Wang. (negative)

7 The negative adverb 不 *(bù)* (not, no)

In Chinese, there are two main negative adverbs. One of the two, 不 *(bù)* (not, no), occurs in this lesson.

A 我不是北京人。

Wǒ bú shì Běijīng rén.

I am not from Beijing.

B 李友不是中國人。

Lǐ Yǒu bú shì Zhōngguó rén.

Li You is not Chinese.

C 老師不姓王。

Lǎoshī bú xìng Wáng.

The teacher's family name is not Wang.

D 我不叫李中。

Wǒ bú jiào Lǐ Zhōng.

My name is not Li Zhong.

EXERCISES

Give negative answers to these questions. Use exercise 1 as an example.

More exercises

1 Q: 李友是中國人嗎？

→ A: 李友不是中國人。

2 Q: 王朋是老師嗎？

3 Q: 李友是北京人嗎？

8 The adverb 也 (*yě*) (too, also)

The adverb 也 (*yě*) basically means "too" or "also." In Chinese, adverbs, especially one-syllable adverbs, normally appear after subjects and before verbs. The adverb 也 (*yě*) cannot be put before the subject or at the very end of a sentence.

A 我也是學生。

Wǒ yě shì xuésheng.

I'm a student, too.

B 王朋是學生，李友也是學生。

Wáng Péng shì xuésheng, Lǐ Yǒu yě shì xuésheng.

Wang Peng is a student. Li You is a student, too.

C 你是中國人，我也是中國人。

Nǐ shì Zhōngguó rén, wǒ yě shì Zhōngguó rén.

You are Chinese. I am Chinese, too.

[⊗ ……我是中國人也。]

[⊗ ……也我是中國人。]

When the adverb 也 (*yě*) is used together with the negative adverb 不 (*bù*) (not, no), 也 (*yě*) is placed before 不 (*bù*).

D 王朋不是老師，李友也不是老師。

Wáng Péng bú shì lǎoshī, Lǐ Yǒu yě bú shì lǎoshī.

Wang Peng is not a teacher. Li You is not a teacher, either.

E 你不是紐約人，我也不是紐約人。

Nǐ bú shì Niǔyuē rén, wǒ yě bú shì Niǔyuē rén.

You are not from New York. I am not from New York, either.

EXERCISES

Use these sentences to form question-and-answers, inserting 也 where appropriate.

Use exercise 1 as an example.

1 王朋是學生。

→ Q: 王朋是學生，你呢? A: 我也是學生。

2 李友是美國人。

3 李友不是老師。

Chinese Chat

A friend you just met online is chatting with you on Google Hangouts. How would you reply?

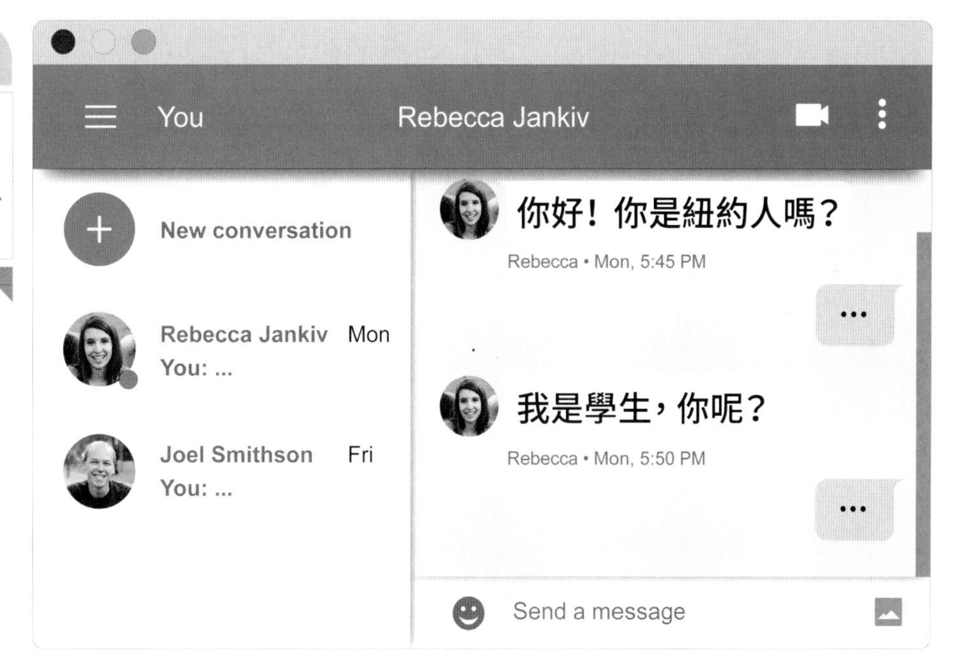

Language Practice

C Getting to know you

INTERPERSONAL

In pairs, form a question-and-answer, inserting 是 *(shì)* in the ◇ and 嗎 *(ma)* when needed, e.g.:

王朋 ◇ 學生

Wáng Péng ◇ xuésheng

Q: 王朋是學生嗎? *Wáng Péng shì xuésheng ma?*

A: 王朋是學生。 *Wáng Péng shì xuésheng.*

1 李友◇美國人 *Lǐ Yǒu ◇ Měiguó rén*

2 王朋◇中國人 *Wáng Péng ◇ Zhōngguó rén*

3 李友◇美國學生 *Lǐ Yǒu ◇ Měiguó xuésheng*

4 王朋◇北京人 *Wáng Péng ◇ Běijīng rén*

5 李友◇紐約人 *Lǐ Yǒu ◇ Niǔyuē rén*

6 你◇學生 *nǐ ◇ xuésheng*

D On the contrary

INTERPERSONAL

In pairs, ask and answer the following questions, using 不 *(bú)* where appropriate, e.g.:

Q: 李小姐叫李朋嗎? *Lǐ xiǎojiě jiào Lǐ Péng ma?*

A: 李小姐不叫李朋。 *Lǐ xiǎojiě bú jiào Lǐ Péng.*

1 李友是中國人嗎? *Lǐ Yǒu shì Zhōngguó rén ma?*

2 你是王朋嗎? *Nǐ shì Wáng Péng ma?*

3 王朋是紐約人嗎? *Wáng Péng shì Niǔyuē rén ma?*

4 王先生叫王友嗎？ *Wáng xiānsheng jiào Wáng Yǒu ma?*

5 你叫李友嗎？ *Nǐ jiào Lǐ Yǒu ma?*

E What about you? INTERPERSONAL

In pairs, ask and answer the following questions with a partner, using 也 *(yě)* where appropriate.

1 王朋是中國人，你也是中國人嗎？

Wáng Péng shì Zhōngguó rén, nǐ yě shì Zhōngguó rén ma?

2 李友是紐約人，你也是紐約人嗎？

Lǐ Yǒu shì Niǔyuē rén, nǐ yě shì Niǔyuē rén ma?

3 王朋不是老師，你呢？

Wáng Péng bú shì lǎoshī, nǐ ne?

4 李友不是中國人，你呢？

Lǐ Yǒu bú shì Zhōngguó rén, nǐ ne?

5 王朋姓王，你也姓王嗎？

Wáng Péng xìng Wáng, nǐ yě xìng Wáng ma?

Characterize it!

What do the characters mean?

What is the common radical?

What does the radical mean?

How does the radical relate to the overall meaning of the characters?

1 呢 2 叫 3 嗎 4 名

More characters

F Where are you from? INTERPERSONAL

Interview your classmates to find out what country, state, or city they're from. Attach the word 人 *(rén)* (person) to the name of the country, state, or city to indicate nationality or place of residence, e.g.:

我是美國 *(Wǒ shì Měiguó)*/California/Boston 人 *(rén)* 。

Student A 我是美國人，你呢？

Wǒ shì Měiguó rén, nǐ ne?

Student B ……

...

Student A 你是 (state) 人嗎？

Nǐ shì (state) *rén ma?*

Student B 我是……人。/
我不是……人，我是……人。

Wǒ shì . . . rén./Wǒ bú shì . . . rén, wǒ shì . . . rén.

Student A 你是 (city) 人嗎？

Nǐ shì (city) *rén ma?*

Student B 我是…… 人。你呢？

Wǒ shì . . . rén, nǐ ne?

Student A 我是…… 人。

Wǒ shì . . . rén.

Pronunciation

Practice your pronunciation with the audio exercises below.

1 Initials:

	b	p	d	t
1	*bǎo*	*pǎo*	*dā*	*tā*
2	*bān*	*pān*	*dí*	*tí*
3	*bù*	*pù*	*duì*	*tuì*
4	*bō*	*pō*	*dīng*	*tīng*
5	*bēng*	*pēng*	*dēng*	*tēng*

2 Initials:

	j	q	z	c
1	*jiāo*	*qiāo*	*zāi*	*cāi*
2	*jǐng*	*qǐng*	*zǎo*	*cǎo*
3	*jīn*	*qīn*	*zì*	*cì*
4	*jiè*	*qiè*	*zè*	*cè*
5	*jiàn*	*qiàn*	*zhè*	*chè*

3 Initials:

	sh	s	x
1	*shà*	*sà*	*xià*
2	*shàn*	*sàn*	*xiàn*
3	*shēn*	*sēn*	*xīn*
4	*shēng*	*sēng*	*xīng*

4 Tones:

1. *tiāntiān*
2. *jīnnián*
3. *jīnglǐ*
4. *shēngqì*
5. *xīngqī*
6. *fādá*
7. *fāzhǎn*
8. *shēngdiào*

5 Tone combinations:

1. *nǐ hǎo*
2. *Lǐ Yǒu*
3. *lǎohǔ*
4. *zhǎnlǎn*
5. *hǎo duō*
6. *nǐ lái*
7. *hǎo shū*
8. *qǐng wèn*

6 The neutral tone:

1. *xiānsheng*
2. *míngzi*
3. *xiáojie*
4. *shénme*
5. *wǒ de*
6. *nǐ de*
7. *tā de*
8. *shéi de*

CULTURAL LITERACY

Continue
to explore

FAMILY names 姓氏

Most Chinese family names, 姓 *(xìng)*, are monosyllabic. There are, however, a few disyllabic family names such as 歐陽 *(Ōuyáng)* and 司徒 *(Sītú)*. The number of Chinese family names is fairly limited. According to the most recent census, the most common family names are 王 *(Wáng)*, 李 *(Lǐ)*, 張 *(Zhāng)*, 劉 *(Liú)*, and 陳 *(Chén)*. Family names precede official titles and other forms of address: 王先生 *(Wáng xiānsheng)* (Mister Wang), 李老師 *(Lǐ lǎoshī)* (Teacher Li), etc. When addressing strangers, it is proper to say 先生 *(xiānsheng)* (Mr.) or 小姐 *(xiǎojiě)* (Miss) following their family name.

In China, family names were originally passed down along maternal lines. Indeed, some of the most ancient Chinese family names, such as 姬 *(Jī)*, 媯 *(Guī)*, 姒 *(Sì)*, 姚 *(Yáo)*, and 姜 *(Jiāng)*, as well as the character 姓 *(xìng)*, contain the female radical 女 *(nǚ)*. Aristocratic men and women were born with a 姓 *(xìng)*, which came to indicate paternal lineage in subsequent ages. However, with the expansion of clans, aristocratic men would adopt a 氏 *(shì)* as a secondary family name. By the Western Han period (207 BCE–8 CE), 姓 *(xìng)* and 氏 *(shì)* had become indistinguishable, and even commoners had acquired family names. Thus, family names, 姓 *(xìng)*, are sometimes called 姓氏 *(xìngshì)*.

When talking about family names, many Chinese people will reference the *Hundred Family Names*, 百家姓 *(Bǎi Jiā Xìng)*, which records the known family names of the Northern Song Dynasty in the tenth century. The more than four hundred family names included are arranged in four-character lines, with every other line rhymed. This book was a popular reading primer for schoolchildren.

COMPARE & CONTRAST

1. Search for the idiom 張三李四 (*Zhāng Sān Lǐ Sì*) using the keywords "張三李四" and "English." Why do you think the family names 張 (*Zhāng*) and 李 (*Lǐ*) are singled out? What is the English equivalent of this idiomatic Chinese expression, and what are some of the most common family names in English?
2. Chinese personal names often carry special meanings. Give examples of personal names with special meanings from other cultures.

FULL names

In Chinese, family names always precede personal or given names, 名 (*míng*). Personal names usually carry auspicious meanings. They can be either monosyllabic, written in one character, or disyllabic, written in two characters. A person is seldom referred to by his or her family name alone. For example, Wang Peng, 王朋 (*Wáng Péng*), should not be referred to as Wang. Additionally, when introducing oneself or someone else, one does not usually mention a monosyllabic personal name alone. For example, Wang Peng would not say ⊗ 我叫朋 (*Wǒ jiào Péng*) or ⊗ 她叫友 (*Tā jiào Yǒu*) when introducing Li You. Instead, he would typically say 我叫王朋 (*Wǒ jiào Wáng Péng*) and 她叫李友 (*Tā jiào Lǐ Yǒu*).

When meeting someone for the first time, it is polite to first ask for a family name. Then the question 你叫什麼名字? (*Nǐ jiào shénme míngzi?*) (What is your name?) can be asked to find out the person's given name or full name.

In Chinese culture, the use of given names often suggests a much higher degree of intimacy than is the case in the West. If one's given name is monosyllabic, its use is even more limited and is usually confined to couples. For example, Wang Peng's girlfriend could address him as Peng, but most people would call him Wang Peng.

Lesson Wrap-Up

Make It Flow!

Rearrange the following sentences into a logical sequence. Then combine them into a coherent self-introduction. Remember to omit repetitive elements where appropriate.

____ 我是北京人。

____ 我叫王朋。

__1__ 我姓王。

Role-Play

You are at the first event hosted by your school's Chinese-American Student Association. Be friendly! Meet and greet and introduce yourself.

Student A You are an American student from New York City.

Student B You are a Chinese student from Beijing.

Student C You are an American teacher from Boston.

Student D You are a Chinese student from Shanghai.

Video

Make a short video introducing yourself in Chinese and post it on social media.

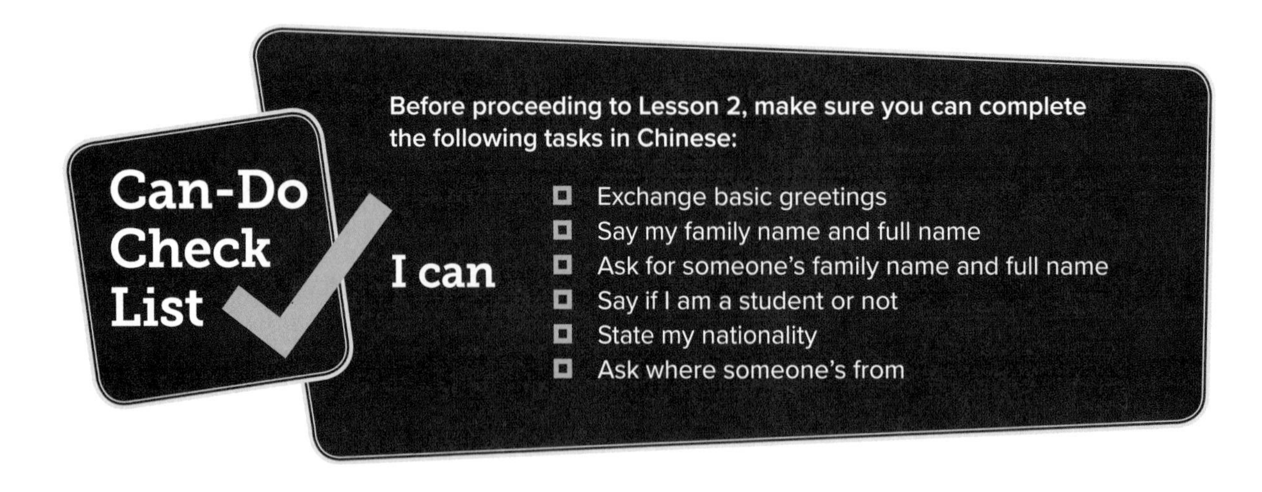

Lesson 2

第二課

Dì èr kè

家庭

Jiātíng

FAMILY

Learning Objectives

In this lesson, you will learn to:

- Use basic kinship terms for family members
- Describe a family photo
- Ask about someone's profession
- Name some common professions

Relate & Get Ready

In your own culture/community:

- What is the typical family structure?
- Do adults consider their parents' house their home?
- Do adults live with their parents?
- When talking about family members, do people mention their father or mother first?
- Is it appropriate to ask about people's professions when you first meet them?

Looking at a Family Photo

Dialogue 1

Wang Peng is in Gao Wenzhong's room and points to a picture on the desk.

Audio

Video

 高文中，那是你的[1]照片嗎？

They walk toward the picture and stand in front of it.

 是。這是我爸爸，這是我媽媽。

 這[a]個[2]女孩子是誰[3]？

 她是我姐姐。

 這個男孩子是你弟弟嗎？

 不是，他是我大哥的兒子[b]。

 你大哥有[4]女兒嗎？

 他沒有女兒。

Pinyin Dialogue

Wang Peng is in Gao Wenzhong's room and points to a picture on the desk.

 *Gāo Wénzhōng, nà shì nǐ de*[1] *zhàopiàn ma?*

They walk toward the picture and stand in front of it.

 *Shì. Zhè shì wǒ bàba, zhè shì wǒ māma.*

 *Zhè*[a] *ge*[2] *nǚ háizi shì shéi*[3]*?*

 *Tā shì wǒ jiějie.*

 *Zhè ge nán háizi shì nǐ dìdi ma?*

 *Bú shì, tā shì wǒ dàgē de érzi*[b]*.*

 *Nǐ dàgē yǒu*[4] *nǚ'ér ma?*

 *Tā méiyǒu nǚ'ér.*

a 這，那

In colloquial Chinese, 這 can also be pronounced as *zhèi* and 那 as *nèi* when they are followed by a measure word or a numeral and a measure word.

b 兒子 *(érzi)*，女兒 *(nǚ'ér)*

Do not refer to someone's son, 兒子 *(érzi)*, as 男孩子 *(nán háizi)* (boy), or someone's daughter, 女兒 *(nǚ'ér)*, as 女孩子 *(nǚ háizi)* (girl).

Vocabulary

Audio

Flashcards

No.	Word	Pinyin	Part of Speech	Definition
1	那	*nà*	pr	that
2	的	*de*	p	(a possessive or descriptive particle) [See Grammar 1.]
3	照片	*zhàopiàn*	n	picture, photo
4	這	*zhè*	pr	this
5	爸爸	*bàba*	n	father, dad
6	媽媽	*māma*	n	mother, mom
7	個	*gè/ge*	m	(measure word for many common everyday objects) [See Grammar 2.]
8	女	*nǚ*	adj	female
9	孩子	*háizi*	n	child
10	誰	*shéi*	qpr	who, whom [See Grammar 3.]

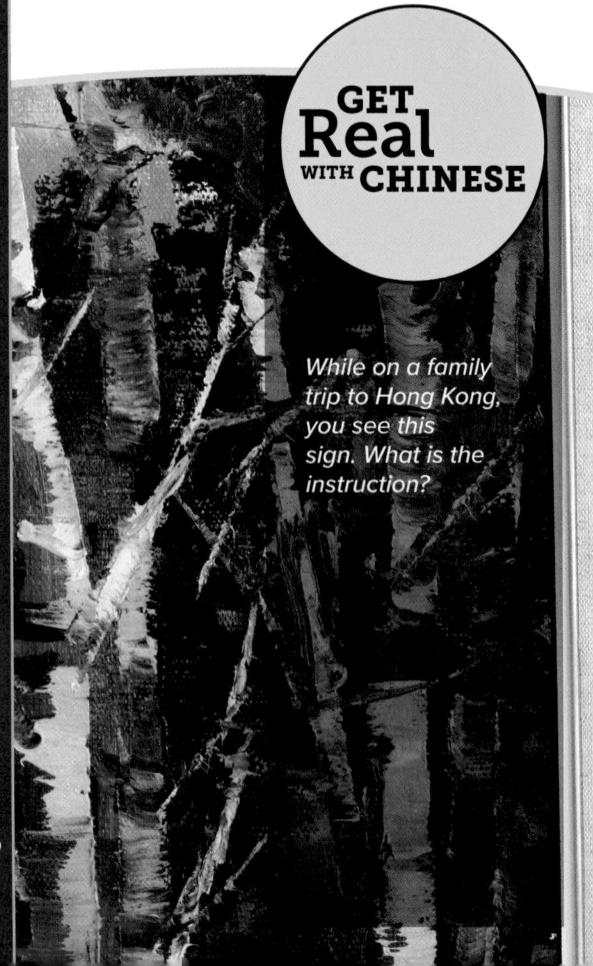

GET Real WITH CHINESE

While on a family trip to Hong Kong, you see this sign. What is the instruction?

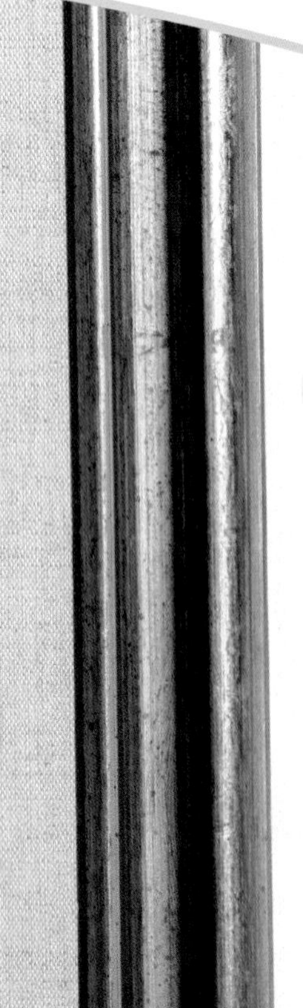

No.	Word	Pinyin	Part of Speech	Definition
11	她	*tā*	pr	she, her
12	姐姐	*jiějie*	n	older sister
13	男	*nán*	adj	male
14	弟弟	*dìdi*	n	younger brother
15	他	*tā*	pr	he, him
16	大哥	*dàgē*	n	eldest/oldest brother
17	兒子	*érzi*	n	son
18	有	*yǒu*	v	to have, to exist [See Grammar 4 and Grammar 5.]
19	女兒	*nǚ'ér*	n	daughter
20	沒	*méi*	adv	not
21	高文中	*Gāo Wénzhōng*	pn	(a personal name)
	高	*gāo*	pn/adj	(a family name); tall, high

這是誰？

Zhè shì shéi?

Who is this?

How About You?

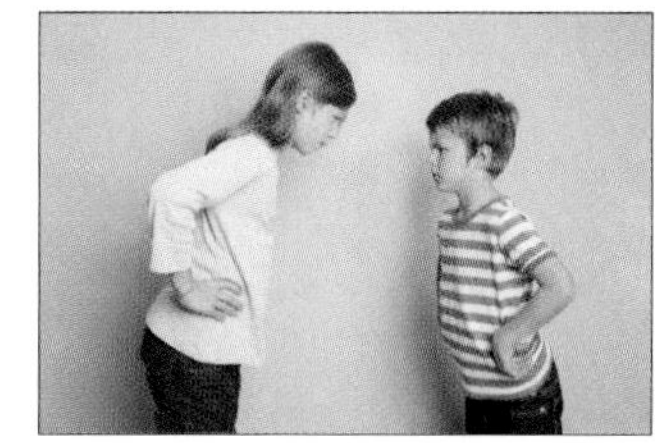

這是 ________ 。

Zhè shì ________.

Bring a family photo to class, like the ones above, and identify your family members.

Grammar

1 The particle 的 *(de)* (I)

To indicate a possessive relationship, the particle 的 is used between the "possessor" and the "possessed." To that extent, it is equivalent to the "'s" structure in English, as in 老師的名字 *(lǎoshī de míngzi)* (teacher's name). The particle 的 *(de)* is often omitted in colloquial speech after a personal pronoun. Therefore, we say "王朋的媽媽" *(Wáng Péng de māma)* (Wang Peng's mother) but "我媽媽" *(wǒ māma)* (my mother). [See also Grammar 4, Lesson 3.]

More exercises

EXERCISES

Translate these phrases containing the particle 的.

1 李友的爸爸

2 哥哥的女兒

2 Measure words (I)

In Chinese, a numeral is usually not followed immediately by a noun. Instead, a measure word is inserted between the number and the noun, as in (A), (B), and (C). Similarly, a measure word is often inserted between a demonstrative pronoun and a noun, as in (D) and (E). There are over one hundred measure words in Chinese, but you will come across only two or three dozen in everyday speech. Many nouns are associated with specific measure words, which are often related in meaning to the nouns.

個 *(gè/ge)* is the single most common measure word in Chinese. It is also sometimes used as a substitute for other measure words.

A 一個人

yí ge rén

a person

B 一個學生

yí ge xuésheng

a student

C 一個老師

yí ge lǎoshī

a teacher

D 這個孩子

zhè ge háizi

this child

E 那個男學生

nà ge nán xuésheng

that male student

EXERCISES

Translate these phrases containing the measure word 個.

More exercises

1 一個中國人

2 三個弟弟

3 Question pronouns

Question pronouns include 誰 *(shéi)* (who/whom), 什麼 *(shénme)* (what), 哪 *(nǎ/něi)* (which) [see Lesson 6], 哪兒 *(nǎr)* (where) [see Lesson 5], and 幾 *(jǐ)* (how many). In a question with a question pronoun, the word order is exactly the same as that in a declarative sentence. Therefore, when forming a question with a question pronoun, start with a declarative sentence and then replace the relevant part with the appropriate question pronoun.

A 那個女孩子是李友。

Nà ge nǚ háizi shì Lǐ Yǒu.

That girl is Li You.

那個女孩子 *(Nà ge nǚ háizi)* can be replaced with 誰 *(shéi)* to form the question below.

誰是李友？

Shéi shì Lǐ Yǒu?

Who is Li You?

Here 誰 *(shéi)* functions as the subject of the sentence and occupies the same position as 那個女孩子 *(Nà ge nǚ háizi)* in the corresponding statement. 李友 *(Lǐ Yǒu)* in (A) can also be replaced with 誰 *(shéi)* to form the question below.

那個女孩子是誰？

Nà ge nǚ háizi shì shéi?

Who is that girl?

誰 *(shéi)* functions as the object of the sentence and occupies the same position as 李友 *(Lǐ Yǒu)*.

B Q: 誰是老師？
Shéi shì lǎoshī?
Who is a teacher?

A: 李先生是老師。
Lǐ xiānsheng shì lǎoshī.
Mr. Li is a teacher.

C Q: 那個女孩子姓什麼？
Nà ge nǚ háizi xìng shénme?
What's that girl's family name?

A: 那個女孩子姓王。
Nà ge nǚ háizi xìng Wáng.
That girl's family name is Wang.

D Q: 誰有姐姐？
Shéi yǒu jiějie?
Who has older sisters?

A: 高文中有姐姐。
Gāo Wénzhōng yǒu jiějie.
Gao Wenzhong has an older sister.

EXERCISES

Use the question pronoun 誰 to survey your classmates.

1 Q: 誰是________？ A: 我是________。

2 Q: 誰有________？ A: 我有________。

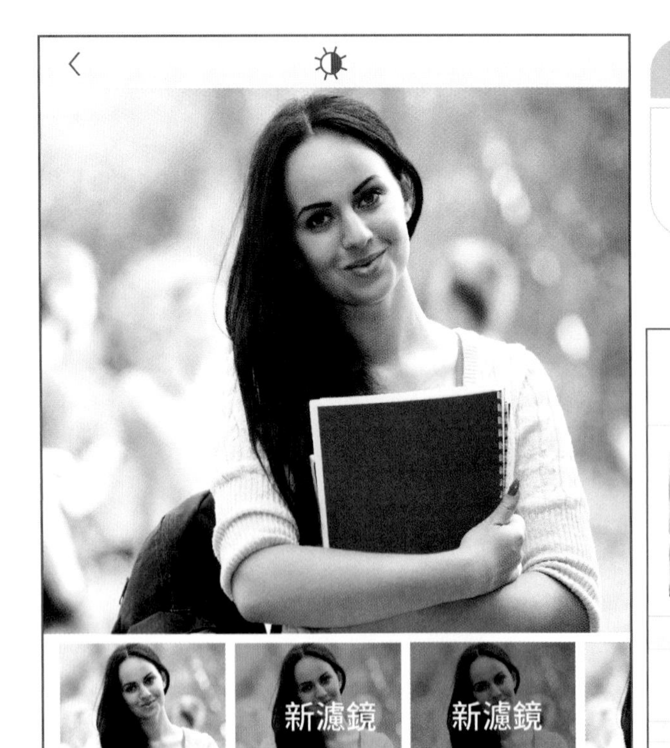

Chinese Chat

You're about to post this picture of a family member on Instagram. What caption would you write? Use the hashtag #姐姐.

新帖子

撰寫說明......

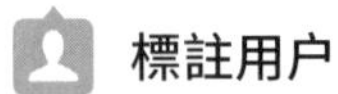

新增地點

4 Indicating possession using 有 *(yǒu)*

有 *(yǒu)* is always negated with 沒 *(méi)*, not 不 *(bù)*.

A Q: 王先生有弟弟嗎？

Wáng xiānsheng yǒu dìdi ma?

Does Mr. Wang have a younger brother?

A: 王先生沒有弟弟。

Wáng xiānsheng méiyǒu dìdi.

Mr. Wang doesn't have any younger brothers.

B Q: 我有三個姐姐，你呢？

Wǒ yǒu sān ge jiějie, nǐ ne?

I have three older sisters. How about you?

A: 我沒有姐姐。

Wǒ méiyǒu jiějie.

I don't have any older sisters.

EXERCISES

In pairs, complete either the question or the answer, inserting 有 where appropriate.

More exercises

1 Q: 高文中________________？

A: 高文中有姐姐。

2 Q: 你有哥哥嗎？

A: 我________________。

Language Practice

A Who's this? INTERPERSONAL

In pairs, identify the IC characters below using 誰 *(shéi)*, e.g.:

Q: 這個人/男孩子是誰？ *Zhè ge rén/nán háizi shì shéi?*

A: 這個人/男孩子是王朋。 *Zhè ge rén/nán háizi shì Wáng Péng.*

1

2 

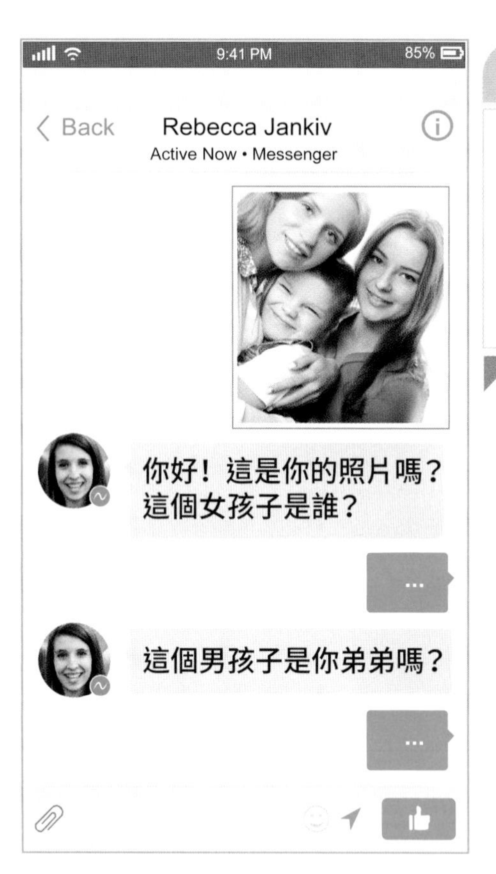

Chinese Chat

You've just shared a family photo with a friend on Facebook Messenger and she's asking you about it. How would you reply?

Characterize it!

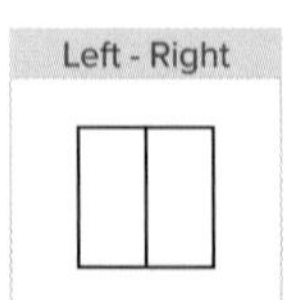

1  那

2  的

3  爸

4  高

5  他

Which of these characters are formed with the pattern on the left?

More characters

B Family matters

INTERPERSONAL

Form a question-and-answer about family members, inserting 有 *(yǒu)* or 沒有 *(méiyǒu)* in the ◇ and 嗎 *(ma)* where appropriate, e.g.:

高大哥 ◇ 女兒

Gāo dàgē ◇ *nǚ'ér*

Q: 高大哥有女兒嗎？

Gāo dàgē yǒu nǚ'ér ma?

A: 他沒有女兒。

Tā méiyǒu nǚ'ér.

1 高文中 ◇ 姐姐

Gāo Wénzhōng ◇ *jiějie*

2 高大哥 ◇ 兒子

Gāo dàgē ◇ *érzi*

3 你 ◇ 姐姐

nǐ ◇ *jiějie*

4 你 ◇ 弟弟

nǐ ◇ *dìdi*

5 你的老師 ◇ 女兒

nǐ de lǎoshī ◇ *nǚ'ér*

C Family portrait

INTERPERSONAL PRESENTATIONAL

In pairs, share and discuss family photos.

Q: 這是誰？

Zhè shì shéi?

A: 這是我________。

Zhè shì wǒ ______________.

Now present your family photo to the class and describe the people in the picture.

這是我爸爸，這是我媽媽，……

Zhè shì wǒ bàba, zhè shì wǒ māma, . . .

Discussing Family

Dialogue 2

Li You and Bai Ying'ai are chatting about their family members and what each of them does.

Audio

Video

白英愛，你家[a]有[5]幾口[b]人？

我家有六口人，我爸爸、我媽媽、一[c]個哥哥、兩[6]個妹妹和[d]我[e]。李友，你家有幾口人？

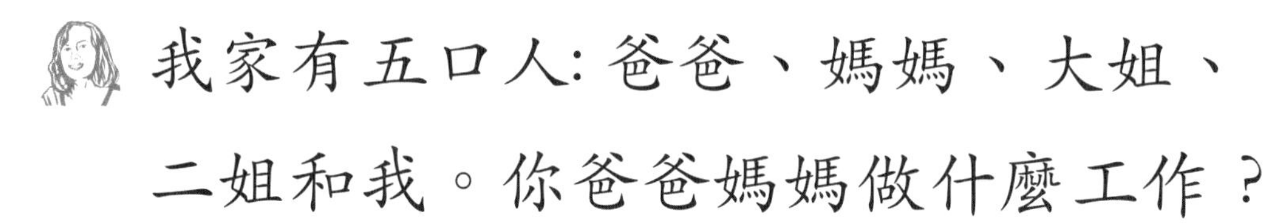

我家有五口人：爸爸、媽媽、大姐、二姐和我。你爸爸媽媽做什麼工作？

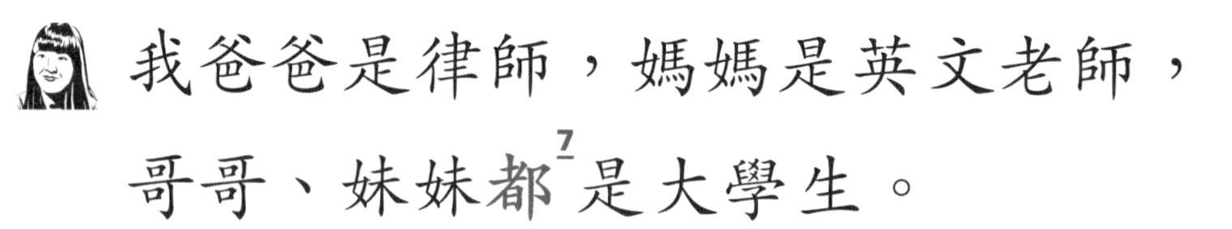

我爸爸是律師，媽媽是英文老師，哥哥、妹妹都[7]是大學生。

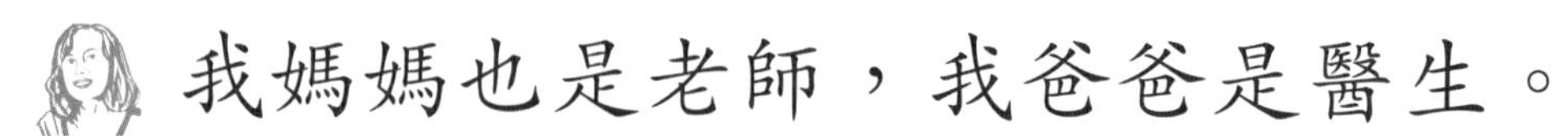

我媽媽也是老師，我爸爸是醫生。

Pinyin Dialogue

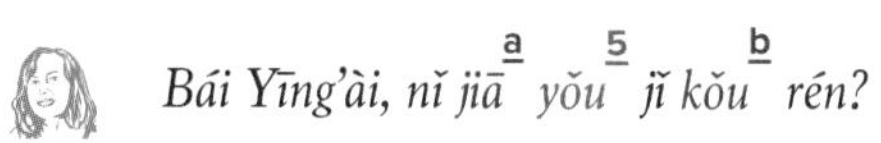

Bái Yīng'ài, nǐ jiā[a] yǒu[5] jǐ kǒu[b] rén?

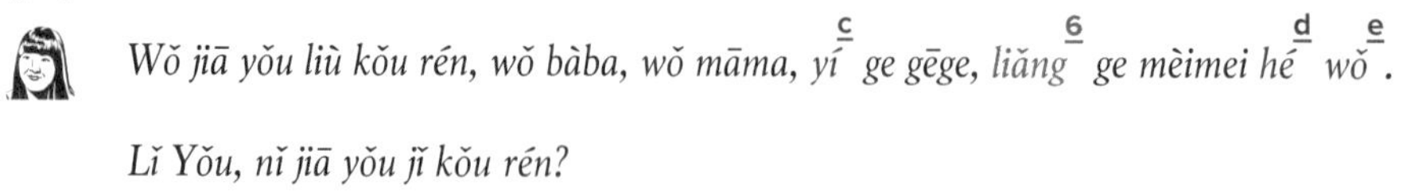

Wǒ jiā yǒu liù kǒu rén, wǒ bàba, wǒ māma, yí[c] ge gēge, liǎng[6] ge mèimei hé[d] wǒ[e].

Lǐ Yǒu, nǐ jiā yǒu jǐ kǒu rén?

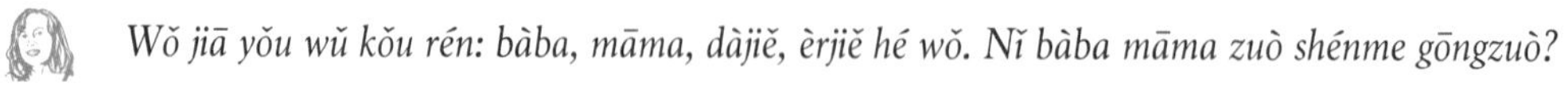

Wǒ jiā yǒu wǔ kǒu rén: bàba, māma, dàjiě, èrjiě hé wǒ. Nǐ bàba māma zuò shénme gōngzuò?

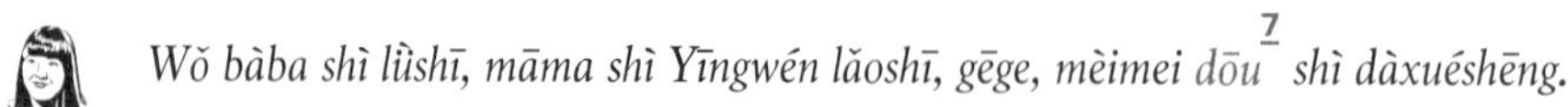

Wǒ bàba shì lǜshī, māma shì Yīngwén lǎoshī, gēge, mèimei dōu[7] shì dàxuéshēng.

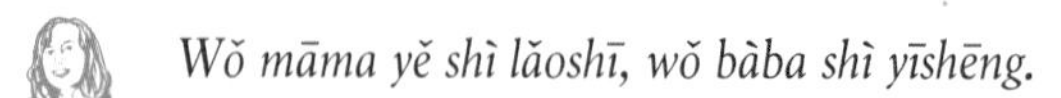

Wǒ māma yě shì lǎoshī, wǒ bàba shì yīshēng.

a 家 *(jiā)*

This word can refer to one's family or home. 我家有四口人 *(Wǒ jiā yǒu sì kǒu rén)* (There are four people in my family) can be used to describe the number of people in your family and 這是我家 *(Zhè shì wǒ jiā)* (This is my home) can be used to point out your house.

b 口 *(kǒu)*

This is the idiomatic measure word used in northern China for number of family members. In the south, people say 個 *(gè/ge)* instead.

c 一 *(yī/yí)*

The numeral 一 *(yī)* (one) is pronounced in the first tone *(yī)* in the following cases: when it stands alone; when it implies an ordinal number, e.g., 一樓 *(yī lóu)* (first floor); and when it comes at the end of a phrase. Otherwise, its tone changes according to the following rules:

- Before a fourth-tone word, it becomes second tone: 一個 *(yí gè)*.
- Before a first-, second-, or third-tone word, it is pronounced in the fourth tone, e.g., 一張 *(yì zhāng)* (a sheet), 一盤 *(yì pán)* (one plate), 一本 *(yì běn)* (one volume).

d 和 *(hé)*

Unlike "and," 和 *(hé)* cannot link two clauses or two sentences: 我爸爸是老師 *(Wǒ bàba shì lǎoshī)*，❌ 和我媽媽是醫生.

e 、

The pause mark or series comma, 、, is often used to link two, three, or even more parallel words or phrases, e.g., 爸爸、媽媽、兩個妹妹和我 *(bàba, māma, liǎng ge mèimei hé wǒ)* (dad, mom, two younger sisters, and I). [See Language Note A, Dialogue 1, Lesson 4.]

Vocabulary

Audio

Flashcards

No.	Word	Pinyin	Part of Speech	Definition
1	家	*jiā*	n	family, home
2	幾	*jǐ*	nu	how many, some, a few
3	口	*kǒu*	m	(measure word for number of family members)
4	哥哥	*gēge*	n	older brother
5	兩	*liǎng*	nu	two, a couple of [See Grammar 6.]
6	妹妹	*mèimei*	n	younger sister
7	和	*hé*	conj	and
8	大姐	*dàjiě*	n	eldest/oldest sister
9	二姐	*èrjiě*	n	second oldest sister

GET Real WITH CHINESE

Chinese custom is to present business cards with both hands, ensuring the writing faces the recipient. What type of professional gave out this card?

No.	Word	Pinyin	Part of Speech	Definition
10	做	*zuò*	v	to do
11	工作	*gōngzuò*	n/v	job; to work
12	律師	*lǜshī*	n	lawyer
13	英文	*Yīngwén*	n	the English language
14	都	*dōu*	adv	both, all [See Grammar 7.]
15	大學生	*dàxuéshēng*	n	college student
	大學	*dàxué*	n	university, college
16	醫生	*yīshēng*	n	doctor, physician
17	白英愛	*Bái Yīng'ài*	pn	(a personal name)

他/她做什麼工作？你呢?

Tā zuò shénme gōngzuò? Nǐ ne?

What does he/she do? How about you?

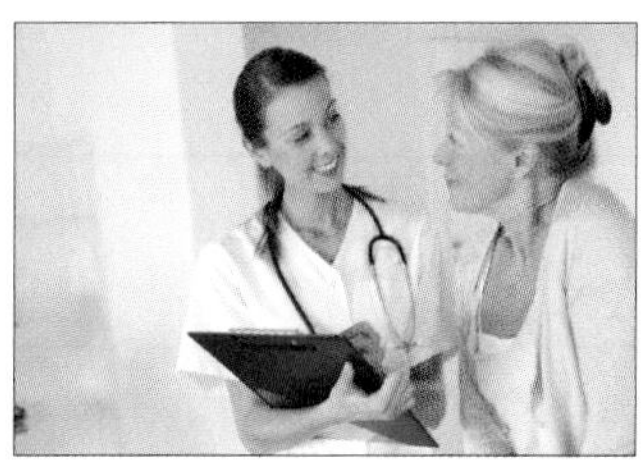

How About You?

他/她是______，我是______。

Tā shì ______ , wǒ shì______.

See index for corresponding vocabulary or research another term.

Grammar

5 Indicating existence using 有 (*yǒu*)

A 我家有五口人。

Wǒ jiā yǒu wǔ kǒu rén.

There are five people in my family.

B 小高家有兩個大學生。

Xiǎo Gāo jiā yǒu liǎng ge dàxuéshēng.

There are two college students in Little Gao's family.

More exercises

EXERCISES

Complete the question or the answer, inserting 有 where appropriate.

1 Q: 你家 ______________________ ?

A: 我家有五口人。

2 Q: 白英愛家有幾口人?

A: 白英愛家 __________________ 。

6 Using 二 (*èr*) and 兩 (*liǎng*)

二 (*èr*) and 兩 (*liǎng*) both mean "two," but they differ in usage. 兩 (*liǎng*) is used in front of common measure words to express a quantity, e.g., 兩個人 (*liǎng ge rén*) (two people). When counting numbers, however, 二 (*èr*) is used, e.g., 一, 二, 三, 四 (*yī, èr, sān, sì*) (one, two, three, four). In compound numerals, 二 (*èr*) is always used in the last two digits, e.g., 二十二 (*èrshí'èr*) (22) and 一百二十五 (*yìbǎi èrshíwǔ*) (125). But 二百二十二 (*èrbǎi èrshí'èr*) (222) can also be expressed as 兩百二十二 (*liǎngbǎi èrshí'èr*) (222).

7 The adverb 都 (dōu) (both, all)

The word 都 *(dōu)* (both, all) indicates inclusiveness. As it always occurs in front of a verb, it is classified as an adverb. Because it refers to things or people just mentioned, it must be used at the end of an enumeration.

A 王朋、李友和高文中都是學生。

Wáng Péng, Lǐ Yǒu hé Gāo Wénzhōng dōu shì xuésheng.

Wang Peng, Li You, and Gao Wenzhong are all students.

[都 *(dōu)* refers back to Wang Peng, Li You, and Gao Wenzhong, and therefore appears after them.]

B 王朋和李友都不是律師。

Wáng Péng hé Lǐ Yǒu dōu bú shì lǜshī.

Neither Wang Peng nor Li You is a lawyer.

C 王朋和白英愛都有妹妹。

Wáng Péng hé Bái Yīng'ài dōu yǒu mèimei.

Both Wang Peng and Bai Ying'ai have younger sisters.

D 高文中和李友都沒有弟弟。

Gāo Wénzhōng hé Lǐ Yǒu dōu méiyǒu dìdi.

Neither Gao Wenzhong nor Li You has any younger brothers.

沒 *(méi)* is always used to negate 有 *(yǒu)*. However, to say "not all of . . . have," we say 不都有 *(bù dōu yǒu)* rather than ✖ 沒都有. Whether the negative precedes or follows the word 都 *(dōu)* makes the difference between partial negation and complete negation. Compare the following examples. Note: 他們 *(tāmen)* (they).

E 他們不都是中國人。

Tāmen bù dōu shì Zhōngguó rén.

Not all of them are Chinese.

F 他們都不是中國人。

Tāmen dōu bú shì Zhōngguó rén.

None of them are Chinese.

G 他們不都有弟弟。

Tāmen bù dōu yǒu dìdi.

Not all of them have younger brothers.

H 他們都沒有弟弟。

Tāmen dōu méiyǒu dìdi.

None of them have any younger brothers.

More exercises

EXERCISES

Join these sentences to indicate inclusiveness, inserting 都 where appropriate. Use exercise 1 as an example.

1 白英愛的媽媽是老師。
李友的媽媽是老師。
→ 白英愛的媽媽和李友的媽媽都是老師。

2 白英愛沒有弟弟。
李友沒有弟弟。

3 我姐姐有兩個女兒。
小李的姐姐有兩個女兒。

Language Practice

E

INTERPERSONAL | **One big family?** | PRESENTATIONAL

Interview your classmates to find out how many family members they have and report back to the class. Use 有 *(yǒu)*, e.g.:

Q: 請問，你家有幾口人？

Qǐng wèn, nǐ jiā yǒu jǐ kǒu rén?

A: 我家有四口人。

Wǒ jiā yǒu sì kǒu rén.

F

All about the cast

Complete the following questions-and-answers by inserting 誰 *(shéi)* or another appropriate question pronoun, e.g.:

Q: 這是誰？

Zhè shì shéi?

A: 這是王朋。

Zhè shì Wáng Péng.

1 Q: ______有兒子？

______ *yǒu érzi?*

A: 高文中的大哥有兒子。

Gāo Wénzhōng de dàgē yǒu érzi.

2 Q: 李友家有______口人？

Lǐ Yǒu jiā yǒu ______ *kǒu rén?*

A: 李友家有五口人。

Lǐ Yǒu jiā yǒu wǔ kǒu rén.

3 Q: 白英愛有______個妹妹？

Bái Yīng'ài yǒu _______ ge mèimei?

A: 白英愛有兩個妹妹。

Bái Yīng'ài yǒu liǎng ge mèimei.

4 Q: 李友的爸爸做______工作？

Lǐ Yǒu de bàba zuò _______ gōngzuò?

A: 李友的爸爸是醫生。

Lǐ Yǒu de bàba shì yīshēng.

5 Q: 白英愛的媽媽做______工作？

Bái Yīng'ài de māma zuò _______ gōngzuò?

A: 白英愛的媽媽是英文老師。

Bái Yīng'ài de māma shì Yīngwén lǎoshī.

G World traveler

INTERPERSONAL

You're staying at a hostel in China. Using the images below, ask your international roommates where they're from and what they do.

你是______人嗎？

Nǐ shì _______ rén ma?

or

你做什麼工作？你是______嗎？

Nǐ zuò shénme gōngzuò? Nǐ shì_______ ma?

1 

2 

3  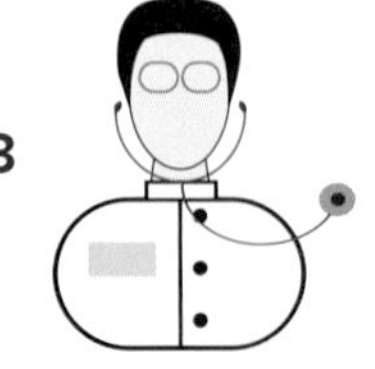

4  

5 

H Common denominator

Based on the information given, rephrase the sentences using 都 *(dōu)*, e.g.:

王朋是學生，李友也是學生。

Wáng Péng shì xuésheng, Lǐ Yǒu yě shì xuésheng.

王朋和李友都是學生。

Wáng Péng hé Lǐ Yǒu dōu shì xuésheng.

1 白英愛的媽媽是老師，李友的媽媽也是老師。

Bái Yīng'ài de māma shì lǎoshī, Lǐ Yǒu de māma yě shì lǎoshī.

____

2 李友有姐姐，高文中也有姐姐。

Lǐ Yǒu yǒu jiějie, Gāo Wénzhōng yě yǒu jiějie.

____

3 王朋不是紐約人，高文中也不是紐約人。

Wáng Péng bú shì Niǔyuē rén, Gāo Wénzhōng yě bú shì Niǔyuē rén.

____

4 王朋沒有哥哥，李友也沒有哥哥。

Wáng Péng méiyǒu gēge, Lǐ Yǒu yě méiyǒu gēge.

____

I To have or have not

PRESENTATIONAL

The following chart shows the similarities and differences among Wang Peng, Li You, Gao Wenzhong, and Bai Ying'ai. Based on the information given, make negative sentences using 都 *(dōu)* with 不 *(bù)* or 沒有 *(méiyǒu)* appropriately. Note: 他們 *(tāmen)* (they).

	律師 *lǜshī*	弟弟 *dìdi*	照片 *zhàopiàn*	姐姐 *jiějie*
	✗	✗	✓	✗
	✗	✗	✓	✗
	✗	✗	✓	✓
	✗	✗	✗	✗

J #1 fan

PRESENTATIONAL

Who is your favorite celebrity? As a true fan *(fěnsī)*, introduce him or her to your friends through a post on social media. Include biographical information such as name, nationality, and family details.

Characterize it!

What do the characters mean?

What is the common radical?

What does the radical mean?

How does the radical relate to the overall meaning of the characters?

More characters

1 

2 姐

3 

4 

5 

Pronunciation

Audio

Practice your pronunciation with the audio exercises below.

1 Initials:

1	*zhè*	*chè*	*shè*	*rè*
2	*zhǎo*	*chǎo*	*shǎo*	*rǎo*
3	*zhèn*	*chèn*	*shèn*	*rèn*
4	*zhāng*	*chāng*	*shāng*	*rāng*

2 The final "e":

1	*gē*	*dé*	*zhè*	*hē*
2	*kē*	*tè*	*chē*	*shé*
3	*zé*	*cè*	*sè*	*rè*

3 Compound finals:

1	*dōu*	*duō*	*tóu*	*tuó*
2	*duī*	*diū*	*shuǐ*	*xuě*
3	*shùn*	*xùn*	*jiū*	*zhuī*
4	*lüè*	*nüè*	*juè*	*què*

4 Tones:

1	*chénggōng*	5	*Chángjiāng*
2	*chángcháng*	6	*Chángchéng*
3	*rénkǒu*	7	*míngxiǎn*
4	*xuéxiào*	8	*chídào*

5 The neutral tone:

1	*māma*	5	*bàba*
2	*dìdi*	6	*gēge*
3	*jiějie*	7	*jǐ ge*
4	*mèimei*	8	*zhè ge*

Chinese Chat

Your friend just posted a photo of her family with a short description on Instagram.
What comment would you leave?

Instagram

andreacameron_86 20min

♥ 75 likes

andreacameron_86 這是我家人的照片。 我家有三口人：媽媽、姐姐和我。 我媽媽是醫生，姐姐是律師。 我是學生。 你家有幾口人？ 有照片嗎？

20 MINUTES AGO

Comment

CULTURAL LITERACY

文化
Continue to explore

Kinship terms

When expressing kinship terms, the Chinese customarily put male before female: 爸爸媽媽 *(bàba māma)* (dad and mom), 哥哥姐姐 *(gēge jiějie)* (older brothers and sisters), and 弟弟妹妹 *(dìdi mèimei)* (younger brothers and sisters). When pairing up kinship terms for the same gender, the one with seniority is mentioned first: 哥哥弟弟 *(gēge dìdi)* (older and younger brothers), 姐姐妹妹 *(jiějie mèimei)* (older and younger sisters).

Siblings are 兄弟姐妹 *(xiōng dì jiě mèi)*. To ask whether someone has any siblings, say 你有兄弟姐妹嗎? *(Nǐ yǒu xiōng dì jiě mèi ma?)* (Do you have any brothers or sisters?). Oldest siblings are called 大哥 *(dàgē)* (oldest brother) and 大姐 *(dàjiě)* (oldest sister); the youngest are 小弟 *(xiǎodì)* (youngest brother) and 小妹 *(xiǎomèi)* (youngest sister). The rest are ranked by numerals according to their birth order, e.g., 二姐 *(èrjiě)* (second oldest sister), 三弟 *(sāndì)* (third youngest brother). Younger siblings generally do not refer to their older brothers and sisters by name but use the appropriate kinship terms instead. Because of the one-child policy, however, many Chinese people have only cousins but no siblings.

Family structure

In traditional Chinese society, multiple generations often lived in the same house, thus the term 四代同堂 *(sì dài tóng táng)* (four generations under the same roof). It was common for the head of the household to live with his sons and daughters-in-law, grandchildren, and even his great-grandchildren. Nowadays, while some couples still live with the husband's parents, nuclear families living independently are more and more common. Due to family planning policies in China since the late 1970s, many Chinese people do not have any brothers or sisters. In 2015, the government abandoned the one-child policy and allowed every couple to have two children. The new policy came into effect on January 1, 2016.

COMPARE & CONTRAST

1 How does the family structure of traditional and modern China compare and contrast with that of your society or culture?

2 Below is a Chinese government poster. Look up 一樣 *(yíyàng)* in the Vocabulary Index. What does the headline 男孩女孩一樣好 *(Nánhái nǚhái yíyàng hǎo)* mean? What orientation is the government trying to change? Does the same orientation exist in your culture?

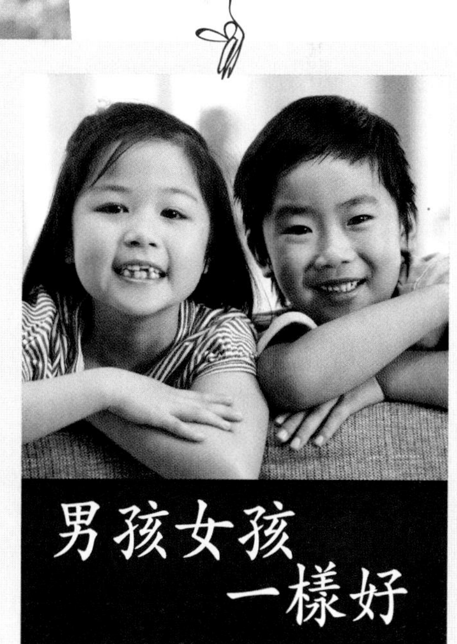

Lesson Wrap-Up

Make It Flow!

Rearrange the following sentences into a logical sequence. Then combine them into a coherent narrative. Remember to omit repetitive elements and substitute subjects with personal pronouns where appropriate. Don't forget to incorporate the adverb 都 (*dōu*).

_____白英愛的妹妹是大學生。

_____白英愛的哥哥是大學生。

__1__白英愛的爸爸是律師。

_____白英愛的媽媽是英文老師。

Role-Play

In groups, create your own "family," assigning roles to each person. Then, as a group, introduce yourselves to the class by stating your new names and family roles.

Family Photo

After you have introduced your new "family" to the class, take a family photo. Then, label the picture with everyone's Chinese name and family role and post it on social media.

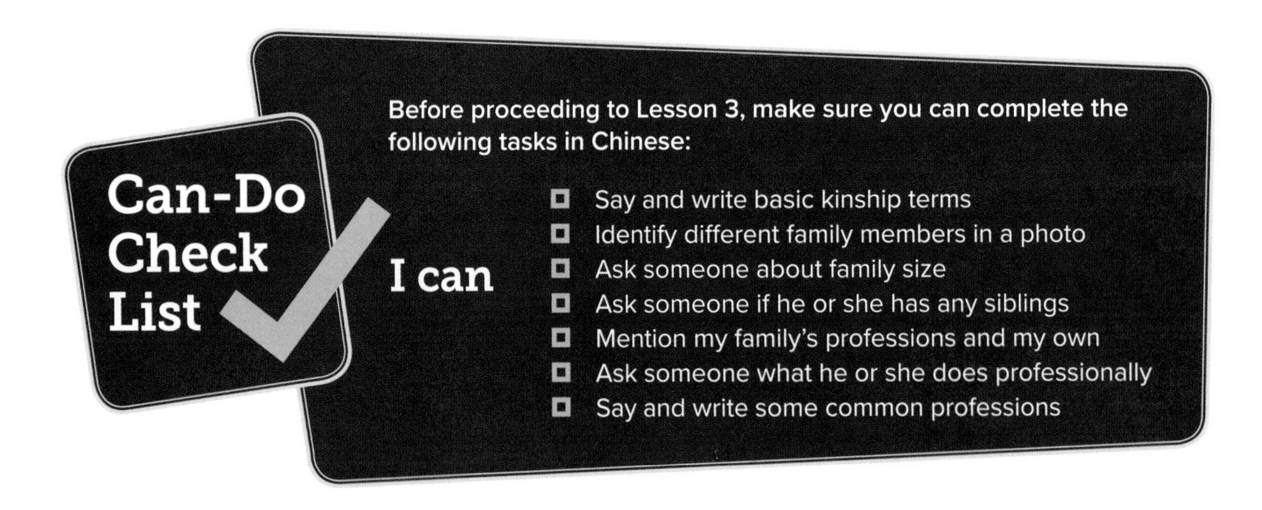

Lesson 3

第三課

Dì sān kè

時間

Shíjiān

TIME AND DATE

Learning Objectives

In this lesson, you will learn to:

- Discuss times and dates
- Talk about ages and birthdays
- Arrange a dinner date with someone

Relate & Get Ready

In your own culture/community:

- Do people write the month before the day or vice versa?
- Is it appropriate to ask someone's age and birthday?
- What do people typically do to celebrate their birthday?

Out for a Birthday Dinner

Dialogue 1

Gao Wenzhong is talking to Bai Ying'ai about a special day coming up.

Audio

Video

白英愛，九月十二[1][a]號[2]是星期幾[2]？

是星期四。

那天[b]是我的[3]生日。

是嗎？你今年多大[c]？

十八歲[d]。

我星期四請你吃飯[4]，怎麼樣？

太好了[e]！謝謝，謝謝[f]。

你喜歡吃中國菜還是[5]美國菜？

我是英國人，可是我喜歡吃中國菜。

好，我們吃中國菜。

星期四幾點？

七點半怎麼樣？

好，星期四晚上見。

再見！

 *Bái Yīng'ài, jiǔyuè shí'èr*[1a] *hào*[2] *shì xīngqījǐ*[2] *?*

 *Shì xīngqīsì.*

 *Nà tiān*[b] *shì wǒ de*[3] *shēngrì.*

 *Shì ma? Nǐ jīnnián duō dà*[c] *?*

 *Shíbā suì*[d] *.*

 *Wǒ xīngqīsì qǐng nǐ chī fàn*[4] *, zěnmeyàng?*

 *Tài hǎo le*[e] *! Xièxie, xièxie*[f] *.*

 *Nǐ xǐhuan chī Zhōngguó cài háishi*[5] *Měiguó cài?*

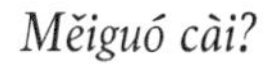

 *Wǒ shì Yīngguó rén, kěshì wǒ xǐhuan chī Zhōngguó cài.*

 *Hǎo, wǒmen chī Zhōngguó cài.*

 *Xīngqīsì jǐ diǎn?*

 *Qī diǎn bàn zěnmeyàng?*

 *Hǎo, xīngqīsì wǎnshang jiàn.*

 *Zàijiàn!*

a 時間 *(Shíjiān)*

Chinese time expressions proceed from the largest to the smallest unit, e.g., 二〇一九年八月十二日晚上七點 *(èr líng yī jiǔ nián bāyuè shí'èr rì wǎnshang qī diǎn)* (2019, August 12, 7:00 p.m.).

b 天 *(tiān)* and 年 *(nián)*

These nouns do not require a measure word because they function as measure words on their own.

c 你今年多大？

(Nǐ jīnnián duō dà?)

Say this to find out someone's age. If you're asking a child, use 你今年幾歲？ *(Nǐ jīnnián jǐ suì?)*. To ask an older person, use the polite forms 您多大年紀了？ *(Nín duō dà niánjì le?)* or 您多大歲數了？ *(Nín duō dà suìshù le?)*.

d 十八歲 *(shíbā suì)*

State your age by saying 我十八歲 *(wǒ shíbā suì)* (I'm eighteen years old). The verb 是 *(shì)* is usually not needed, and the word 歲 *(suì)* (years of age) can often be dropped. However, if the age is ten or under, the word 歲 *(suì)* cannot be omitted: ⊗ 我十 or ⊗ 我八. Note that it is incorrect to say, ⊗ 我十八年.

e 太…了 *(tài . . . le)*

When 太…了 *(tài . . . le)* is used in an exclamation (as in the case here), the stress usually falls on 太 *(tài)*, and it can typically be translated as "so" or "really."

f 謝謝 *(xièxie)*

To express gratitude, say 謝謝 *(xièxie)*, or 謝謝，謝謝 *(xièxie, xièxie)*, which is more polite and exuberant.

Vocabulary

Audio

Flashcards

No.	Word	Pinyin	Part of Speech	Definition
1	九月	*jiǔyuè*	n	September
2	月	*yuè*	n	month
3	十二	*shí'èr*	nu	twelve
4	號	*hào*	m	(measure word for position in a numerical series, day of the month)
5	星期	*xīngqī*	n	week
6	星期四	*xīngqīsì*	n	Thursday
7	天	*tiān*	n	day
8	生日	*shēngrì*	n	birthday
	生	*shēng*	v	to give birth to, to be born
	日	*rì*	n	day, sun
9	今年	*jīnnián*	t	this year
	年	*nián*	n	year
10	多	*duō*	adv	how many/much, to what extent
11	大	*dà*	adj	big, old
12	十八	*shíbā*	nu	eighteen
13	歲	*suì*	n	year (of age)
14	吃	*chī*	v	to eat
15	飯	*fàn*	n	meal, (cooked) rice
16	怎麼樣	*zěnmeyàng*	qpr	Is it OK? How is that? How does that sound?
17	太⋯了	*tài . . . le*		too, extremely
18	謝謝	*xièxie*	v	to thank

No.	Word	Pinyin	Part of Speech	Definition
19	喜歡	*xǐhuan*	v	to like
20	菜	*cài*	n	dish, cuisine
21	還是	*háishi*	conj	or [See Grammar 6.]
22	可是	*kěshì*	conj	but
23	我們	*wǒmen*	pr	we, us
24	點	*diǎn*	m	o'clock (lit. dot, point, thus "points on the clock")
25	半	*bàn*	nu	half, half an hour
26	晚上	*wǎnshang*	t	evening, night
27	見	*jiàn*	v	to see
28	再見	*zàijiàn*	v	goodbye, see you again
	再	*zài*	adv	again
29	英國	*Yīngguó*	pn	Britain

How About You?

你喜歡吃什麼菜？

Nǐ xǐhuan chī shénme cài?

What do you like to eat?

我喜歡吃＿＿＿＿＿＿。

Wǒ xǐhuan chī __________.

See index for vocabulary corresponding to national cuisine or research another term.

Grammar

1 Numbers up to 100

The characters below serve as the basis for the Chinese numeration system.

〇 *(líng)* zero	一 *(yī)* one	二 *(èr)* two	三 *(sān)* three	四 *(sì)* four	五 *(wǔ)* five
六 *(liù)* six	七 *(qī)* seven	八 *(bā)* eight	九 *(jiǔ)* nine	十 *(shí)* ten	

All other double-digit numbers can be formed using numbers from 一 *(yī)* to 十 *(shí)*, following the patterns below.

Pattern	Application	Example
十 *(shí)* + Single Digit	11, 12–18, 19	十五 *(shíwǔ)* (15)
Single Digit + 十 *(shí)*	20, 30–80, 90	四十 *(sìshí)* (40)
Single Digit + 十 *(shí)* + Single Digit	21, 22–98, 99	八十三 *(bāshísān)* (83)

When counting by hundreds, the pattern is single digit + 百 *(bǎi)* (hundred), e.g.: 一百 *(yìbǎi)* (one hundred), 二百/兩百 *(èrbǎi/liǎngbǎi)* (two hundred).

More exercises

EXERCISES

Say the following numbers in Chinese.

9 18 27 36 90 100

2 Dates

Days of the week

星期幾 *(xīngqījǐ)* is the standard way to ask the day of the week. To answer the question, simply replace the word 幾 *(jǐ)* (how many) with the number indicating the day of the week. The following table shows varying degrees of formality. Note that 週 *(zhōu)* (week) is formal, 星期 *(xīngqī)* (week) is standard, and 禮拜 *(lǐbài)* (week) is informal.

ENGLISH	CHINESE		
	Standard	Informal[a]	Formal
Monday	星期一 (xīngqīyī)	禮拜一 (lǐbàiyī)	週一 (zhōuyī)
Tuesday	星期二 (xīngqī'èr)	禮拜二 (lǐbài'èr)	週二 (zhōu'èr)
Wednesday	星期三 (xīngqīsān)	禮拜三 (lǐbàisān)	週三 (zhōusān)
Thursday	星期四 (xīngqīsì)	禮拜四 (lǐbàisì)	週四 (zhōusì)
Friday	星期五 (xīngqīwǔ)	禮拜五 (lǐbàiwǔ)	週五 (zhōuwǔ)
Saturday	星期六 (xīngqīliù)	禮拜六 (lǐbàiliù)	週六 (zhōuliù)
Sunday	星期日 (xīngqīrì) or 星期天[b] (xīngqītiān)	禮拜日 (lǐbàirì) or 禮拜天 (lǐbàitiān)	週日 (zhōurì)
Weekend			週末[c] (zhōumò)

[a]The expression 禮拜 (lǐbài) is generally used in spoken Chinese and is more colloquial than 星期 (xīngqī).
[b]星期日 (xīngqīrì) is used more in written Chinese, whereas 星期天 (xīngqītiān) is used more in spoken Chinese.
[c]週末 (zhōumò) is used in standard, informal, and formal Chinese. [See Lesson 4.]

Months

English	Chinese	Pinyin
January	一月	yīyuè
February	二月	èryuè
March	三月	sānyuè
April	四月	sìyuè
May	五月	wǔyuè
June	六月	liùyuè
July	七月	qīyuè
August	八月	bāyuè
September	九月	jiǔyuè
October	十月	shíyuè
November	十一月	shíyīyuè
December	十二月	shí'èryuè

Dates

In spoken Chinese, 號 *(hào)* (number) is used to refer to dates. However, in written Chinese, 日 *(rì)* (day) is used instead.

A

二月五號 (spoken)

èryuè wǔ hào

February 5

二月五日 (written)

èryuè wǔ rì

February 5

Year

The word 年 *(nián)* (year) always follows the number referring to a specific year. Years are read one digit at a time.

B

一七八六年

yī qī bā liù nián

1786

二〇三九年

èr líng sān jiǔ nián

2039

Word order for dates

To specify a date in Chinese, observe the following order.

C

二〇一九年七月二十六號/日星期五

èr líng yī jiǔ nián qīyuè èrshíliù hào/rì, xīngqīwǔ

Friday, July 26, 2019

EXERCISES

Say the following dates in Chinese.

1 Saturday, October 1, 1949

2 Friday, September 9, 1988

3 Tuesday, May 12, 2020

3

Time

The terms used to tell the time are: 點 *(diǎn)*/點鐘 *(diǎnzhōng)* (o'clock), 半 *(bàn)* (half hour), 刻 *(kè)* (quarter hour), and 分 *(fēn)* (minute).

Hour

A

兩點（鐘）

liǎng diǎn (zhōng)

2:00

十一點（鐘）

shíyī diǎn (zhōng)

11:00

鐘 *(zhōng)* can be omitted from 點鐘 *(diǎnzhōng)*. ⊗ 二點（鐘） is not used.

Minute

B

十二點四十（分）

shí'èr diǎn sìshí (fēn)

12:40

五點二十（分）

wǔ diǎn èrshí (fēn)

5:20

兩點〇五（分）

liǎng diǎn líng wǔ (fēn)

2:05

八點十分

bā diǎn shí fēn

8:10

When telling the time, 〇 *(líng)* (zero) is usually added before a single-digit number and 分 *(fēn)* (minute), e.g., 兩點〇五分 *(liǎng diǎn líng wǔ fēn)* (2:05). 分 *(fēn)* can be omitted from the end of the expression if the number for the minutes appears in two syllables. Another way of looking at this is that 分 *(fēn)* has to be added if the number for the minutes appears in one syllable.

C

一點四十

yī diǎn sìshí

1:40

一點十分

yī diǎn shí fēn

1:10

[⊗ 一點十]

兩點〇五

liǎng diǎn líng wǔ

2:05

兩點五分

liǎng diǎn wǔ fēn

2:05

[⊗ 兩點五]

Quarter hour

D

兩點一刻
liǎng diǎn yí kè
2:15

十一點三刻
shíyī diǎn sān kè
11:45

[⊗ 兩刻 (two quarters) is not used]

Half hour

E

兩點半
liǎng diǎn bàn
2:30

十二點半
shí'èr diǎn bàn
12:30

Evening

F

晚上七點（鐘）
wǎnshang qī diǎn (zhōng)
7:00 p.m.

晚上八點〇五（分）
wǎnshang bā diǎn líng wǔ (fēn)
8:05 p.m.

晚上九點一刻
wǎnshang jiǔ diǎn yí kè
9:15 p.m.

晚上十點半
wǎnshang shí diǎn bàn
10:30 p.m.

Observe the temporal progression from general to specific and from largest to smallest unit.

More exercises

EXERCISES

Say the following times in Chinese.

1 3:45
2 4:00
3 9:09 p.m.

4 Pronouns as modifiers and the particle 的 *(de)* (II)

When personal pronouns such as 我 *(wǒ)* (I), 我們 *(wǒmen)* (we), 你 *(nǐ)* (you), 他 *(tā)* (he), and 她 *(tā)* (she) are followed by a term indicating a close personal relationship, the particle 的 *(de)* can be omitted, e.g., 我媽媽 *(wǒ māma)* (my mother), 你弟弟 *(nǐ dìdi)* (your younger brother), 我們家 *(wǒmen jiā)* (our family). Otherwise 的 *(de)* is generally required, e.g., 他的醫生 *(tā de yīshēng)* (his doctor), 我的照片 *(wǒ de zhàopiàn)* (my photo).

5 The sentence structure of 我請你吃飯 *(wǒ qǐng nǐ chī fàn)*

In the sentence 我請你吃飯 *(wǒ qǐng nǐ chī fàn)* (I will treat you to dinner), 你 *(nǐ)* (you) is the object of the verb 請 *(qǐng)* (to treat) as well as the subject of the second verb, 吃 *(chī)* (to eat).

A 明天李先生請你吃中國菜。

Míngtiān Lǐ xiānsheng qǐng nǐ chī Zhōngguó cài.

Mr. Li is inviting you to have Chinese food tomorrow.

B 今天晚上我請你和你妹妹吃美國菜，怎麼樣？

Jīntiān wǎnshang wǒ qǐng nǐ hé nǐ mèimei chī Měiguó cài, zěnmeyàng?

I'll treat you and your younger sister to American food tonight. How about it?

EXERCISES

Rearrange the words to form a question, and then answer it.

More exercises

1 誰　七點半　白英愛　吃飯　請　星期四

2 怎麼樣　吃飯　星期五　請　你　我

6 Alternative questions

The structure (是)…還是… *([shì] . . . háishi . . .)* (. . . or . . .) is used to form an alternative question. If there is another verb used in the predicate, the first 是 *(shì)* (to be) can often be omitted.

A 你哥哥是老師還是學生？

Nǐ gēge shì lǎoshī háishi xuésheng?

Is your older brother a teacher or a student?

B Q: 他（是）喜歡吃中國菜還是喜歡吃美國菜？

Tā (shì) xǐhuan chī Zhōngguó cài háishi xǐhuan chī Měiguó cài?

Does he like to eat Chinese or American food?

A: 中國菜、美國菜他都喜歡（吃）。

Zhōngguó cài, Měiguó cài tā dōu xǐhuan (chī).

He likes both Chinese food and American food.

C 你是中國人還是美國人？

Nǐ shì Zhōngguó rén háishi Měiguó rén?

Are you Chinese or American?

D Q: 他（是）姓高還是姓王？

Tā (shì) xìng Gāo háishi xìng Wáng?

Is his family name Gao or Wang?

A: 他不姓高，也不姓王。他姓李。

Tā bú xìng Gāo, yě bú xìng Wáng. Tā xìng Lǐ.

His family name is not Gao or Wang. His family name is Li.

More exercises

EXERCISES

In pairs, ask and answer these alternative questions.

1 你是中國人還是美國人？

2 李友有姐姐還是有妹妹？

Language Practice

A March madness

INTERPERSONAL

三月

日	一	二	三	四	五	六
				1 十二	2 十三	3 十四
4 十五	5 十六	6 驚蟄	7 十八	8 十九	9 二十	10 廿一
11 廿二	12 廿三	13 廿四	14 廿五	15 廿六	16 廿七	17 廿八
18 廿九	19 二月	20 初二	21 春分	22 初四	23 初五	24 初六
25 初七	26 初八	27 初九	28 初十	29 十一	30 十二	31 十三

In pairs, form a question-and-answer about dates based on the calendar above, e.g.:

三月二十一號

sānyuè èrshíyī hào

Q: 三月二十一號（是）星期幾？
Sānyuè èrshíyī hào (shì) xīngqījǐ?

A: 三月二十一號（是）星期三。
Sānyuè èrshíyī hào (shì) xīngqīsān.

1 三月十八號 *sānyuè shíbā hào*

2 三月二十號 *sānyuè èrshí hào*

3 三月二十三號 *sānyuè èrshísān hào*

4 三月二十四號 *sānyuè èrshísì hào*

B See you then

INTERPERSONAL

Based on the visual clues given, ask your partner what time you will meet, e.g.:

7:30 Q: 我們幾點見？
Wǒmen jǐ diǎn jiàn?

A: 我們七點半見。
Wǒmen qī diǎn bàn jiàn.

1

2 

3 

4 

C When's your birthday?

INTERPERSONAL

Find out when people's birthdays are, e.g.:

Q: 高文中的生日（是）幾月幾號？
Gāo Wénzhōng de shēngrì (shì) jǐ yuè jǐ hào?

A: 高文中的生日（是）九月十二號。
Gāo Wénzhōng de shēngrì (shì) jiǔyuè shí'èr hào.

1 你
nǐ

2 你爸爸
nǐ bàba

3 你媽媽
nǐ māma

4 你哥哥/姐姐/弟弟/妹妹
nǐ gēge/jiějie/dìdi/mèimei

5 你們（的）老師
nǐmen (de) lǎoshī

D Which is it? INTERPERSONAL

In pairs, form a question-and-answer by inserting 還是 *(háishi)* in the ◇, e.g.:

高大哥有兒子◇女兒

Gāo dàgē yǒu érzi ◇ nǚ'ér

Q: 高大哥有兒子還是有女兒？ *Gāo dàgē yǒu érzi háishi yǒu nǚ'ér?*

A: 高大哥有兒子。 *Gāo dàgē yǒu érzi.*

1 王朋是學生◇老師 *Wáng Péng shì xuésheng ◇ lǎoshī*

2 高文中今年十八歲◇十九歲 *Gāo Wénzhōng jīnnián shíbā suì ◇ shíjiǔ suì*

3 白英愛的爸爸是醫生◇律師 *Bái Yīng'ài de bàba shì yīshēng ◇ lǜshī*

4 李友是美國人◇英國人 *Lǐ Yǒu shì Měiguó rén ◇ Yīngguó rén*

5 你喜歡星期五◇星期六 *Nǐ xǐhuan xīngqīwǔ ◇ xīngqīliù*

6 你喜歡吃美國菜◇中國菜 *Nǐ xǐhuan chī Měiguó cài ◇ Zhōngguó cài*

E Form a birthday dragon INTERPERSONAL

Mobilize the class to ask each other's birthday and form a line. Students whose birthdays are earlier in the year will line up before people whose birthdays are later. After the line is formed, the teacher will ask the first student: 你的生日（是）幾月幾號？ *(Nǐ de shēngrì [shì] jǐ yuè jǐ hào?)*. After answering the question, the first student will ask the second student the same question, the second student will answer and ask the third, and so on. Then sing the "Happy Birthday" song in Chinese to the student with the most recent birthday:

祝你生日快樂 *zhù nǐ shēngrì kuàilè*
祝你生日快樂 *zhù nǐ shēngrì kuàilè*
祝你生日快樂 *zhù nǐ shēngrì kuàilè*
祝你生日快樂 *zhù nǐ shēngrì kuàilè*

F INTERPERSONAL

D.O.B.

PRESENTATIONAL

Share your and your family's birthdays with a partner or the class. Your teacher will then ask questions about the information reported.

Chris

我的生日（是）______月______號，
我爸爸的生日（是）______月______號，
……

Wǒ de shēngrì (shì)______yuè______hào,

wǒ bàba de shēngrì (shì)______yuè______hào,

…

Teacher

Chris 的生日（是）幾月幾號？
Chris 爸爸的生日（是）幾月幾號？

Chris *de shēngrì (shì) jǐ yuè jǐ hào?* Chris *bàba de shēngrì (shì) jǐ yuè jǐ hào?*

G

Let's eat!

INTERPERSONAL

In pairs, ask and answer the following questions about food preferences.

Q: 你喜歡吃什麼菜？
英國菜還是美國菜？
Nǐ xǐhuan chī shénme cài?
Yīngguó cài háishi Měiguó cài?

A: 我喜歡吃______菜。
Wǒ xǐhuan chī ______cài.

Q: 你喜歡吃______菜嗎？
Nǐ xǐhuan chī ______cài ma?

A: 我也喜歡吃/我不喜歡吃______菜。
Wǒ yě xǐhuan chī/Wǒ bù xǐhuan chī ______cài.

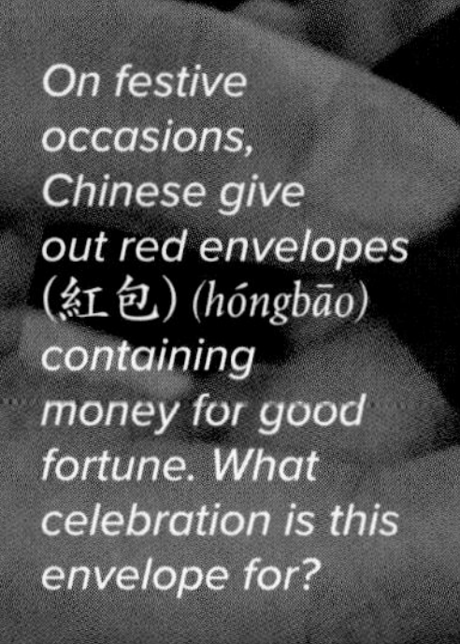

On festive occasions, Chinese give out red envelopes (紅包) (hóngbāo) containing money for good fortune. What celebration is this envelope for?

GET Real WITH CHINESE

Characterize it!

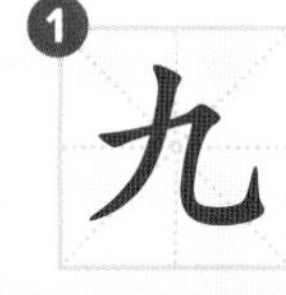

1 九 2 星 3 多 4 日 5 歲

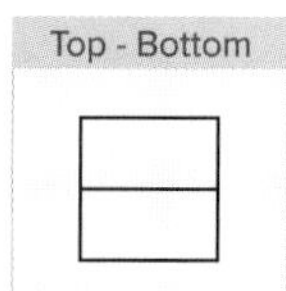

Top - Bottom

Which of these characters are formed with the pattern on the right?

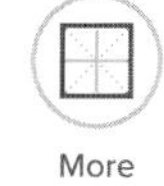

More characters

Chinese Chat

You're discussing your upcoming birthday on WeChat with a friend. How would you reply to her question?

Dinner Invitation

Dialogue 2

Bai Ying'ai asks Wang Peng about his plans for tomorrow.

Audio

Video

 白英愛，現在幾點？

 五點三刻。

 我六點一刻有事兒。

 你今天很忙[a]，明天忙不忙[6]？

 我今天很忙，可是明天不忙。
有事兒嗎？

 明天我請你吃晚飯，怎麼樣？

 你為什麼請我吃飯？

 因為明天是高文中的生日。

 是嗎？好。還[7]請誰？

 還請我的同學李友。

 那太好了，我認識李友，
她也是我的朋友。明天幾點？

 明天晚上七點半。

 好，明天七點半見。

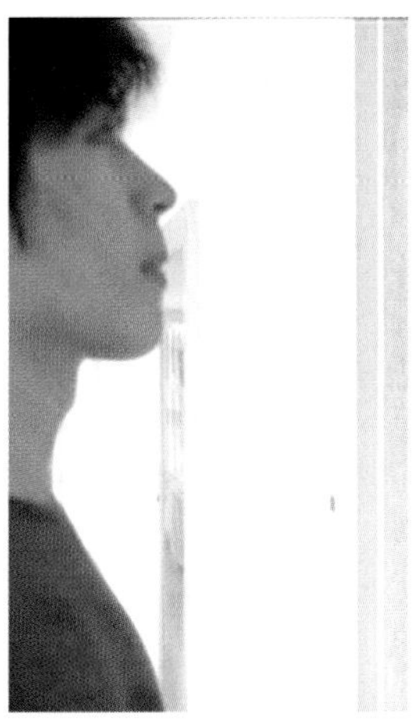

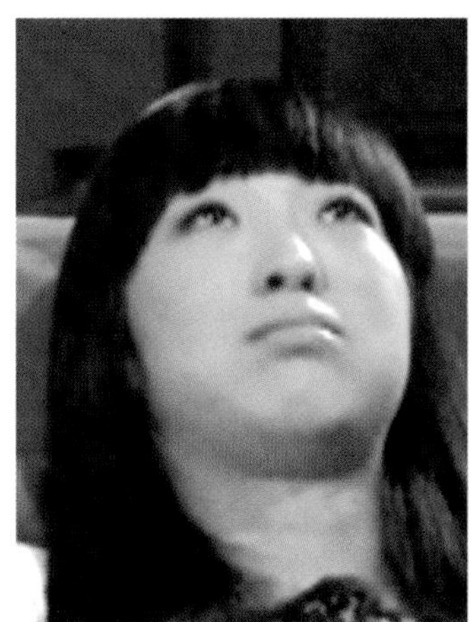

 *Bái Yīng'ài, xiànzài jǐ diǎn?*

 *Wǔ diǎn sān kè.*

 *Wǒ liù diǎn yí kè yǒu shìr.*

 *Nǐ jīntiān hěn máng*[a]*, míngtiān máng bu máng*[6]*?*

 *Wǒ jīntiān hěn máng, kěshì míngtiān bù máng. Yǒu shìr ma?*

 *Míngtian wǒ qǐng nǐ chī wǎnfàn, zěnmeyàng?*

 *Nǐ wèishénme qǐng wǒ chī fàn?*

 *Yīnwèi míngtiān shì Gāo Wénzhōng de shēngrì.*

 *Shì ma? IIǎo, hái*[7] *qǐng shéi?*

 *Hái qǐng wǒ de tóngxué Lǐ Yǒu.*

 *Nà tài hǎo le! Wǒ rènshi Lǐ Yǒu, tā yě shì wǒ de péngyou. Míngtiān jǐ diǎn?*

 *Míngtiān wǎnshang qī diǎn bàn.*

 *Hǎo, míngtiān qī diǎn bàn jiàn.*

Language Note

a 很 *(hěn)*

When an adjective functions as a predicate, it is usually preceded by adverbial modifiers such as 很 *(hěn)* (very). [See Grammar 2, Lesson 5.]

Vocabulary

Audio

Flashcards

No.	Word	Pinyin	Part of Speech	Definition
1	現在	*xiànzài*	t	now
2	刻	*kè*	m	quarter (of an hour)
3	事（兒）	*shì(r)*	n	matter, affair, event
4	今天	*jīntiān*	t	today
5	很	*hěn*	adv	very
6	忙	*máng*	adj	busy
7	明天	*míngtiān*	t	tomorrow
8	晚飯	*wǎnfàn*	n	dinner, supper
9	為什麼	*wèishénme*	qpr	why
	為	*wèi*	prep	for
10	因為	*yīnwèi*	conj	because
11	還	*hái*	adv	also, too, as well [See Grammar 8.]
12	同學	*tóngxué*	n	classmate
13	認識	*rènshi*	v	to be acquainted with, to recognize
14	朋友	*péngyou*	n	friend

How About You?

你的生日是幾月幾號？

Nǐ de shēngrì shì jǐ yuè jǐ hào?

When is your birthday?

我的生日是＿＿＿月＿＿＿號。

Wǒ de shēngrì shì＿＿＿yuè＿＿＿hào.

See Grammar 1 and 2 for vocabulary corresponding to dates.

Grammar

7 Affirmative + negative (A-not-A) questions (I)

Besides adding the question particle 嗎 *(ma)* to a declarative sentence, another common way of forming a question is to repeat the verb or adjective in its affirmative and negative form.

A Q: 你今天忙不忙？

Nǐ jīntiān máng bu máng?

Are you busy today?

A: 我今天很忙。

Wǒ jīntiān hěn máng.

I am very busy today.

B Q: 你媽媽喜歡不喜歡吃中國菜？

Nǐ māma xǐhuan bu xǐhuan chī Zhōngguó cài?

Does your mother like to eat Chinese food or not?

A: 我媽媽不喜歡吃中國菜。

Wǒ māma bù xǐhuan chī Zhōngguó cài.

My mother doesn't like to eat Chinese food.

C Q: 請問，王律師今天有沒有事兒？

Qǐng wèn, Wáng lǜshī jīntiān yǒu méi yǒu shìr?

Excuse me, is Lawyer Wang free today or not?

A: 王律師今天沒有事兒。

Wáng lǜshī jīntiān méi yǒu shìr.

Lawyer Wang is free today.

EXERCISES

Change the …嗎 questions below into A-not-A questions. Use exercise 1 as an example.

More exercises

1 王朋是北京人嗎？→ 王朋是不是北京人？

2 高文中的哥哥有兒子嗎？

3 白英愛的爸爸是律師嗎？

8 The adverb 還 *(hái)* (also, too, as well)

As an adverb, 還 *(hái)* (also, too, as well) indicates that the action or situation denoted by the verb involves someone or something else.

A 白英愛請高文中和王朋，還請李友。

Bái Yīng'ài qǐng Gāo Wénzhōng hé Wáng Péng, hái qǐng Lǐ Yǒu.

Bai Ying'ai is inviting Gao Wenzhong and Wang Peng, and Li You, too.

B 王朋喜歡吃中國菜，還喜歡吃美國菜。

Wáng Péng xǐhuan chī Zhōngguó cài, hái xǐhuan chī Měiguó cài.

Wang Peng likes to eat Chinese food, and American food, too.

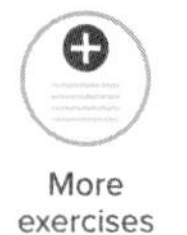
More exercises

EXERCISES

Add more information to the sentences by inserting 還 where appropriate. Use exercise 1 as an example.

1 高文中有姐姐。 哥哥

→ 高文中有姐姐，還有哥哥。

2 白英愛明天請高文中吃飯。 王朋

3 王朋認識白英愛。 李友

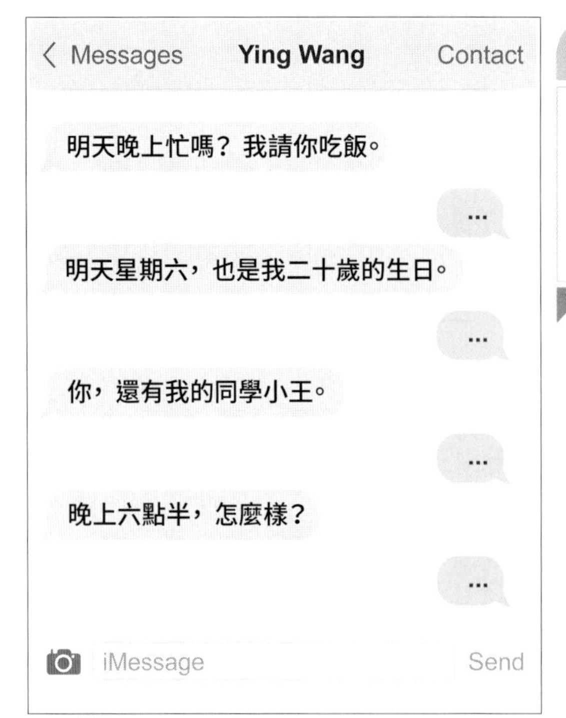

Chinese Chat

You and a friend are using iMessage to set up a dinner date. How would you respond to finalize your plans?

Language Practice

H Just double-checking

INTERPERSONAL

In pairs, take turns rearranging the declarative sentence into an A-not-A question for your partner to answer, e.g.:

王朋是◇北京人 — *Wáng Péng shì ◇ Běijīng rén*

Q: 王朋是不是北京人？ — *Wáng Péng shì bu shì Běijīng rén?*

A: 王朋是北京人。 — *Wáng Péng shì Běijīng rén.*

1 今天是◇星期五 — *jīntiān shì ◇ xīngqīwǔ*

---

2 高大哥有◇女兒 — *Gāo dàgē yǒu ◇ nǚ'ér*

---

3 你喜歡◇高文中 — *nǐ xǐhuan ◇ Gāo Wénzhōng*

---

4 王朋認識◇白英愛 — *Wáng Péng rènshi ◇ Bái Yīng'ài*

---

5 我們的老師忙◇ — *wǒmen de lǎoshī máng ◇*

---

6 美國大◇ — *Měiguó dà ◇*

I This and that

INTERPERSONAL

In pairs, ask and answer the following questions. Use 還 *(hái)*, e.g.:

Q: 白英愛喜歡吃什麼菜？

Bái Yīng'ài xǐhuan chī shénme cài?

A: 白英愛喜歡吃美國菜，還喜歡吃中國菜。

Bái Yīng'ài xǐhuan chī Měiguó cài, hái xǐhuan chī Zhōngguó cài.

1 Q: 白英愛請誰吃飯？

Bái Yīng'ài qǐng shéi chī fàn?

A: ______________________________

2 Q: 李友認識誰？

Lǐ Yǒu rènshi shéi?

A: ______________________________

J When are you free?

INTERPERSONAL PRESENTATIONAL

Find out when your partner is free this week, e.g.:

Q: 你星期一忙不忙？ *Nǐ xīngqīyī máng bu máng?*

A: 我星期一很忙/不忙。 *Wǒ xīngqīyī hěn máng/bù máng.*

How about Tuesday?

Q: 星期二呢？你忙不忙？ *Xīngqī'èr ne? Nǐ máng bu máng?*

A: …… ...

Go through the days of the week. Then report to the class when your partner is free.

Emma 星期一、__________、__________……很忙，星期二、__________、__________……不忙。

Emma *xīngqīyī, ________, ________ . . . hěn máng, xīngqī'èr, ________, ________ . . . bù máng.*

K Making dinner plans

INTERPERSONAL

Ask your friend out to dinner.

我星期＿＿＿請你吃晚飯，怎麼樣？

Wǒ xīngqī____qǐng nǐ chī wǎnfàn, zěnmeyàng?

Your friend is busy that day, and suggests an alternative time:

星期＿＿＿，我很忙。

Xīngqī____, wǒ hěn máng.

星期＿＿＿，怎麼樣？

Xīngqī____, zěnmeyàng?

Your response:

____

Your friend wants to find out who else will be there, and asks:

你還請誰？

Nǐ hái qǐng shéi?

Your answer:

我還請＿＿＿＿＿＿＿＿＿＿＿＿＿＿＿＿＿＿＿。

Wǒ hái qǐng ________________________________.

Chinese Chat

Li You just posted this on Twitter during an evening out with friends. How do you think she is feeling?

Li You @liyou_88 • Aug 10

今天是我的生日，朋友請我吃飯！

25 28

Pronunciation

Practice your pronunciation with the audio exercises below.

1 The initial r:

1. *shēngrì*
2. *rìjì*
3. *rèqíng*
4. *rénmín*
5. *réngrán*
6. *ránhòu*
7. *ruìlì*
8. *ràngbù*

2 Finals:

1	*ie*	*jiè*	*xiě*	*qié*	*tiě*
2	*ue*	*jué*	*xué*	*quē*	*qiē*
3	*uo*	*duō*	*tuō*	*zuò*	*cuò*
4	*ou*	*dōu*	*tóu*	*zǒu*	*còu*
5	*u*	*zhū*	*chū*	*zū*	*cū*

3 Two-syllable words:

1. *dāndāng*
2. *shōuhuò*
3. *qūchú*
4. *yúnwù*
5. *jiǎozhà*
6. *chūnqiū*
7. *juébié*
8. *kuìjiù*

4 The neutral tone:

1. *zhè ge*
2. *nà ge*
3. *wǒmen*
4. *nǐmen*
5. *wǎnshang*
6. *xièxie*
7. *xǐhuan*
8. *rènshi*

5 Tone sandhi:

[See D.2, Basics]

1. *zhǎnlǎn*
2. *lǚguǎn*
3. *yǔsǎn*
4. *qǔshě*
5. *shǒufǎ*
6. *yǔnxǔ*
7. *xuǎnjǔ*
8. *guǎngchǎng*

GET Real WITH CHINESE

In addition to widely circulated papers like China's official People's Daily, vibrant local media serve Chinese communities worldwide. When was this issue of The China Press Weekly published?

Characterize it!

What do the characters mean?

What is the common radical?

What does the radical mean?

How does the radical relate to the overall meaning of the characters?

1 

2 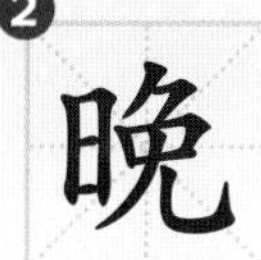

3 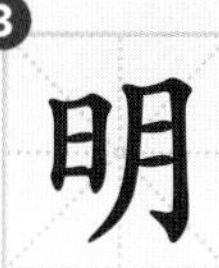

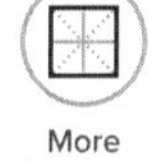

More characters

Chinese Chat

You receive a group message from Bai Ying'ai about dinner plans on WeChat（微信）(*Wēixìn*), one of the most popular messaging apps in China. What would you need to ask in order to add the event to your calendar?

9:41 PM 85%

Cancel	New Event	Add

高文中生日

Dumpling Cafe

All-day

Starts — Date / Time

Ends — Time

文化

Continue to explore

Calendars

When you open a Chinese calendar, you will most likely see two different dates for any given day of the year, one according to the traditional lunar calendar and the other according to the international solar calendar. Typically, the lunar calendar date lags about one month behind its corresponding date in the solar calendar. In most years, the Lunar New Year falls in late January or early February.

Age

The traditional Chinese manner of counting age, which is still in use among many (mainly older) people on non-official occasions, is based on the number of calendar years one has lived in, rather than the length of time in actual years that one has lived. For example, a child born in January 2016 is said to have turned two in January 2017, since the child has by then lived during two calendar years, 2016 and 2017. But for official purposes, for instance in the census, the child would still be considered one year old. The former is called the child's nominal age, 虛歲 *(xūsuì)*, and the latter his/her actual age, 實歲 *(shísuì)*.

COMPARE & CONTRAST

1 Research holidays and festivals observed in Chinese-speaking countries. Are similar holidays and festivals observed in your own country or culture?

2 Certain numbers in Chinese are considered auspicious because they sound similar to words with lucky meanings. Look up the word 久 *(jiǔ)* in a dictionary. What number is it a homophone of, and why do you think this number is popular at weddings? Can you think of another culture in which numbers carry auspicious meaning?

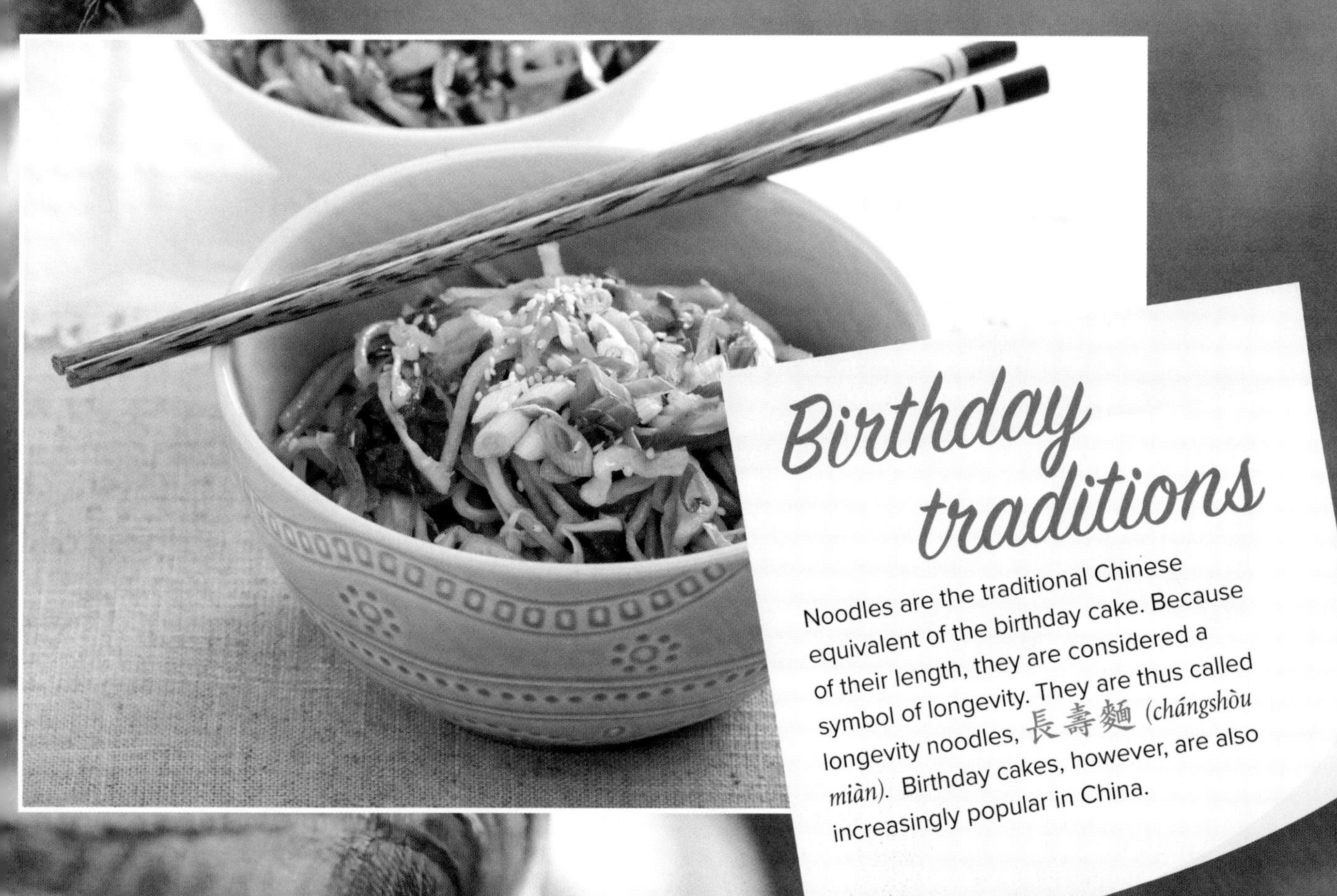

Birthday traditions

Noodles are the traditional Chinese equivalent of the birthday cake. Because of their length, they are considered a symbol of longevity. They are thus called longevity noodles, 長壽麵 *(chángshòu miàn)*. Birthday cakes, however, are also increasingly popular in China.

Lesson Wrap-Up

Make It Flow!

Rearrange the following sentences into a logical sequence. Then combine them into a coherent narrative. Try to replace a proper noun with a personal pronoun and 星期四 *(xīngqīsì)* with 那天 *(nà tiān)* wherever appropriate.

_____星期四是高文中的生日。

__1__高文中今年十八歲。

_____白英愛星期四請高文中吃飯。

_____白英愛和高文中吃中國菜。

Birthday Party

Share your date of birth with your classmates. If anyone is celebrating his or her birthday this or next month, organize a party to celebrate! Find out when everyone is free and what type of food they like. When everyone has agreed on the time, confirm it: 好 *(hǎo)*，______見 *(jiàn)*！

Birthday Card

Write your friend's Chinese or English name and age, combined with 祝你生日快樂！*(Zhù nǐ shēngrì kuài lè!)* (Happy Birthday), on a birthday card. Don't forget to date and sign it before delivery.

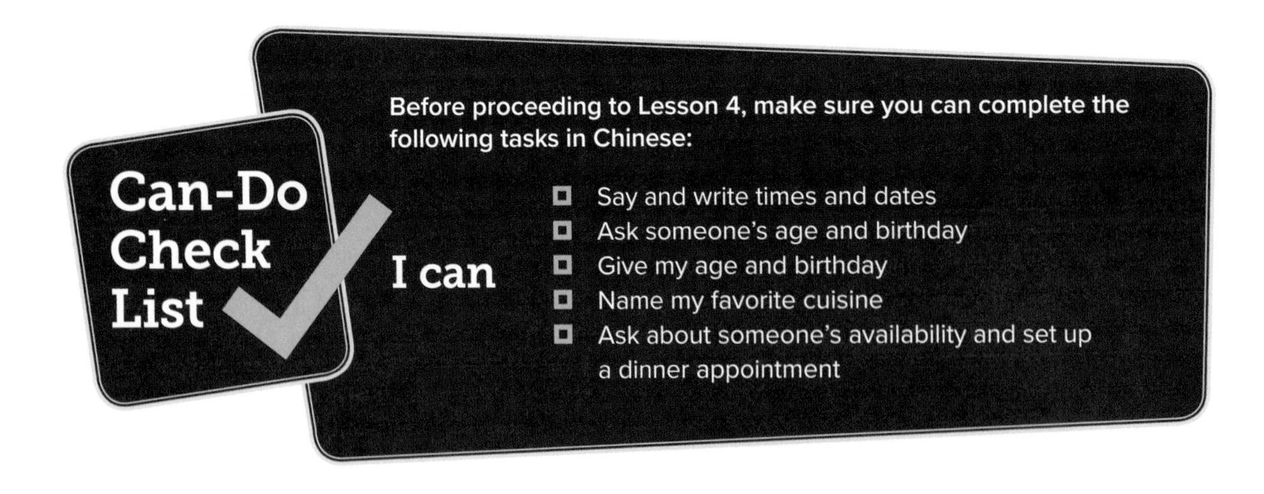

Lesson 4

第四課

Dì sì kè

愛好

Àihào

HOBBIES

Learning Objectives

In this lesson, you will learn to:

- Name common hobbies
- Ask about someone's hobbies
- Make plans for the weekend with friends

Relate & Get Ready

In your own culture/community:

- What are people's favorite pastimes?
- What do people usually do on weekends?

Discussing Hobbies

Dialogue 1

Gao Wenzhong asks Bai Ying'ai about her weekend plans and wants to invite her to a movie; however . . .

Audio

Video

白英愛，你週末喜歡做什麼[1]？

我喜歡打球、看電視[a]。你呢？

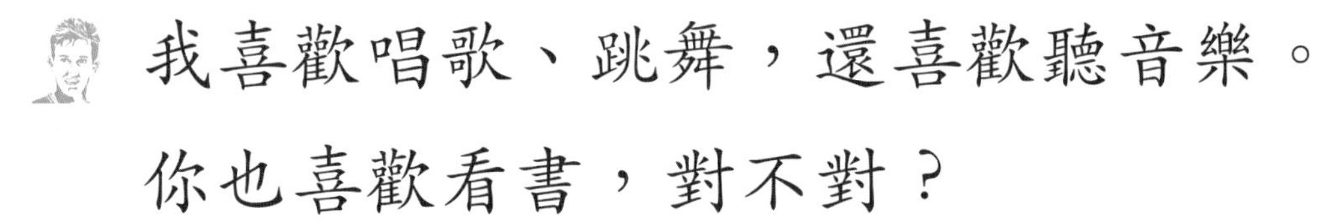

我喜歡唱歌、跳舞，還喜歡聽音樂。
你也喜歡看書，對不對？

對，有的時候也喜歡看書。

你喜歡不喜歡[2]看電影？

喜歡。我週末常常看電影。

那[3]我們今天晚上去看[4]一個外國電影，
怎麼樣？我請客。

為什麼你請客？

因為昨天你請我吃飯，所以今天我
請你看電影。

那你也請王朋、李友，好嗎[5]？

……好。

Pinyin Dialogue

 *Bái Yīng'ài, nǐ zhōumò xǐhuan zuò shénme*[1]*?*

 *Wǒ xǐhuan dǎ qiú, kàn diànshì*[a]*. Nǐ ne?*

 *Wǒ xǐhuan chàng gē, tiào wǔ, hái xǐhuan tīng yīnyuè.*

Nǐ yě xǐhuan kàn shū, duì bu duì?

 *Duì, yǒude shíhou yě xǐhuan kàn shū.*

 *Nǐ xǐhuan bu xǐhuan*[2] *kàn diànyǐng?*

 *Xǐhuan. Wǒ zhōumò chángcháng kàn diànyǐng.*

 *Nà*[3] *wǒmen jīntiān wǎnshang qù kàn*[4] *yí ge wàiguó diànyǐng, zěnmeyàng? Wǒ qǐng kè.*

 *Wèishénme nǐ qǐng kè?*

 *Yīnwèi zuótiān nǐ qǐng wǒ chī fàn, suǒyǐ jīntiān wǒ qǐng nǐ kàn diànyǐng.*

 *Nà nǐ yě qǐng Wáng Péng, Lǐ Yǒu, hǎo ma*[5]*?*

 *. . . Hǎo.*

Language Note

a 、

When nouns or pronouns occur in a series, " 、 " is used to separate them. The conjunction 和 *(hé)* connects the last two items in the series, e.g., 我、你和她 *(wǒ, nǐ hé tā)* (me, you, and her); 中國、美國、英國和法國 *(Zhōngguó, Měiguó, Yīngguó hé Fǎguó)* (China, United States, Britain, and France). The series comma can also be used between two or more verbs or adjectives, as in 我常常打球、跳舞、看電視 *(Wǒ chángcháng dǎ qiú, tiào wǔ, kàn diànshì)* (I often play ball, dance, and watch TV).

Vocabulary

Audio

Flashcards

No.	Word	Pinyin	Part of Speech	Definition
1	週末	*zhōumò*	n	weekend
2	打球	*dǎ qiú*	vo	to play ball
	打	*dǎ*	v	to hit
	球	*qiú*	n	ball
3	看	*kàn*	v	to watch, to look, to read
4	電視	*diànshì*	n	television
	電	*diàn*	n	electricity
	視	*shì*	n	vision
5	唱歌（兒）	*chàng gē(r)*	vo	to sing (a song)
	唱	*chàng*	v	to sing
	歌	*gē*	n	song
6	跳舞	*tiào wǔ*	vo	to dance
	跳	*tiào*	v	to jump
	舞	*wǔ*	n	dance
7	聽	*tīng*	v	to listen
8	音樂	*yīnyuè*	n	music
9	書	*shū*	n	book
10	對	*duì*	adj	right, correct
11	有的	*yǒude*	pr	some
12	時候	*shíhou*	n	(a point in) time, moment, (a duration of) time
13	電影	*diànyǐng*	n	movie
	影	*yǐng*	n	shadow
14	常常	*chángcháng*	adv	often

Your friend in Shanghai is taking you out for the night and gives you this ticket. Where will you be going?

GET Real WITH CHINESE

No.	Word	Pinyin	Part of Speech	Definition
15	那	*nà*	conj	in that case, then
16	去	*qù*	v	to go
17	外國	*wàiguó*	n	foreign country
18	請客	*qǐng kè*	vo	to invite someone (to dinner, coffee, etc.), to play the host
19	昨天	*zuótiān*	t	yesterday
20	所以	*suǒyǐ*	conj	so

你週末喜歡做什麼？

Nǐ zhōumò xǐhuan zuò shénme?

What do you like to do on weekends?

How About You?

我喜歡 ________。

Wǒ xǐhuan ________.

See index for corresponding vocabulary or research another term.

Grammar

1 Word order

The basic word order in a Chinese sentence is as follows.

Subject (agent of the action)	Adverbial (time, place, manner, etc.)	Verb	(Object) (receiver of the action)
白醫生 *Bái yīshēng*	星期六、星期天 *xīngqīliù, xīngqītiān*	工作 *gōngzuò*	
Dr. Bai works on Saturdays and Sundays.			
王朋 *Wáng Péng*	週末/常常 *zhōumò/chángcháng*	聽 *tīng*	音樂 *yīnyuè*
Wang Peng often listens to music on weekends.			
李友 *Lǐ Yǒu*	明天 *míngtiān*	吃 *chī*	中國菜 *Zhōngguó cài*
Li You will have Chinese food tomorrow.			
高文中 *Gāo Wénzhōng*	今天下午五點半 *jīntiān xiàwǔ wǔ diǎn bàn*	去看 *qù kàn*	外國電影 *wàiguó diànyǐng*
Gao Wenzhong will go to see a foreign movie at 5:30 this afternoon.			

While this is the most common word order in a Chinese sentence, the norm varies depending on context.

2 Affirmative + negative (A-not-A) questions (II)

In this type of question, there can be no adverbials before the verb other than time words, as in (A) and (B). If there is an adverbial—such as 都 *(dōu)* (both, all) or 常常 *(chángcháng)* (often)—before the verb, the 嗎 *(ma)* type question must be used instead, as in (C) and (D). If there is more than one verb, the question form applies to the first verb, as seen in (E) and (F).

A 你明天去不去？

Nǐ míngtiān qù bu qù?

Are you going tomorrow?

B 她今天晚上看不看電視？

Tā jīntiān wǎnshang kàn bu kàn diànshì?

Is she going to watch TV tonight?

C 他們都是學生嗎？ [⊗ 他們都是不是學生？]

Tāmen dōu shì xuésheng ma?

Are they all students?

D 你常常看電影嗎？ [⊗ 你常常看不看電影？]

Nǐ chángcháng kàn diànyǐng ma?

Do you often go to the movies?

E 你喜歡不喜歡跳舞？ [⊗ 你喜歡跳不跳舞？]

Nǐ xǐhuan bu xǐhuan tiào wǔ?

Do you like dancing?

F 你的同學去不去打球？

Nǐ de tóngxué qù bu qù dǎ qiú?

Are your classmates going to play ball?

[⊗ 你的同學去打不打球？]

EXERCISES

In pairs, form an A-not-A question-and-answer based on the information below. Use exercise 1 as an example.

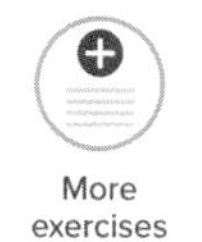

1 白英爱 明天 去跳舞

→ Q: 白英愛明天去不去跳舞？

A: 白英愛明天去/不去跳舞。

2 李友 今天晚上 聽中國音樂

3 白英愛 明天晚上 請李友吃飯

3 The conjunction 那（麼）*(nà [me])* (then, in that case)

In conversation, immediately following a statement by speaker A, speaker B can often start with 那（麼）*(nà [me])* (then, in that case), which links up the sentences by the two speakers.

A

Student A 今天晚上沒事兒。

Jīntiān wǎnshang méi shìr.

We have nothing to do tonight.

Student B 那麼我們去看電影，怎麼樣？

Nàme wǒmen qù kàn diànyǐng, zěnmeyàng?

In that case, let's go to see a movie. How about that?

Student A 好，我請客。

Hǎo, wǒ qǐng kè.

OK, my treat.

Student B 是嗎？太好了！

Shì ma? Tài hǎo le.

Really? Great!

B

Student A 我今天很忙，晚上不去吃晚飯。

Wǒ jīntiān hěn máng, wǎnshang bú qù chī wǎnfàn.

I'm very busy today, and will not go to dinner tonight.

Student B 那明天呢？

Nà míngtiān ne?

Then how about tomorrow?

C **Student A** 你喜歡不喜歡吃美國菜？

Nǐ xǐhuan bu xǐhuan chī Měiguó cài?

Do you like to eat American food or not?

Student B 不喜歡。

Bù xǐhuan.

No, I don't.

Student A 那我們吃中國菜，怎麼樣？

Nà wǒmen chī Zhōngguó cài, zěnmeyàng?

Then let's eat Chinese food. How about that?

Student B 我也不喜歡。

Wǒ yě bù xǐhuan.

I don't like that either.

EXERCISES

Form questions based on the context, inserting 那（麼） where appropriate. Use exercise 1 as an example.

More exercises

1 **Student A** 我今天不忙。

Student B 那我們去看電影，怎麼樣？

2 **Student A** 我不喜歡跳舞。

Student B ______________________________？

3 **Student A** 王朋星期六很忙。

Student B ______________________________？

4 去 *(qù)* (to go) + action

If the performance of an action involves a change of location, then use the construction below.

A 我們明天去看電影。

Wǒmen míngtiān qù kàn diànyǐng.

We are going to see a movie tomorrow.

B 週末我去跳舞，你去不去？

Zhōumò wǒ qù tiào wǔ, nǐ qù bu qù?

I'll go dancing this weekend. Are you going?

C 晚上我不去跳舞。

Wǎnshang wǒ bú qù tiào wǔ.

I will not go dancing tonight.

More exercises

EXERCISES

Answer these questions, inserting the given verb phrases and 去 where appropriate.

Use exercise 1 as an example.

1 Q: 李友明天晚上做什麼？ 看中國電影

→ A: 李友明天晚上去看中國電影。

2 Q: 白英愛星期天晚上做什麼？ 打球

3 Q: 王朋和李友今天晚上做什麼？ 吃美國菜

5 Questions with 好嗎 *(hǎo ma)* (OK?)

To solicit someone's opinion, we can ask 好嗎 *(hǎo ma)* (OK?) after stating an idea or suggestion. As an alternative, we can also say 好不好 *(hǎo bu hǎo)* (all right?).

A 我們去看電影，好嗎？

Wǒmen qù kàn diànyǐng, hǎo ma?

We'll go see a movie, OK?

B 我們今天晚上吃中國菜，好嗎？

Wǒmen jīntiān wǎnshang chī Zhōngguó cài, hǎo ma?

We'll eat Chinese food tonight, OK?

Language Practice

A **What a week!** PRESENTATIONAL

Using the images below, take turns describing Little Wang's schedule this week, e.g.:

小王星期一看書。

Xiǎo Wáng xīngqīyī kàn shū.

1 星期一 *(xīngqīyī)* 

2 星期二 *(xīngqī'èr)* 

3 星期三 *(xīngqīsān)* 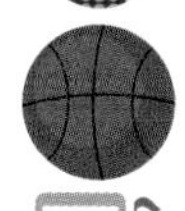

4 星期四 *(xīngqīsì)* 

5 星期五 *(xīngqīwǔ)* 

6 星期六 *(xīngqīliù)* 

7 星期天 *(xīngqītiān)* 

What does your calendar look like? Share your schedule with the class, e.g.:

我星期一去跳舞。 *Wǒ xīngqīyī qù tiào wǔ.*

B **Shall we?** INTERPERSONAL

In pairs, use the images to find out what your partner likes to do and invite him/her out tomorrow night by using 去 *(qù)* and 好嗎 *(hǎo ma)*, e.g.:

Q: 你喜歡看電影嗎？
我們明天晚上去看電影，好嗎？

Nǐ xǐhuan kàn diànyǐng ma?

Wǒmen míngtiān wǎnshang qù kàn diànyǐng, hǎo ma?

A: 好！(agreeing, confirming, accepting)

Hǎo!

A: 我明天很忙，也不喜歡看電影。(declining)

Wǒ míngtiān hěn máng, yě bù xǐhuan kàn diànyǐng.

1 

2 

3 

4 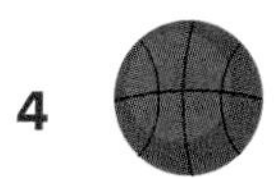

C That's why!

INTERPERSONAL

In pairs, form a question-and-answer about why you will or won't do something by using 因為…所以… (*yīnwèi . . . suǒyǐ . . .*), e.g.:

Q: 你為什麼不去看電影？ (很忙)
Nǐ weìshénme bú qù kàn diànyǐng? (*hěn máng*)

A: 因為我很忙，所以不去看電影。
Yīnwèi wǒ hěn máng, suǒyǐ bú qù kàn diànyǐng.

1 你為什麼不去打球？ (有事兒)
Nǐ wèishénme bú qù dǎ qiú? (*yǒu shìr*)

2 你為什麼不去看外國電影？ (不喜歡)
Nǐ wèishénme bú qù kàn wàiguó diànyǐng? (*bù xǐhuan*)

3 你為什麼星期五請我吃晚飯？ (你的生日)
Nǐ wèishénme xīngqīwǔ qǐng wǒ chī wǎnfàn? (*nǐ de shēngrì*)

4 你為什麼不去跳舞？ (不喜歡)
Nǐ wèishénme bú qù tiào wǔ? (*bù xǐhuan*)

5 你為什麼不聽音樂？ (很忙)
Nǐ wèishénme bù tīng yīnyuè? (*hěn máng*)

Characterize it!

Semi - Enclosing

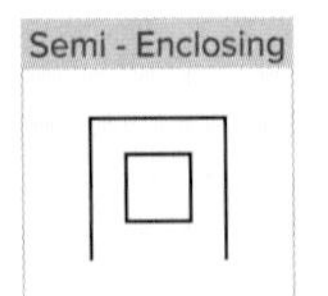

1 歌

2 

3 

4 

5 

Which of these characters are formed with the pattern on the left?

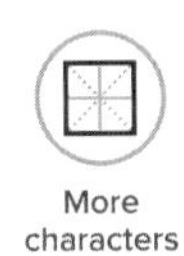

More characters

D Weekend warrior

INTERPERSONAL PRESENTATIONAL

In pairs, find out what your partner likes to do on weekends, e.g.:

Q: 你週末喜歡做什麼？

Nǐ zhōumò xǐhuan zuò shénme?

A: 我週末喜歡＿＿＿＿＿＿＿＿＿＿。

Wǒ zhōumò xǐhuan ＿＿＿＿＿＿＿＿＿＿.

Report to the class and be prepared to answer the teacher's questions.

Juan 週末喜歡做什麼？

Juan *zhōumò xǐhuan zuò shénme?*

Kristen 呢？ Kristen 週末喜歡不喜歡看書？……

Kristen *ne?* Kristen *xǐhuan bù xǐhuan kàn shū?*...

E Trending now

INTERPERSONAL

Survey your classmates about their favorite singers, movie stars, athletes, and dancers using the questions below.

你喜歡聽誰的歌？
你喜歡看誰的電影？
你喜歡看誰打球？
你喜歡看誰跳舞？

Let's Play Ball

Dialogue 2

Wang Peng visits Gao Wenzhong and invites him to play ball over the weekend.

Audio

Video

小高[a]，好久不見[b]，你好嗎[c]？

我很好。你怎麼樣？

我也不錯。這個週末你想[6]做什麼？想不想去打球？

打球？我不喜歡打球。

那我們去看球，怎麼樣？

看球？我覺得看球也沒有意思[d]。

那你這個週末想做什麼？

我只想吃飯、睡覺[7][e]。

算了，我去找別人。

Pinyin Dialogue

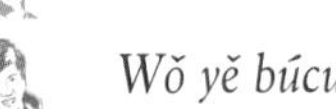

Xiǎo Gāo[a]*, hǎo jiǔ bú jiàn*[b]*, nǐ hǎo ma*[c]*?*

Wǒ hěn hǎo. Nǐ zěnmeyàng?

Wǒ yě búcuò. Zhè ge zhōumò nǐ xiǎng[6] *zuò shénme? Xiǎng bu xiǎng qù dǎ qiú?*

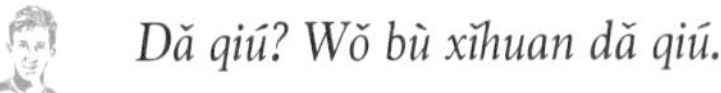

Dǎ qiú? Wǒ bù xǐhuan dǎ qiú.

Nà wǒmen qù kàn qiú, zěnmeyàng?

Kàn qiú? Wǒ juéde kàn qiú yě méiyǒu yìsi[d]*.*

Nà nǐ zhè ge zhōumò xiǎng zuò shénme?

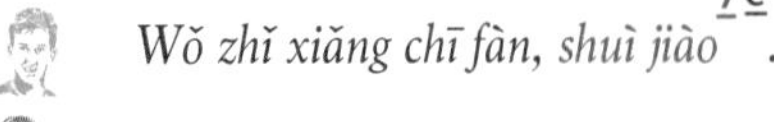

Wǒ zhǐ xiǎng chī fàn, shuì jiào[7][e]*.*

Suàn le, wǒ qù zhǎo biérén.

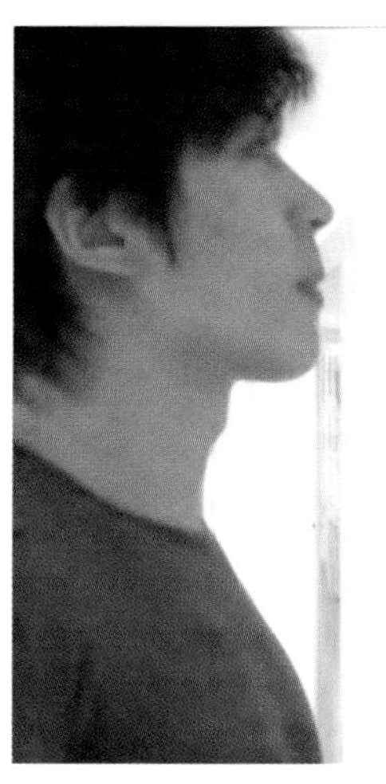

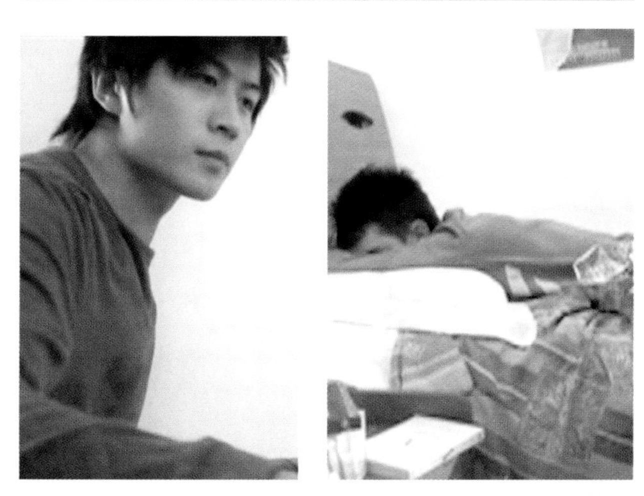

<u>a</u> 小 *(xiǎo)*

A familiar and affectionate way of addressing a young person is to add 小 *(xiǎo)* (little, small) to the family name, e.g., 小王 *(Xiǎo Wáng)* (Little Wang). Similarly, to address an older acquaintance, 老 *(lǎo)* (old) can be used with the family name, e.g., 老王 *(Lǎo Wáng)* (Old Wang). However, such terms are rarely used to address a relative or a superior.

<u>b</u> 好久不見 *(hǎo jiǔ bú jiàn)*

Now you know where the expression "Long time no see" comes from.

<u>c</u> 你好嗎？ *(Nǐ hǎo ma?)*

This question (meaning "How are you?") is typically asked of people you already know. The answer is usually 我很好 *(Wǒ hěn hǎo)* (I am fine).

<u>d</u> 覺得沒有意思 *(juéde méiyǒu yìsi)*

The position of negatives in Chinese is not always the same as it is in English. An English speaker would say: "I don't think going to the movies is much fun," but a Chinese speaker would say 我覺得看電影沒有意思 *(Wǒ juéde kàn diànyǐng méiyǒu yìsi)*, which literally means, "I think going to the movies is not much fun."

<u>e</u> 覺 *(jué/jiào)*

The character 覺 is pronounced in two different ways and has two different meanings: *jué* as in 覺得 *(juéde)* (to feel) and *jiào* as in 睡覺 *(shuì jiào)* (to sleep).

Vocabulary

Audio

Flashcards

No.	Word	Pinyin	Part of Speech	Definition
1	小	*xiǎo*	adj	small, little
2	好久	*hǎo jiǔ*		a long time
	好	*hǎo*	adv	very
	久	*jiǔ*	adj	long (of time)
3	不錯	*búcuò*	adj	pretty good
	錯	*cuò*	adj	wrong
4	想	*xiǎng*	mv	to want to, would like to [See Grammar 6.]
5	覺得	*juéde*	v	to feel, to think [See Grammar 6.]

Your roommate puts this on before lying down on the couch. What is she trying to tell you?

No.	Word	Pinyin	Part of Speech	Definition
6	有意思	*yǒu yìsi*	adj	interesting
	意思	*yìsi*	n	meaning
7	只	*zhǐ*	adv	only
8	睡覺	*shuì jiào*	vo	to sleep
	睡	*shuì*	v	to sleep
	覺	*jiào*	n	sleep
9	算了	*suàn le*		forget it, never mind
10	找	*zhǎo*	v	to look for
11	別人	*biérén*	n	other people, another person
	別（的）	*bié (de)*	adj	other

How About You?

這個週末你想做什麼？

Zhè ge zhōumò nǐ xiǎng zuò shénme?

What would you like to do this weekend?

我想＿＿＿＿＿＿。

Wǒ xiǎng ＿＿＿＿＿＿.

See index for corresponding vocabulary or research another term.

Grammar

6 The modal verb 想 *(xiǎng)* (want to, would like to)

想 *(xiǎng)* has several meanings. In this lesson, it is a modal verb indicating a desire to do something. It must be followed by a verb or a clause.

A 你想聽音樂嗎？

Nǐ xiǎng tīng yīnyuè ma?

Would you like to listen to some music?

B 白老師想打球，可是王老師不想打。

Bái lǎoshī xiǎng dǎ qiú, kěshì Wáng lǎoshī bù xiǎng dǎ.

Teacher Bai felt like playing ball, but Teacher Wang didn't.

C 你想不想看中國電影？

Nǐ xiǎng bu xiǎng kàn Zhōngguó diànyǐng?

Do you feel like going to see a Chinese movie?

D 你想不想聽外國音樂？

Nǐ xiǎng bu xiǎng tīng wàiguó yīnyuè?

Do you feel like listening to some foreign music?

想 *(xiǎng)* vs. 喜歡 *(xǐhuan)*

想 *(xiǎng)* can be translated as "would like to" or "to have a desire to." 喜歡 *(xǐhuan)* is "to like," meaning "to be fond of." 想 *(xiǎng)* and 喜歡 *(xǐhuan)* are different, and are not interchangeable.

想 *(xiǎng)* vs. 覺得 *(juéde)*

Both 想 *(xiǎng)* and 覺得 *(juéde)* can be translated as "to think," but the former is used to express a desire, whereas the latter is to express an opinion or comment on something.

EXERCISES

In pairs, form a question-and-answer about your partner's intent, inserting 想 where appropriate. Use exercise 1 as an example.

1 吃中國菜

→ Q: 你晚上想吃中國菜嗎？

A: 我想吃中國菜。(affirmative)

A: 我不想吃中國菜。(negative)

2 請同學去看電影

3 去聽中國音樂

7 Verb + object as a detachable compound

Even though 睡覺 *(shuì jiào)* (to sleep), 唱歌 *(chàng gē)* (to sing), and 跳舞 *(tiào wǔ)* (to dance) are each treated as a word, grammatically speaking, they are all verb-object compounds. When an attributive element modifies the object, such as an adjective or a number-measure word combination, it must be inserted between the verb and the noun. Such a compound does not take an object, and is called a "detachable compound."

A

睡覺	睡一個好覺
shuì jiào	*shuì yí ge hǎo jiào*
to sleep	have a good sleep

B

唱歌	唱英文歌
chàng gē	*chàng Yīngwén gē*
to sing	sing an English song

C

跳舞	跳中國舞
tiào wǔ	*tiào Zhōngguó wǔ*
to dance	do a Chinese dance

In later lessons, you will see examples of other elements, like aspect markers, being inserted between the verb and the object in a detachable compound.

Language Practice

F Let the weekend begin!

INTERPERSONAL

In pairs, discuss what you'd like to do over the weekend by using 想 *(xiǎng)*, e.g.:

Q: 你週末想不想打球？

Nǐ zhōumò xiǎng bu xiǎng dǎ qiú?

A: 我（週末）想打球。(affirmative)

Wǒ zhōumò xiǎng dǎ qiú.

A: 我（週末）不想打球。(negative)

Wǒ zhōumò bu xiǎng dǎ qiú.

1 

2

3

4

5

G How interesting

INTERPERSONAL PRESENTATIONAL

In pairs, determine your partner's interest level in these activities and report to the class by using 很有意思 *(hěn yǒu yìsi)* or 沒有意思 *(méiyǒu yìsi)*, e.g.:

打球（小高） 小高覺得打球很有意思。

dǎ qiú (Xiǎo Gāo) *Xiǎo Gāo juéde dǎ qiú hěn yǒu yìsi.*

1 跳舞

tiào wǔ

2 聽中國音樂

tīng Zhōngguó yīnyuè

3 看外國電影

kàn wàiguó diànyǐng

4 看英文書

kàn Yīngwén shū

5 看電視

kàn diànshì

H

Weekend ahead

INTERPERSONAL

In pairs, complete these sentences and role-play the discussion about the weekend ahead.

Q: 你這個週末想做什麼？

Nǐ zhè ge zhōumò xiǎng zuò shénme?

A: 我這個週末想________________。

Wǒ zhè ge zhōumò xiǎng ________________.

Then find out if your partner feels like doing something else this weekend.

Q: 你想________________嗎？

Nǐ xiǎng ________________ ma?

A: 我想________________。 (affirmative)

Wǒ xiǎng ________________.

A: 我不想________________。 (negative)

Wǒ bù xiǎng ________________.

What types of activities does your partner think are interesting?

Q: 你覺得（看電影、打球，etc.）有意思嗎？

Nǐ juéde (kàn diànyǐng, dǎ qiú, etc.*) yǒu yìsi ma?*

A: 我覺得________________很有意思。 (affirmative)

Wǒ juéde ________________hěn yǒu yìsi.

A: 我覺得________________沒有意思。 (negative)

Wǒ juéde ________________méi yǒu yìsi.

Characterize it!

What do the characters mean?
What is the common radical?
What does the radical mean?
How does the radical relate to the overall meaning of the characters?

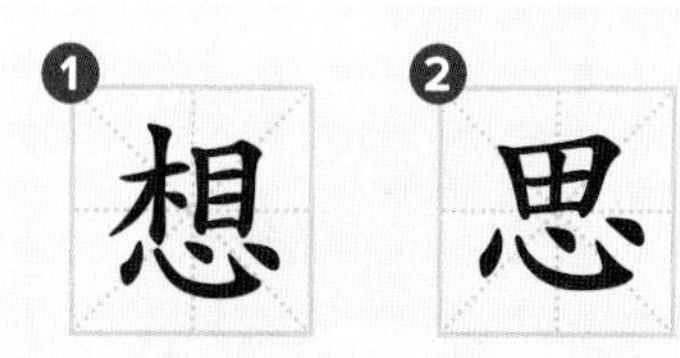

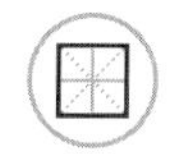

More characters

文化
Continue to explore

MAHJONG

Mahjong, 麻將 *(májiàng)*, is one of the most popular Chinese pastimes, involving four players. To win, one has to draw various tiles to form different combinations, which have all been assigned scores based on pre-set rules. The more difficult the combination, the higher the score. There are usually four games in each round, and the players can decide how many rounds they wish to play. Normally, people play either eight or twelve rounds.

The two teams of Chinese chess pieces are identified by colors, typically black and red. They are set up as shown. Since you have learned the character/radical meaning "horse," can you find where the "horse" is on the board?

Chinese chess, 象棋 *(xiàngqí)*, is another popular pastime especially among senior citizens. While international chess has such pieces as king, queen, rook, knight, and pawn, Chinese chess has commander-in-chief, general, chariot, horse, and soldier. Both mahjong and Chinese chess go back centuries. Community centers and clubhouses in China often have a 棋牌室 *(qípáishì)*, or chess-and-poker room, where residents, especially retirees, meet for chess and mahjong marathons. In neighborhood parks, it is also common to find onlookers gathering around chess players

CHINESE CHESS

1 Organize a lunch or dinner with two or three friends. Use the end of Dialogue 1 as a model. Decide if you want to treat or to split the bill with your friends by using 今天我請客 (*Jīntiān wǒ qǐngkè*) or 我們今天AA制 (*Wǒmen jīntiān AA zhì*), explained below. How often do people treat in your culture?

2 Nowadays, binge-watching is a hobby for many people. Dramas produced in Mainland China and Taiwan have been gaining popularity in many Chinese-speaking countries, and even among viewers who do not speak Chinese. Research some of the most popular Chinese dramas. How do they compare with popular dramas in your own country?

Arguably less popular but more prestigious is the game of Encirclement, 圍棋 (*wéiqí*), better known in the West by its Japanese name, Go. It is a deceptively simple game played with counters or stones on a board. The objective of the game is to surround and capture the opponent's counters. Every year, major corporations sponsor tournaments with master players from China, Japan, and South Korea participating and TV stations providing live coverage of important matches.

When Chinese people go out to eat with friends, they rarely split the check. Usually, someone will insist on picking up the tab by saying 今天我請客 (*Jīntiān wǒ qǐngkè*) (It's my treat today). The unspoken expectation is that someone else will offer to pay the next time. Often, more than one person will reach for the bill and there might be a little struggle over who gets to pay. Among young urban white-collar professionals and college students, it is increasingly common to separate the check or adopt the AA制 (*AA zhì*) except on celebratory or festive occasions.

Lesson Wrap-Up

Make It Flow!

Rearrange the following sentences into a logical sequence according to Gao Wenzhong and Bai Ying'ai's likes and dislikes. Then combine them into a coherent narrative. If the subject is the same, remember not to repeat it in subsequent clauses. Replace the proper noun in the previous clause with a personal pronoun if beginning a new sentence.

_____高文中不喜歡打球。

_____白英愛還喜歡看電影。

_____高文中覺得看球沒有意思。

__1__高文中喜歡唱歌、跳舞。

_____白英愛喜歡打球、看電視。

_____白英愛有的時候也喜歡看書。

_____高文中還喜歡聽音樂。

_____白英愛週末常常去看電影。

_____高文中也不喜歡看球。

Interview

Interview your classmates about what their families like to do.

你爸爸、媽媽喜歡做什麼？

你哥哥、姐姐、弟弟、妹妹喜歡做什麼？

Hang Out

Do your classmates share your interests? Survey them about their hobbies on social media: 你喜歡……？ (*Nǐ xǐhuan . . . ?*). Arrange a time to hang out with classmates who share your interests.

Lesson 5

第五課

Dì wǔ kè

看朋友

Kàn péngyou

VISITING FRIENDS

Learning Objectives

In this lesson, you will learn to:

- Welcome a visitor
- Introduce one person to another
- Be a gracious guest
- Ask for beverages as a guest
- Offer beverages to a visitor
- Briefly describe a visit to a friend's place

Relate & Get Ready

In your own culture/community:

- Is it common to visit a friend's place without advance notice?
- Do people bring anything when visiting a friend's home?
- What food and drinks do hosts commonly offer guests?

Visiting a Friend's Place

Dialogue

Audio

Video

Wang Peng and Li You visit Gao Wenzhong and meet his sister, Gao Xiaoyin.
(The doorbell rings.)

 誰呀？

 是我，王朋，還有李友。

 請進，請進，快進來！來，我介紹一下[1]，這是我姐姐，高小音。

  小音，你好。認識你很高興。

 認識你們我也很高興。

 你們家很大[2]，也很漂亮。

 是嗎？[a]請坐，請坐。

 小音，你在[3]哪兒[b]工作？

 我在學校工作。你們想喝點兒[1]什麼？喝茶還是喝咖啡？

 我喝茶吧[4]。

 我要一瓶可樂，可以嗎？

 對不起，我們家沒有可樂。

 那給我一杯水吧。

(The doorbell rings.)

 *Shéi ya?*

 *Shì wǒ, Wáng Péng, hái yǒu Lǐ Yǒu.*

 *Qǐng jìn, qǐng jìn, kuài jìn lai! Lái, wǒ jièshào yí xià*[1]*, zhè shì wǒ jiějie, Gāo Xiǎoyīn.*

 *Xiǎoyīn, nǐ hǎo. Rènshi nǐ hěn gāoxìng.*

 *Rènshi nǐmen wǒ yě hěn gāoxìng.*

 *Nǐmen jiā hěn dà*[2]*, yě hěn piàoliang.*

 *Shì ma?*[a] *Qǐng zuò, qǐng zuò.*

 *Xiǎoyīn, nǐ zài*[3] *nǎr*[b] *gōngzuò?*

 *Wǒ zài xuéxiào gōngzuò. Nǐmen xiǎng hē diǎnr*[1] *shénme? Hē chá háishi hē kāfēi?*

 *Wǒ hē chá ba*[4]*.*

 *Wǒ yào yì píng kělè, kěyǐ ma?*

 *Duìbuqǐ, wǒmen jiā méi yǒu kělè.*

 *Nà gěi wǒ yì bēi shuǐ ba.*

Language Notes

a 是嗎? *(Shì ma?)*

"Is that so?" or "Really?" It is a rhetorical question here. This is a modest way to respond to a compliment.

b 哪兒 *(nǎr)*

A question word meaning "where." Do not confuse it with 那兒 *(nàr)* (there). "Here" is 這兒 *(zhèr)*.

Vocabulary

Audio

Flashcards

No.	Word	Pinyin	Part of Speech	Definition
1	呀	*ya*	p	(interjectory particle used to soften a question)
2	進	*jìn*	v	to enter
3	快	*kuài*	adv/adj	fast, quick; quickly
4	進來	*jìn lai*	vc	to come in
5	來	*lái*	v	to come
6	介紹	*jièshào*	v	to introduce
7	一下	*yí xià*	n+m	once, a bit [See Grammar 1.]
8	高興	*gāoxìng*	adj	happy, pleased
9	漂亮	*piàoliang*	adj	pretty
10	坐	*zuò*	v	to sit
11	在	*zài*	prep	at, in, on [See Grammar 3.]
12	哪兒	*nǎr*	qpr	where
13	學校	*xuéxiào*	n	school
14	喝	*hē*	v	to drink
15	點（兒）	*diǎn(r)*	m	a little, a bit, some [See Grammar 1.]
16	茶	*chá*	n	tea
17	咖啡	*kāfēi*	n	coffee
18	吧	*ba*	p	(a sentence-final particle) [See Grammar 4.]
19	要	*yào*	v	to want
20	瓶	*píng*	m	(measure word for bottled liquid, etc.)
21	可樂	*kělè*	n	cola

China's booming soft drinks market offers consumers a variety of choices. Can you identify these flavors?

GET Real WITH CHINESE

No.	Word	Pinyin	Part of Speech	Definition
22	可以	*kěyǐ*	mv	can, may
23	對不起	*duìbuqǐ*	v	sorry
24	給	*gěi*	v	to give
25	杯	*bēi*	m	(measure word for things contained in a cup or glass)
26	水	*shuǐ*	n	water
27	高小音	*Gāo Xiǎoyīn*	pn	(a personal name)

你喜歡喝什麼?

Nǐ xǐhuan hē shénme?

What do you like to drink?

How About You?

我喜歡喝 ________。

Wǒ xǐhuan hē ________.

See index for corresponding vocabulary or research another term.

Grammar

1 Moderating tone of voice: 一下 *(yí xià)* and （一）點兒 *(|yì| diǎnr)*

Following a verb, both 一下 *(yí xià)* (lit. "once") and （一）點兒 *(|yì| diǎnr)* ("a bit") can soften the tone of a question or an imperative sentence, making it more polite. When used in this way, 一下 *(yí xià)* modifies the verb, while （一）點兒 *(|yì| diǎnr)* modifies the object.

A 你看一下，這是誰的照片？

Nǐ kàn yí xià, zhè shì shéi de zhàopiàn?

Take a look. Whose photo is this?

B 你想吃點兒什麼?

Nǐ xiǎng chī diǎnr shénme?

What would you like to eat?

C 你進來一下。

Nǐ jìn lai yí xià.

Come in for a minute.

D 你喝一點兒茶吧。

Nǐ hē yì diǎnr chá ba.

Have some tea.

More exercises

EXERCISES

Moderate the tone of these sentences by inserting 一下 or （一）點兒.
Use exercise 1 as an example.

1 我看_______你的照片 → 我看一下你的照片。

2 我看_______你的書。

3 你喝_______咖啡。

2 Adjectives as predicates using 很 *(hěn)* (very)

When an adjective functions as a predicate, it is not preceded by the verb 是 *(shì)* (to be). It is usually modified by 很 *(hěn)* (very)—as in (A), (B), (C), and (D)—or some other adverbial modifier. Although usually translated as "very," 很 *(hěn)* is not quite as strong as its English equivalent when not stressed. It acts as an affirmative indicator. When forming a question with an adjective as the predicate, 很 *(hěn)* is not used, as in (E) and (F).

A 我今天很高興。

Wǒ jīntiān hěn gāoxìng.

I'm very happy today.

B 他妹妹很漂亮。

Tā mèimei hěn piàoliang.

His younger sister is very pretty.

C 那個電影很好。

Nà ge diànyǐng hěn hǎo.

That movie is very good.

D 你們大學很大。

Nǐmen dàxué hěn dà.

Your university is very large.

E Q: 你弟弟高嗎？

Nǐ dìdi gāo ma?

Is your younger brother tall?

A: 他很高。

Tā hěn gāo.

He is very tall.

F Q: 你家大嗎？

Nǐ jiā dà ma?

Is your house big?

A: 我家不大，很小。

Wǒ jiā bú dà, hěn xiǎo.

My house is not big; it's very small.

Chinese adjectives without 很 *(hěn)* or any sort of modifier before them can often imply comparison or contrast, as in (G) and (H).

G Q: 姐姐忙還是妹妹忙?

Jiějie máng háishi mèimei máng?

Who's busier, the older sister or the younger sister?

A: 妹妹忙。

Mèimei máng.

The younger sister is busier.

H 哥哥的中文好，我的中文不好。

Gēge de Zhōngwén hǎo, wǒ de Zhōngwén bù hǎo.

My older brother's Chinese is good. My Chinese is not good.

More exercises

EXERCISES

Use adjectives as predicates by inserting 很. Use exercise 1 as an example.

1 我弟弟＿＿＿＿高。→ 我弟弟很高。

2 我妹妹今天＿＿＿＿高興。

3 王律師的中文＿＿＿＿好。

3 The preposition 在 *(zài)* (at, in, on)

在 *(zài)* is a verb in (A).

A Q: 我的書在哪兒？

Wǒ de shū zài nǎr?

Where is my book?

A: 在那兒。

Zài nàr.

It's over there.

It is a preposition when a "在 *(zài)* + location" appears before a verb, as in (B), (C), and (D).

B Q: 你在哪兒工作?

Nǐ zài nǎr gōngzuò?

Where do you work?

A: 我在這兒工作。

Wǒ zài zhèr gōngzuò.

I work here.

C 我在這個大學學中文。

Wǒ zài zhè ge dàxué xué Zhōngwén.

I study Chinese at this university.

D 我不在家看電影。

Wǒ bú zài jiā kàn diànyǐng.

I don't watch movies at home.

EXERCISES

Form a question-and-answer about where each of the activities occurs, inserting 在 where appropriate. Use exercise 1 as an example.

More exercises

1 白英愛 跳舞 學校

→ Q: 白英愛在哪兒跳舞？ A: 她在學校跳舞。

2 白英愛這個週末 喝茶 高文中家

3 高文中明天 吃中國飯 老師家

4 The particle 吧 *(ba)*

吧 *(ba)* is a sentence-final particle often used to soften the tone of a command or suggestion.

A 你喝咖啡吧。

Nǐ hē kāfēi ba.

Why don't you have some coffee?

B 請進來吧。

Qǐng jìn lai ba.

Come in, please.

C 我們跳舞吧。

Wǒmen tiào wǔ ba.

Let's dance.

More exercises

EXERCISES

Soften the tone of these suggestions by inserting 吧. Use exercise 1 as an example.

1. 你喝點兒水＿＿＿＿。→ 你喝點兒水吧。
2. 我們明天去看中國電影＿＿＿＿。
3. 你今天晚上去聽音樂＿＿＿＿。

Chinese Chat

Gao Wenzhong just published a new post on Weibo (微博) (*Wēibó*), a popular Chinese microblogging platform. Based on his tone, can you tell how he's feeling?

高文中

02-13 17:54 來自iPhone 客戶端

晚上朋友請客！太高興了！去哪吃呀？
@白英愛

轉發 1　評論 7　讚 79

GET Real WITH CHINESE

Chinese lanterns are sometimes used as advertisements. What are these lanterns promoting?

photo courtesy of ShuWen Zhang

Language Practice

A If you ask politely . . .

Complete the sentences by using 一下 (*yí xià*) to moderate the tone of voice, e.g.:

You'd like to see a picture of your brother's girlfriend, so you ask him . . .

哥哥，我看一下你女朋友的照片，好嗎?

Gēge, wǒ kàn yí xià nǐ nǚpéngyou de zhàopiàn, hǎo ma?

1 You'd like your friend Little Bai to introduce you to Miss Li, so you say . . .

小白，我想認識李小姐。請你________。

Xiǎo Bái, wǒ xiǎng rènshi Lǐ xiǎojiě. Qǐng nǐ ________.

2 You're at the doctor's office for your appointment; the nurse tells you the doctor is busy, and asks you to take a seat, so she says . . .

對不起，醫生現在有事兒，請你________。

Duìbuqǐ, yīshēng xiànzài yǒu shìr, qǐng nǐ ________.

3 Your roommate is streaming an album and suggests that you listen to it, so she says . . .

這個音樂不錯。你________。

Zhè ge yīnyuè búcuò. Nǐ ________.

4 Your teacher wants to talk to you after class and asks you to come with him, so he says . . .

我有事兒找你。你________。

Wǒ yǒu shìr zhǎo nǐ. Nǐ ________.

Characterize it!

What do the characters mean?
What is the common radical?
What does the radical mean?
How does the radical relate to the overall meaning of the characters?

1 

2 

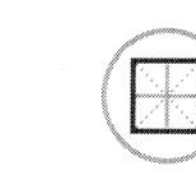

More characters

B What do you think?

INTERPERSONAL

In pairs, use the sentences to form questions about each other's personal opinions. Answer in the affirmative by inserting 很 (*hěn*) in the ◇, and then in the negative, e.g.:

高文中的家◇漂亮 *Gāo Wénzhōng de jiā ◇ piàoliang*

If people ask your opinion of Gao Wenzhong's house,

Q: 高文中的家漂亮嗎？ *Gāo Wénzhōng de jiā piàoliang ma?*

and you think Gao Wenzhong's house is beautifully decorated (affirmative), you can say . . .

A: 高文中的家很漂亮。 *Gāo Wénzhōng de jiā hěn piàoliang.*

But, if you don't think Gao's house is beautifully decorated (negative), you can say . . .

A: 高文中的家不漂亮。 *Gāo Wénzhōng de jiā bú piàoliang.*

1. 你的醫生◇忙 *nǐ de yīshēng ◇ máng*
2. 你的學校◇大 *nǐ de xuéxiào ◇ dà*
3. 你的同學◇高興 *nǐ de tóngxué ◇ gāoxìng*
4. 你的老師◇好 *nǐ de lǎoshī ◇ hǎo*
5. 你的書◇有意思 *nǐ de shū ◇ yǒu yìsi*

C Hanging out

INTERPERSONAL

Where are Wang Peng and Li You and what are they doing there? Use the visual information and 在 (*zài*) to form different answers to the question, e.g.:

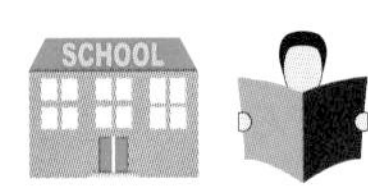

王朋和李友在學校看書。

Wáng Péng hé Lǐ Yǒu zài xuéxiào kàn shū.

1 

2 

3 

Then ask your classmates where they like to do certain activities, e.g.:

你喜歡在哪兒看書/打球/聽音樂 ?

Nǐ xǐhuan zài nǎr kàn shū/dǎ qiú/tīng yīnyuè?

D May I offer you a refreshment? INTERPERSONAL

In groups of five, act out a brief scenario. One of you is hosting a party for Gao Wenzhong, Wang Peng, Li You, and Bai Ying'ai. Find out what your guests would like to drink, and have them answer by using 吧 (*ba*), e.g.:

高文中，你想喝點兒什麼？

Gāo Wénzhōng, nǐ xiǎng hē diǎnr shénme?

我喝茶吧。

Wǒ hē chá ba.

1 

2 

3 

E Do you know everyone in your class? INTERPERSONAL

Form a circle and take turns introducing the classmate on your right to the classmate on your left.

Student A 我介紹一下，這是______。

Wǒ jièshào yí xià, zhè shì ______.

Student B 認識你很高興。我介紹一下，這是______。

Rènshi nǐ hěn gāoxìng. Wǒ jièshào yí xià, zhè shì ______.

Student C 認識你很高興。我介紹一下，這是______。

Rènshi nǐ hěn gāoxìng. Wǒ jièshào yí xià, zhè shì ______.

F May I offer you something else? INTERPERSONAL

Form groups of three and role-play the following exchange:

Host 你/你們想喝點兒什麼？

Nǐ/Nǐmen xiǎng hē diǎnr shénme?

Guests 我喝________吧。

Wǒ hē ________ba.

Apologize for not having that beverage and offer an alternative:

Host 對不起，沒有________。________，可以嗎？

Duìbuqǐ, méiyǒu ________. ________, kěyǐ ma?

The guests accept or ask for something else:

Guests 那給我一杯/一瓶 ________吧。

Nà gěi wǒ yì bēi/yì píng ________ ba.

G INTERPERSONAL And the winner is . . . PRESENTATIONAL

In groups, interview your classmates about what they like to drink. Have a representative from each group record the results on the board, in a book, or on a computer, and another report the results to the class. Tally the results from all groups and have someone announce the class's favorite drinks.

你喜歡喝什麼?

Nǐ xǐhuan hē shénme?

你喜歡喝茶嗎?

Nǐ xǐhuan hē chá ma?

你喜歡喝可樂還是咖啡?

Nǐ xǐhuan hē kělè háishi kāfēi?

你喜歡喝水還是喝茶？

Nǐ xǐhuan hē shuǐ háishi hē chá?

At a Friend's Place

Narrative

Wang Peng and Li You visited Gao Wenzhong and Gao Xiayon.

Audio

Video

昨天晚上，王朋和李友去高文中家玩兒。在高文中家，他們認識了[5]高文中的姐姐。她叫高小音，在學校的圖書館工作。她請王朋喝[a]茶，王朋喝了[5]兩杯。李友不喝茶，只喝了一杯水。他們一起聊天兒、看電視。王朋和李友晚上十二點才[6]回家。

Pinyin Narrative

Zuótiān wǎnshang, Wáng Péng hé Lǐ Yǒu qù Gāo Wénzhōng jiā wánr. Zài Gāo Wénzhōng jiā, tāmen rènshi le[5] *Gāo Wénzhōng de jiějie. Tā jiào Gāo Xiǎoyīn, zài xuéxiào de túshūguǎn gōngzuò. Tā qǐng Wáng Péng hē*[a] *chá, Wáng Péng hē le*[5] *liǎng bēi. Lǐ Yǒu bù hē chá, zhǐ hē le yì bēi shuǐ. Tāmen yìqǐ liáo tiānr, kàn diànshì. Wáng Péng hé Lǐ Yǒu wǎnshang shí'èr diǎn cái*[6] *huí jiā.*

Language Note

a 喝 *(hē)*

Unlike its English counterpart, 喝 *(hē)* always functions as a transitive verb, i.e., unless it's clear from the context, the beverage has to be specified. Therefore, 他常常喝 *(Tā chángcháng hē)* is not a complete sentence unless the beverage is understood; e.g., when it occurs as an affirmative answer to a question:

Q: 他常常喝咖啡嗎？
Tā chángcháng hē kāfēi ma?
Does he often drink coffee?

A: 他常常喝。
Tā chángcháng hē.
He often does.

Vocabulary

Audio

Flashcards

No.	Word	Pinyin	Part of Speech	Definition
1	玩（兒）	*wán(r)*	v	to have fun, to play
2	了	*le*	p	(a dynamic particle) [See Grammar 5.]
3	圖書館	*túshūguǎn*	n	library
4	一起	*yìqǐ*	adv	together
5	聊天（兒）	*liáo tiān(r)*	vo	to chat
	聊	*liáo*	v	to chat
	天	*tiān*	n	sky
6	才	*cái*	adv	not until, only then [See Grammar 6.]
7	回家	*huí jiā*	vo	to go home
	回	*huí*	v	to return

How About You?

你在哪兒看書?

Nǐ zài nǎr kàn shū?

Where do you read books?

我在＿＿＿＿＿＿看書。

Wǒ zài ＿＿＿＿＿＿ kàn shū.

See index for corresponding vocabulary or research another term.

Characterize it!

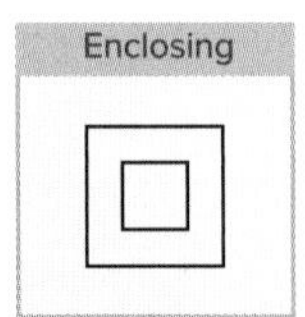

❶ 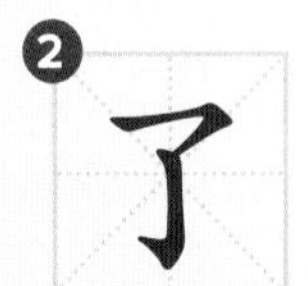

❷ 

❸ 

❹ 

❺ 

Which of these characters are formed with the pattern on the left?

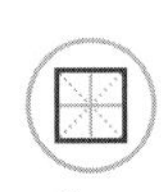
More characters

Grammar

5 The particle 了 *(le)* (I)

The dynamic particle 了 *(le)* signifies : 1) the occurrence or completion of an action or event, or 2) the emergence of a situation. The action, event, or situation usually pertains to the past, but sometimes it can refer to the future. Therefore 了 *(le)* is not a "past tense" marker and should not be taken as the equivalent of the past tense in English. In this lesson, it indicates the occurrence or completion of an action or event. It is usually used directly after a verb. In interrogative and declarative sentences, it sometimes appears after a verb and the object of the verb.

A 今天媽媽喝了三杯水。

Jīntiān Māma hē le sān bēi shuǐ.

Mom drank three glasses of water today.

OCCURRENCE OR COMPLETION OF AN ACTION, IN THE PAST.

B 星期一小高請我喝了一瓶可樂。

Xīngqīyī Xiǎo Gāo qǐng wǒ hē le yì píng kělè.

On Monday, Little Gao bought me a bottle of cola.

OCCURRENCE OR COMPLETION OF AN EVENT, IN THE PAST.

C Q: 昨天晚上你去打球了嗎？

Zuótiān wǎnshang nǐ qù dǎ qiú le ma?

Did you play ball last night?

OCCURRENCE OR COMPLETION OF AN EVENT, IN THE PAST, INTERROGATIVE

A: 昨天晚上我去打球了。

Zuótiān wǎnshang wǒ qù dǎ qiú le.

I went to play ball last night.

OCCURRENCE OR COMPLETION OF AN EVENT, IN THE PAST.

D 明天我吃了晚飯去看電影。

Míngtiān wǒ chī le wǎnfàn qù kàn diànyǐng.

Tomorrow I'll go see a movie after I eat dinner.

OCCURRENCE OR COMPLETION OF AN ACTION IN THE FIRST PART OF THE SENTENCE, IN THE FUTURE

There is often a specific time phrase in a sentence with the dynamic particle 了 *(le)*, such as:

- 今天 *(jīntiān)* (today) in (A)
- 昨天晚上 *(zuótiān wǎnshang)* (last night) in (C)
- 星期一 *(xīngqīyī)* (Monday) in (B)

When 了 *(le)* is used between the verb and the object, the object is usually preceded by a modifier. The following "numeral + measure word" is the most common type of modifier for the object:

- 三杯 *(sān bēi)* (three cups/glasses) in (A)
- 一瓶 *(yì píng)* (one bottle) in (B)

If there are other phrases or sentences following the object of the first clause, then the object does not need a modifier. See (D) above. This v 了 o+v (o) structure can be used to depict a sequence of actions regardless of the time of their occurrence.

If the object following 了 *(le)* is a proper noun, it doesn't need a modifier either. See (E).

E 我昨天看了《星球大戰》，那個電影很好。

Wǒ zuótiān kàn le «Xīngqiú Dàzhàn», nà ge diànyǐng hěn hǎo.

I saw *Star Wars* yesterday. The movie was very good.

To say that an action did not take place in the past, use 沒（有） *(méi [yǒu])* instead of 不...了 *(bù . . . le)* or 沒有...了 *(méiyǒu . . . le)*, as in the example below.

F 昨天我沒有聽音樂。[⊗昨天我不聽音樂了。]
[⊗昨天我沒有聽音樂了。]

Zuótiān wǒ bù tīng yīnyuè le.

I didn't listen to music yesterday.

The following are examples of interrogative forms:

G Q: 你吃飯了嗎? or 你吃饭了沒有? A: 我沒吃。

Nǐ chī fàn le ma? or Nǐ chī fàn le méiyǒu? *Wǒ méi chī.*

Have you eaten? No, I haven't.

H Q: 你喝了幾杯水? A: 我喝了一杯水。

Nǐ hē le jǐ bēi shuǐ? *Wǒ hē le yì bēi shuǐ.*

How many glasses of water did you drink? I drank one glass of water.

EXERCISES

Rearrange the words to form a sentence by inserting 了 after the verb and before the numeral and the measure word. Use exercise 1 as an example.

More exercises

1 我　喝　可樂　一　→　我喝了一瓶可樂。

2 他昨天　看　中國電影　一

3 李友今天　認識　人　四

6 The adverb 才 (*cái*) (not until)

The adverb 才 (*cái*) (not until) indicates the occurrence of an action or situation later than the speaker expects. That lateness is perceived by the speaker, and is not necessarily objective, as in (B) and (C). 才 (*cái*) never takes the particle 了 (*le*), even if it pertains to a past action or situation.

A 我請他六點吃晚飯，他六點半才來。

Wǒ qǐng tā liù diǎn chī wǎnfàn, tā liù diǎn bàn cái lái.

I invited him out to dinner at six o'clock. He didn't arrive until six-thirty.

B 小高常常晚上十二點才回家。

Xiǎo Gāo chángcháng wǎnshang shí'èr diǎn cái huí jiā.

Little Gao often doesn't come home until midnight.

C 她晚上很晚才睡覺。

Tā wǎnshang hěn wǎn cái shuì jiào.

She goes to bed very late at night.

EXERCISES

Indicate perceived lateness by joining these sentences. Insert 才 where appropriate. Use exercise 1 as an example.

More exercises

1 我們六點吃飯。她六點一刻來。

→ 我們六點吃飯，她六點一刻才來。

2 我們十點鐘回家。王朋十一點回家。

3 我們兩點去打球。我弟弟四點去打球。

Language Practice

H You did what?

Little Gao has so much energy! He can do a lot in one day. Based on the images, recap what he did yesterday by using 了 *(le)*, e.g.:

小高昨天喝了四杯咖啡。

Xiǎo Gāo zuótiān hē le sì bēi kāfēi.

1 

2 

3 

4 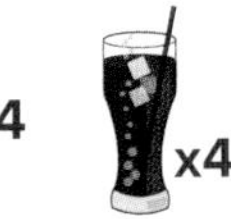

I Fashionably late!

PRESENTATIONAL

Your roommate is a procrastinator and does everything later than you. Present your different schedules to the class using 才 *(cái)*, e.g.:

7:00 vs. 8:00

我七點喝咖啡，她八點才喝（咖啡）。

Wǒ qī diǎn hē kāfēi, tā bā diǎn cái hē (kāfēi).

1 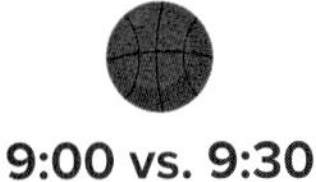

9:00 vs. 9:30

2 

2:15 vs. 2:45

3 

6:00 vs. 7:15

4 

8:00 vs. 8:30

5 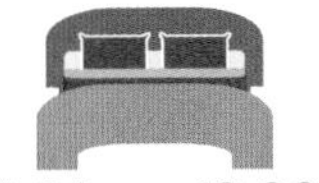

9:30 vs. 12:00

J What did you do last night?

INTERPERSONAL PRESENTATIONAL

Interview your classmates about what they did last night, e.g.:

你昨天晚上去朋友家玩兒了嗎?

Nǐ zuótiān wǎnshang qù péngyou jiā wánr le ma?

If the answer is negative, then ask:

你昨天晚上去哪兒了？你喝什麼了？
你喝了幾杯/幾瓶？

Nǐ zuótiān wǎnshang qù nǎr le? Nǐ hē shénme le? Nǐ hē le jǐ bēi/jǐ píng?

Then report to the class what your partner did last night, e.g.:

Mark 昨天晚上去朋友家玩兒了/沒有去朋友家玩兒……

Mark *zuótiān wǎnshang qù péngyou jiā wánr le/méiyǒu qù péngyou jiā wánr . . .*

K Birthday itinerary

PRESENTATIONAL

Describe what Little Wang did on his birthday, and when, according to these images.

1 

2 

3 

Chinese Chat

A friend is texting you about taking a coffee break. How would you reply?

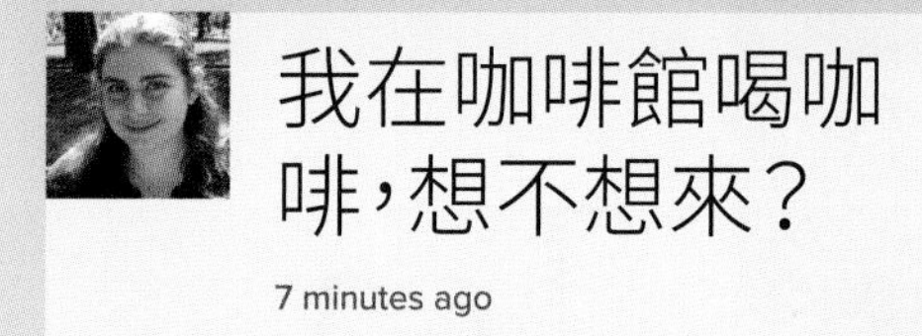

...
6 minutes ago

...
1 minute ago

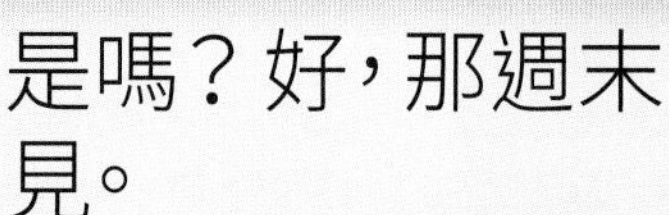

Type your message...

CULTURAL LITERACY

Continue to explore

COMPARE & CONTRAST

1. "Host" and "guest" are 主 (*zhǔ*) and 客 (*kè*). The Chinese often say 客隨主便 (*kè suí zhǔ biàn*), "A good guest goes along with whatever is convenient for the host." A related expression is 入鄉隨俗 (*rù xiāng suí sú*), "Wherever you find yourself, follow local customs." The phrase 反客為主 (*fǎn kè wéi zhǔ*), meanwhile, describes a presumptive guest who usurps the place of the host. Are there similar sayings in your culture?
2. When you visit a friend in China, you should bring a gift. You might be asked to change into slippers and be offered something to drink. Normally, food is served family style to indicate abundance and respect for the guests. Dishes are brought out one course at a time, so the host will not join the meal until all the dishes are served. It is polite to wait for the host to urge you to start eating. If a Chinese friend asks you about visiting etiquette in your culture, what would you say?
3. The tea plant is native to China. The beverage made from its leaves is often called some derivative of the Mandarin or Southern Min dialect pronunciation of the Chinese word for tea. The Russian *chai* comes from Mandarin, whereas tea in English comes from the Southern Min dialect. Do you know what tea is called in any other language?

Tea

茶 (*chá*) can probably be called the national drink of China. Indeed, the practice of drinking tea originated there. According to legend, tea was discovered by the ancient Chinese emperor 神農 (*Shénnóng*) when leaves from a nearby shrub fell into the water he was boiling. It depends on whom you ask, but in general, Chinese tea may be classified into the following categories according to the different methods by which tea leaves are processed: green tea, black tea, Wulong tea, compressed tea, and scented tea.

Chrysanthemum tea, 菊花茶 (*júhuā chá*), is a type of scented tea, whereas Longjing tea, 龍井茶 (*lóngjǐng chá*), belongs to the green tea family. Nowadays, bubble tea, 珍珠奶茶 (*zhēnzhū nǎichá*), is gaining popularity in the West.

Although tea remains the most popular beverage in China, the number of coffee drinkers has been on the rise in recent years. Coffee is now widely available in supermarkets. Coffee shops, including international chains such as Starbucks, 星巴克 (*Xīngbākè*), and Coffee Bean & Tea Leaf, are familiar sights in many Chinese cities.

Do you know where bubble tea originated? 奶茶 (*nǎichá*) literally means milk tea. How about 珍珠 (*zhēnzhū*)? What are they really?

認識你很高興 (*rènshi nǐ hěn gāoxìng*) or 很高興認識你 (*hěn gāoxìng rènshi nǐ*) is basically a translation of "I'm very happy to meet you." This form of greeting is becoming more common, even though to some Chinese it sounds a bit formal.

Greetings

Etiquette

Traditionally, privacy is a somewhat less sacrosanct concept in Chinese culture than it is in the West: you would not necessarily be considered intrusive if you dropped by a friend's place without warning; nor would topics such as age, marital status, and salary necessarily be off limits in a polite conversation. For those who believe in the traditional Chinese notion of friendship or personal loyalty, sharing such personal information is an important gesture of trust. But there is a more prosaic explanation. Until relatively recently, most people lived in close proximity to one another and everyone followed more or less the same prescribed track in life. The income gap was limited. Therefore, there were few secrets. Everyone knew what their neighbors did and how much money they made.

This is changing, however; particularly due to disparity in incomes and urbanization of communities. Chinese citizens have become more conscious of their "right to privacy," or 隱私權 (*yǐnsī quán*). Nowadays, Chinese people consider it more and more important to give notice before visiting friends and to avoid asking about personal information.

Lesson Wrap-Up

Make It Flow!

Rearrange the following sentences into a logical sequence. Then combine them into a coherent narrative. Remember to omit repetitive elements and substitute subjects with personal pronouns where appropriate. Time expressions and place words can also serve as useful connective devices.

_____高文中的姐姐叫高小音。

_____他們一起聊天兒、看電視。

__1__昨天晚上，王朋和李友去高文中家玩兒。

_____晚上十二點王朋和李友才回家。

_____在高文中家王朋和李友認識了高文中的姐姐。

_____高小音在圖書館工作。

Role-Play

Student A You are the host. Introduce your guests and ask what they would like to drink.

Student B Meet and greet the other guest. Compliment the host's home. Ask where the other guest works. Tell the host that you don't drink tea, coffee, or cola. Ask for a glass of water instead.

Student C Meet and greet the other guest. Tell the other guest that you are delighted to meet him/her. Tell the other guest that you don't work; you are a student. Let the host know that you would like a cup of tea.

Email

Email your Chinese-speaking friend about your visit to a friend's place last night. Include the following information:

- Where you went
- Whom you met there, what they did, and whether you found them interesting
- What your friend's home was like, e.g., big, nicely decorated
- What you did
- When you returned home

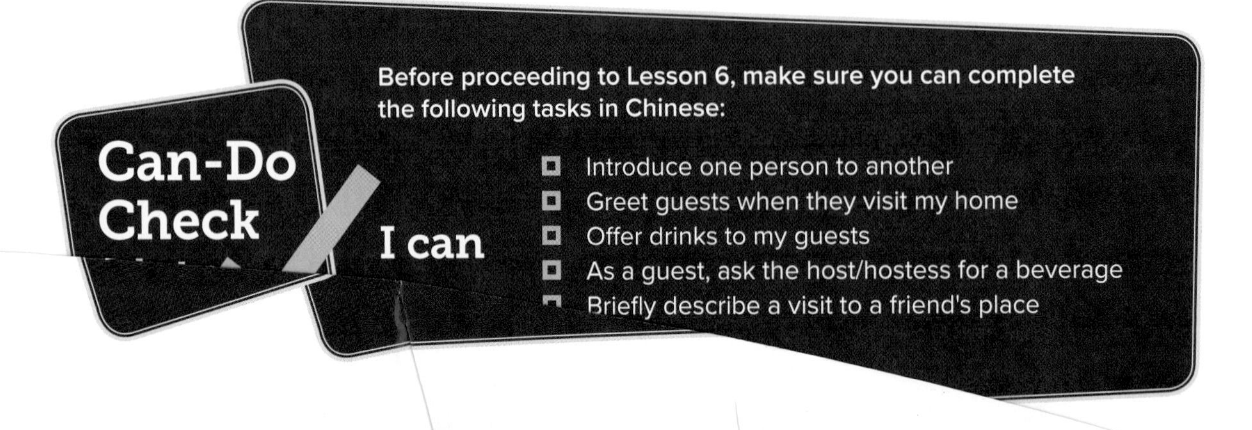

Keeping It Casual (L1–L5)

Before you progress to the next half of the text, we'll review how some of the functional expressions from Lessons 1–5 are used in casual Chinese. After you complete the review, note any other casual expressions you would like to learn, then share the list with your teacher.

1 算了 *(suàn le)* (forget it, never mind)

Say this when you've put someone in an awkward position, or when someone's made a mistake that you're willing to let go. You can also say this when you're dissatisfied with what someone is doing and want him/her to stop. [See Lesson 4.]

A

Student A 明天我們去打球，怎麼樣？
Míngtiān wǒmen qù dǎ qiú, zěnmeyàng?
Let's go play ball tomorrow, all right?

Student B 明天我很忙。
Míngtiān wǒ hěn máng.
I'm very busy tomorrow.

Student A 那算了。
Nà suàn le.
Never mind then.

B

Student A 你今年多大？
Nǐ jīnnián duō dà?
How old are you this year?

Student B 你為什麼問我多大？
Nǐ wèishénme wèn wǒ duō dà?
Why are you asking me how old I am?

Student A 算了，我不問了。
Suàn le, wǒ bú wèn le.
Never mind. I won't ask then.

2 誰呀 *(shéi ya)* (who is it?)

Say this when someone knocks on your door. [See Lesson 5.]

A

(Knocking on the door.)

Wang Peng 誰呀？
Shéi ya?
Who is it?

Li You 是我，李友。
Shì wǒ, Lǐ Yǒu.
It's me, Li You.

Wang Peng 請進。
Qǐng jìn.
Please come in.

B

(Knocking on the door.)

Gao Wenzhong 誰呀？
Shéi ya?
Who is it?

Little Wang 我，小王。
Wǒ, Xiǎo Wáng.
It's me, Little Wang.

Gao Wenzhong 進來。
Jìn lai.
Come in.

3 是嗎 *(shì ma)* (really, is that so?)

Say this when you hear something unexpected. [See Lesson 5.]

A

Student A 我昨天晚上三點半才睡覺。
Wǒ zuótiān wǎnshang sān diǎn bàn cái shuì jiào.
Last night, I didn't go to sleep until 3:30.

Student B 是嗎？為什麼？
Shì ma? Wèishénme?
Really? Why?

Student A 因為昨天我很忙。
Yīnwèi zuótiān wǒ hěn máng.
Because I was so busy yesterday.

B

Student A 週末我去跳舞。
Zhōumò wǒ qù tiào wǔ.
I'm going dancing this weekend.

Student B 是嗎？我也去。
Shì ma? Wǒ yě qù.
Really? I'm going as well.

Lesson 6

第六課

Dì liù kè

約時間

Yuē shíjiān

MAKING APPOINTMENTS

Learning Objectives

In this lesson, you will learn to:

- Answer a phone call and initiate a phone conversation
- Set up an appointment with a teacher on the phone
- Ask a favor
- Ask someone to return your call

Relate & Get Ready

In your own culture/community:

- How do you answer the phone?
- How do students address their teachers?
- How do you ask for a favor?

Calling Your Teacher

Dialogue 1

李友給[1]常老師打電話……

喂？

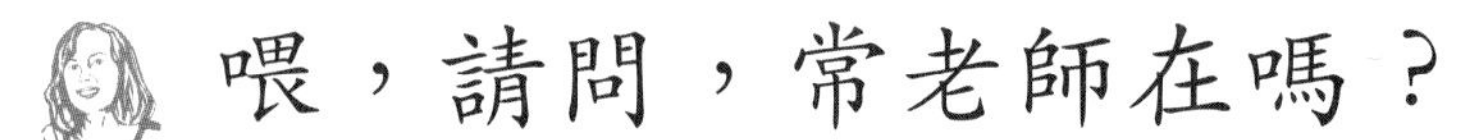

喂，請問，常老師在嗎？

我就是。您[a]是哪位？

老師，您好。我是李友。

李友，有事兒嗎？

老師，今天下午您有時間[b]嗎？我想問[c]您幾個問題。

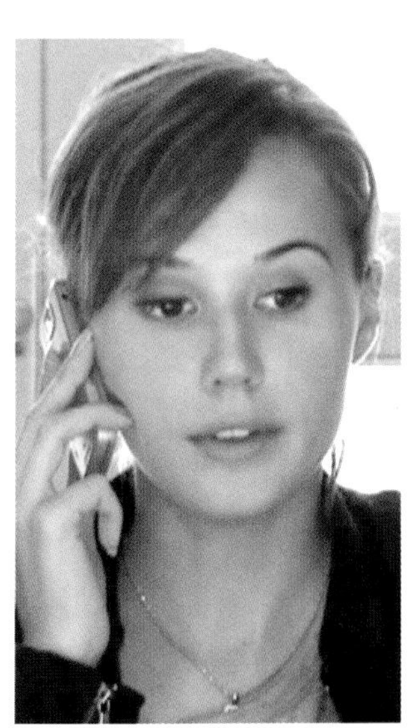

對不起，今天下午我要[2]開會。

明天呢？

明天上午我有兩節[d]課，下午三點要給二年級考試。

您什麼時候[e]有空兒？

明天四點以後[f]才有空兒。

要是[g]您方便，四點半我到您的辦公室去，行嗎？

四點半，沒問題[h]。我在辦公室等你。

謝謝您。

別[3]客氣。

Pinyin Dialogue

Lǐ Yǒu gěi[1] Cháng lǎoshī dǎ diànhuà . . .

Wéi?

Wéi, qǐng wèn, Cháng lǎoshī zài ma?

Wǒ jiù shì. Nín[a] shì nǎ wèi?

 *Lǎoshī, nín hǎo. Wǒ shì Lǐ Yǒu.*

 *Lǐ Yǒu, yǒu shìr ma?*

 *Lǎoshī, jīntiān xiàwǔ nín yǒu shíjiān[b] ma? Wǒ xiǎng wèn[c] nín jǐ ge wèntí.*

 *Duìbuqǐ, jīntiān xiàwǔ wǒ yào[2] kāi huì.*

 *Míngtiān ne?*

 *Míngtiān shàngwǔ wǒ yǒu liǎng jié[d] kè, xiàwǔ sān diǎn yào gěi èr niánjí kǎo shì.*

 *Nín shénme shíhou[e] yǒu kòngr?*

 *Míngtiān sì diǎn yǐhòu[f] cái yǒu kòngr.*

 *Yàoshi[g] nín fāngbiàn, sì diǎn bàn wǒ dào nín de bàngōngshì qù, xíng ma?*

 *Sì diǎn bàn, méi wèntí[h]. Wǒ zài bàngōngshì děng nǐ.*

 *Xièxie nín.*

 *Bié[3] kèqi.*

Language Notes

a 您 *(nín)*

This personal pronoun is often used to address an older person or someone of higher social rank. It is common for strangers to address each other with 您 *(nín)* and then switch to 你 *(nǐ)* as they get acquainted.

b 有時間 *(yǒu shíjiān)*

"To have free time" is 有時間 *(yǒu shíjiān)* or 有空兒 *(yǒu kòngr)*, never 有時候 *(yǒu shíhou)*.

c 問 *(wèn)*

Both 問 *(wèn)* and 請 *(qǐng)* are often translated as "to ask" in English. However, the verb 問 *(wèn)* means "to inquire," e.g., 我問她一個問題 *(Wǒ wèn tā yí ge wèntí)* (I ask her a question), whereas 請 *(qǐng)* means "to invite" or "to request," e.g., 我請她跳舞 *(Wǒ qǐng tā tiào wǔ)* (I invite her to dance).

d 節 *(jié)*

The measure word for academic courses is 門 *(mén)*. Compare: 三門課 *(sān mén kè)* (three courses), 三節課 *(sān jié kè)* (three class periods), and 三課 *(sān kè)* (three lessons).

e 什麼時候 *(shénme shíhou)*

幾點 *(jǐ diǎn)* is used to ask for a specific time of day. To ask about time in general, use the expression 什麼時候 *(shénme shíhou)* (when).

f 以後 *(yǐhòu)*

The Chinese equivalent of "after four o'clock" is 四點以後 *(sìdiǎn yǐhòu)*. Note the difference in word order. Likewise, "before Monday" is 星期一以前 *(xīngqīyī yǐqián)*.

g 要是 *(yàoshi)*

要是 *(yàoshi)* (if) is a conjunction used to introduce a contingent or hypothetical action or situation. Unlike "if," it cannot introduce a subordinate clause: ✖ 我不知道要是他明天來.

h 沒問題 *(méi wèntí)*

This phrase, meaning "no problem," is a reassuring reply to a tentative inquiry. It suggests that the speaker does not foresee any problems. When people thank you and say 謝謝 *(xièxie)*, the appropriate answer is 不謝 *(bú xiè)* or 別客氣 *(bié kèqi)* rather than 沒問題 *(méi wèntí)*.

Vocabulary

Audio

Flashcards

No.	Word	Pinyin	Part of Speech	Definition
1	給	*gěi*	prep	to, for [See Grammar 1.]
2	打電話	*dǎ diànhuà*	vo	to make a phone call
	電話	*diànhuà*	n	telephone
3	喂	*wéi/wèi*	interj	(on the phone) Hello!, Hey!
4	在	*zài*	v	to be present, to be at (a place)
5	就	*jiù*	adv	precisely, exactly
6	您	*nín*	pr	you (honorific for 你)
7	哪	*nǎ/něi*	qpr	which
8	位	*wèi*	m	(polite measure word for people)
9	下午	*xiàwǔ*	t	afternoon
10	時間	*shíjiān*	n	time
11	問題	*wèntí*	n	question, problem
12	要	*yào*	mv	will, to be going to, to want to, to have a desire to [See Grammar 2.]
13	開會	*kāi huì*	vo	to have a meeting
	開	*kāi*	v	to open, to hold (a meeting, party, etc.)
	會	*huì*	n	meeting
14	上午	*shàngwǔ*	t	morning
15	節	*jié*	m	(measure word for class periods)
16	課	*kè*	n	class, course, lesson
17	年級	*niánjí*	n	grade in school
18	考試	*kǎo shì*	vo/n	to give or take a test; test
	考	*kǎo*	v	to give or take a test
	試	*shì*	n/v	test; to try, to experiment
19	以後	*yǐhòu*	t	after, from now on, later on
20	空（兒）	*kòng(r)*	n	free time
21	要是	*yàoshi*	conj	if
22	方便	*fāngbiàn*	adj	convenient
23	到	*dào*	v	to go to, to arrive

Confucius （孔子） (Kǒng Zǐ), considered China's "First Teacher" （先師） (Xiānshī), is associated with wisdom. Why do you think Confucius is referenced on this packaging? How does this pen refill claim to help students?

GET Real WITH CHINESE

No.	Word	Pinyin	Part of Speech	Definition
24	辦公室	*bàngōngshì*	n	office
25	行	*xíng*	v	all right, OK
26	等	*děng*	v	to wait, to wait for
27	別	*bié*	adv	don't [See Grammar 3.]
28	客氣	*kèqi*	adj	polite
29	常老師	*Cháng lǎoshī*	pn	Teacher Chang

How About You?

我們在哪兒見面？

Wǒmen zài nǎr jiànmiàn?

Where will we meet?

我在 ________________ 等你。

Wǒ zài ________________ děng nǐ.

See index for corresponding vocabulary or research another term.

Grammar

1 The preposition 給 (*gěi*) (to, for)

給 (*gěi*) (to, for) can be a verb or a preposition. As a preposition, 給 (*gěi*) is generally combined with nouns or pronouns to form prepositional phrases, which appear before verbs as adverbials.

A 他給我打了一個電話。

Tā gěi wǒ dǎ le yí ge diànhuà.

He gave me a call.

B 他是誰？請你給我們介紹一下。

Tā shì shéi? Qǐng nǐ gěi wǒmen jièshào yí xià.

Who is he? Please introduce us.

C 你有你姐姐的照片嗎？給我看一下，行嗎？

Nǐ yǒu nǐ jiějie de zhàopiàn ma? Gěi wǒ kàn yí xià, xíng ma?

Do you have a picture of your older sister? Can I have a look?

D 我昨天很忙，沒給媽媽打電話。

Wǒ zuótiān hěn máng, méi gěi māma dǎ diànhuà.

I was very busy yesterday. I didn't call my mother.

More exercises

EXERCISES

Rearrange the words to form a sentence by inserting 給 where appropriate. Use exercise 1 as an example.

1 高文中 介紹他姐姐 我們
→ 高文中給我們介紹他姐姐。

2 李老師 介紹中國音樂 他的學生

3 我媽媽 看她的照片 我們

2 The modal verb 要 *(yào)* (will, be going to) (I)

The modal verb 要 *(yào)* (will, be going to) has several meanings. In this lesson, 要 *(yào)* indicates a future action, particularly a scheduled event or an activity that one is committed to. The negative form of 要 *(yào)* is 不 *(bù)* (no, not) rather than 不要 *(bú yào)*.

A 明天下午三點我要給二年級考試。

Míngtiān xiàwǔ sān diǎn wǒ yào gěi èr niánjí kǎo shì.

I'm going to give the second-year class a test at 3:00 p.m. tomorrow.

B 今天晚上妹妹要去看電影。

Jīntiān wǎnshang mèimei yào qù kàn diànyǐng.

My younger sister is going to see a movie tonight.

C Q: 明天我要去小白家玩兒。你呢？

Míngtiān wǒ yào qù Xiǎo Bái jiā wánr. Nǐ ne?

I'm going to visit Little Bai tomorrow. How about you?

A: 明天我不去小白家玩兒，我要開會。

Míngtiān wǒ bú qù Xiǎo Bái jiā wánr, wǒ yào kāi huì.

I'm not going to visit Little Bai tomorrow. I am going to a meeting.

EXERCISES

In pairs, form a question-and-answer about people's scheduled activities by using 要. Use exercise 1 as an example.

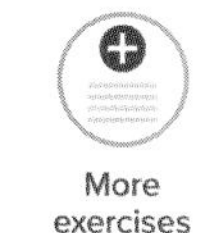

More exercises

1 小李今天晚上 去聽音樂

→ Q: 小李今天晚上要做什麼？

A: 他今天晚上要去聽音樂。

2 王朋星期三 去高文中家玩兒

3 王律師的弟弟明天晚上 去學校看電影

3 The adverb 別 (*bié*) (don't)

別 (*bié*) (don't) is used to advise someone to refrain from doing something. Depending on the context, it can be used to express a polite request, a gentle reminder, or a serious admonition.

A 別客氣。

Bié kèqi.

You're welcome.

B 你別說。

Nǐ bié shuō.

Don't say anything.

C 別進來！

Bié jìn lai!

Don't come in!

D 那個電影沒有意思，你別看了。

Nà ge diànyǐng méi yǒu yìsi, nǐ bié kàn le.

That movie is boring. Don't go see it.

E 別給小王打電話！

Bié gěi Xiǎo Wáng dǎ diànhuà!

Don't call Little Wang!

More exercises

EXERCISES

In pairs, suggest your partner refrain from doing something by using the bracketed phrase and inserting 別 where appropriate. Use exercise 1 as an example.

1 **Student A** 我今天晚上想去看電影。 （沒意思）

Student B 那個電影沒意思，別去看了。

2 **Student A** 我想請小高吃美國菜。 （不喜歡）

Student B 小高 ________________ 。

3 **Student A** 我想給小英打電話。 （很忙）

Student B 小英 ________________ 。

Language Practice

A BFF

PRESENTATIONAL

Recap what Little Gao often does for his friends. Use 給 *(gěi)* where appropriate, e.g.:

打電話	*dǎ diànhuà*
小高常常給他們打電話。	*Xiǎo Gāo chángcháng gěi tāmen dǎ diànhuà.*
1 看他爸爸媽媽的照片	*kàn tā bàba māma de zhàopiàn*
2 聽中國音樂	*tīng Zhōngguó yīnyuè*
3 喝英國茶	*hē Yīngguó chá*
4 介紹新電影	*jièshào xīn diànyǐng*

你呢？Now share what you do for your friends with the class.

B To-do list

INTERPERSONAL

Li You has the next few days all planned out. In pairs, form a question-and-answer about what she will be doing by inserting 要 *(yào)* in the ◇, e.g.:

明天◇去跳舞	*míngtiān ◇ qù tiào wǔ*
Q: 李友明天做什么？	*Lǐ Yǒu míngtiān zuò shénme?*
A: 李友明天要去跳舞。	*Lǐ Yǒu míngtiān yào qù tiào wǔ.*
1 今天晚上◇請朋友喝咖啡	*jīntiān wǎnshang ◇ qǐng péngyou hē kāfēi*
2 明天上午◇ 去同學家練習中文	*míngtiān shàngwǔ ◇* *qù tóngxué jiā liànxí Zhōngwén*
3 明天下午◇ 去老師的辦公室問問題	*míngtiān xiàwǔ ◇* *qù lǎoshī de bàngōngshì wèn wèntí*
4 這個星期五◇ 去學校看電影	*zhè ge xīngqīwǔ ◇* *qù xuéxiào kàn diànyǐng*
5 這個週末◇ 給小高介紹一個朋友	*zhè ge zhōumò ◇* *gěi Xiǎo Gāo jièshào yí ge péngyou*

Then ask about your partner's plans for the next few days.

C I have another suggestion

PRESENTATIONAL

Using the images, practice how to be accommodating. Insert 要是 *(yàoshi)* where appropriate, e.g.:

不喜歡 *(bù xǐhuan)* 喜歡 *(xǐhuan)*

要是你不喜歡唱歌，我們跳舞，怎麼樣？

Yàoshi nǐ bù xǐhuan chàng gē, wǒmen tiào wǔ, zěnmeyàng?

1. 不想 *(bù xiǎng)*  想 *(xiǎng)* 
2. 覺得……沒有意思 *(juéde . . . méiyǒu yìsi)*
   覺得……有意思 *(juéde . . . yǒu yìsi)* 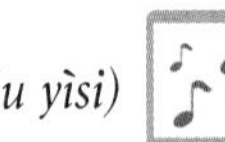
3. 不喜歡 *(bù xǐhuan)*  喜歡 *(xǐhuan)* 
4. 沒有空兒 *(méi yǒu kòngr)* today 有空兒 *(yǒu kòngr)* tomorrow

D What if?

INTERPERSONAL

In pairs, take turns asking and answering the following questions.

1. 要是你有時間，你想去哪兒玩兒？

   Yàoshi nǐ yǒu shíjiān, nǐ xiǎng qù nǎr wánr?

2. 要是朋友請你吃飯，你想吃什麼菜？

   Yàoshi péngyou qǐng nǐ chī fàn, nǐ xiǎng chī shénme cài?

3. 要是同學請你看電影，你想看什麼電影？

   Yàoshi tóngxué qǐng nǐ kàn diànyǐng, nǐ xiǎng kàn shénme diànyǐng?

4. 要是朋友請你去跳舞，你想去哪兒跳舞？

   Yàoshi péngyou qǐng nǐ qù tiào wǔ, nǐ xiǎng qù nǎr tiào wǔ?

5. 要是朋友找你打球，你什麼時候有時間？

   Yàoshi péngyou zhǎo nǐ dǎ qiú, nǐ shénme shíhou yǒu shíjiān?

E Calling up

INTERPERSONAL

You are calling your friend to arrange a time to hang out. In pairs, role-play the conversation between the caller and the person (either your friend or your friend's sibling) who answers.

Caller 喂，請問，________在嗎？ *Wéi, qǐngwèn, ________zài ma?*

Friend 我就是。/ *Wǒ jiù shì. /*

Friend's Sibling ________不在。 *________bú zài.*

Friend/Friend's Sibling 您是哪位？ *Nín shì nǎ wèi?*

Caller 我是________。 *Wǒ shì ________.*

Friend/Friend's Sibling ________，你好！有事兒嗎？ *________, nǐ hǎo! Yǒu shìr ma?*

Caller …… (You ask if you can come over this evening to watch TV.)

Friend/Friend's Sibling …… (They have a ball game, but are free tomorrow night.)

Caller …… (Tomorrow night works for you, so you set a time before saying goodbye.)

Characterize it!

- What do the characters mean?
- What is the common radical?
- What does the radical mean?
- How does the radical relate to the overall meaning of the characters?

1 打 2 找

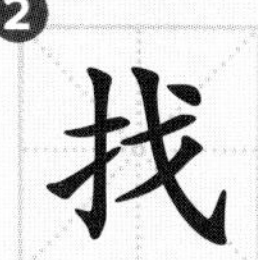

More characters

Chinese Chat

Teacher Chang just posted a tweet. When do you think her students can make an appointment with her?

Teacher Chang
@Teacher_Chang66

Follow

明天上午有兩節課，還要開會……十一點半以後才有空兒。

10:07 PM - 14 Nov 2016

 25 ♥ 28

Calling a Friend for Help

Dialogue 2

李友给王朋打電話……

Audio

Video

喂，請問，王朋在嗎？

我就是。你是李友**吧**[a]？

王朋，我下個星期[4]要考中文，你幫我準備一下，跟我練習說中文，好嗎？

好啊，但是你得[5]請我喝咖啡。

喝咖啡，沒問題。那我什麼時候跟你**見面**[b]？你今天晚上有空兒嗎？

今天晚上白英愛請我吃飯。

是嗎？白英愛請你吃飯？

對。我回來[6]以後給你打電話。

好，我等你的電話。

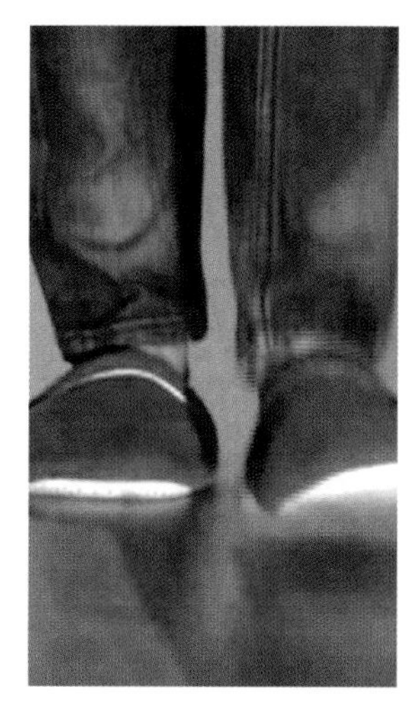

Lǐ Yǒu gěi Wáng Péng dǎ diànhuà . . .

 *Wéi, qǐng wèn, Wáng Péng zài ma?*

 *Wǒ jiù shì. Nǐ shì Lǐ Yǒu ba*[a]*?*

 *Wáng Péng, wǒ xià ge xīngqī*[4] *yào kǎo Zhōngwén, nǐ bāng wǒ zhǔnbèi yí xià, gēn wǒ liànxí shuō Zhōngwén, hǎo ma?*

 *Hǎo a, dànshì nǐ děi*[5] *qǐng wǒ hē kāfēi.*

 *Hē kāfēi, méi wèntí. Nà wǒ shénme shíhou gēn nǐ jiàn miàn*[b]*? Nǐ jīntiān wǎnshang yǒu kòngr ma?*

 *Jīntiān wǎnshang Bái Yīng'ài qǐng wǒ chī fàn.*

 *Shì ma? Bái Yīng'ài qǐng nǐ chī fàn?*

 *Duì. Wǒ huí lai*[6] *yǐhòu gěi nǐ dǎ diànhuà.*

 *Hǎo, wǒ děng nǐ de diànhuà.*

Language Notes

a 吧 *(ba)*

Compare the two particles 吧 *(ba)* and 嗎 *(ma)*:

你是李友吧？

Nǐ shì Lǐ Yǒu ba?

You are Li You, aren't you?

(I think you're Li You. Am I right?)

你是李友嗎？

Nǐ shì Lǐ Yǒu ma?

Are you Li You?

(I am not quite sure.)

b 見面 *(jiàn miàn)*

"A meets B" is "A 跟 *(gēn)* B 見面 *(jiàn miàn)*," not "⊗ A 見面 B."

Vocabulary

Audio

Flashcards

No.	Word	Pinyin	Part of Speech	Definition
1	下個	*xià ge*		next
	下	*xià*		below, next
2	中文	*Zhōngwén*	n	Chinese language
	文	*wén*	n	language, script, written language
3	幫	*bāng*	v	to help
4	準備	*zhǔnbèi*	v	to prepare
5	練習	*liànxí*	v	to practice
6	說	*shuō*	v	to say, to speak
7	啊	*a*	p	(a sentence-final particle of exclamation, interrogation, etc.)
8	但是	*dànshì*	conj	but
9	得	*děi*	av	must, to have to
10	跟	*gēn*	prep	with
11	見面	*jiàn miàn*	vo	to meet up, to meet with
	面	*miàn*	n	face
12	回來	*huí lai*	vc	to come back

我學中文，你呢？

Wǒ xué Zhōngwén, nǐ ne?

I study Chinese. How about you?

How About You?

我（也）學 ________。

Wǒ (yě) xué ________.

See index for corresponding vocabulary or research another term.

Grammar

4 Time expressions

年 *(nián)* (year), 月 *(yuè)* (month), 星期 *(xīngqī)* (week), and 天 *(tiān)* (day) are all nouns, but 年 *(nián)* (year) and 天 *(tiān)* (day) are also measure words. Therefore, they are used differently, following the patterns below.

Pattern	Examples
Numeral + 年/天	一年 *(yì nián)* (one year), 五天 *(wǔ tiān)* (five days)
Numeral + Measure Word + 月/星期	一個月 *(yí ge yuè)* (one month), 三個星期 *(sān ge xīngqī)* (three weeks)

"One week" is 一個星期 *(yí ge xīngqī)*, therefore "one week later" is 一個星期以後 *(yí ge xīngqī yǐhòu)*. "One month" is 一個月 *(yí ge yuè)*, therefore "one month later" is 一個月以後 *(yí ge yuè yǐhòu)*. Please note that "one month" is not 一月 *(yīyuè)* (January). The time expressions 月 *(yuè)* and 星期 *(xīngqī)* can be formed by using 下 *(xià)* (below) and 上 *(shàng)* (above), following the patterns below. "Below" （下） *(xià)* is used to refer to weeks and months in the future, and "above" （上） *(shàng)* to refer to weeks and months in the past.

月[a] *(yuè)* **(month)**	星期[b] *(xīngqī)* **(week)**
上上個月 *(shàng shàng ge yuè)* (the month before last)	上上（個）星期 *(shàng shàng [ge] xīngqī)* (the week before last)
上個月 *(shàng ge yuè)* (last month)	上（個）星期 *(shàng [ge] xīngqī)* (last week)
這個月 *(zhè ge yuè)* (this month)	這（個）星期 *(zhè [ge] xīngqī)* (this week)
下個月 *(xià ge yuè)* (next month)	下（個）星期 *(xià [ge] xīngqī)* (next week)
下下個月 *(xià xià ge yuè)* (the month after next)	下下（個）星期 *(xià xià [ge] xīngqī)* (the week after next)

[a]We don't say ⊗ 上月/下月.
[b]The measure word 個 can be omitted for 星期: 下個星期=下星期; 上個星期=上星期.

The below expressions using 天 *(tiān)* (day) and 年 *(nián)* (year) form two parallel series except for 昨天 *(zuótiān)* (yesterday) and 去年 *(qùnián)* (last year).

天 *(tiān)* **(day)**	年 *(nián)* **(year)**
大前天 *(dàqiántiān)* (three days ago)	大前年 *(dàqiánnián)* (three years ago)
前天 *(qiántiān)* (the day before yesterday)	前年 *(qiánnián)* (the year before last)
昨天 *(zuótiān)* (yesterday)	去年 *(qùnián)* (last year)
今天 *(jīntiān)* (today)	今年 *(jīnnián)* (this year)
明天 *(míngtiān)* (tomorrow)	明年 *(míngnián)* (next year)
後天 *(hòutiān)* (the day after tomorrow)	後年 *(hòunián)* (the year after next)
大後天 *(dàhòutiān)* (three days from today)	大後年 *(dàhòunián)* (three years from now)

More exercises

EXERCISES

Based on the information given, fill in the blanks with the appropriate time expressions. Exercise 1 includes an example.

1 這個月是五月：上個月是四月，______是三月，______是六月，______是七月。

2 今天是星期三：昨天是______，前天是______，明天是______，後天是______。

5 The modal verb 得 *(děi)* (must, have to)

The modal verb 得 *(děi)* means "have to" or "must."

A 我現在得去開會，沒空兒跟你聊天兒。

Wǒ xiànzài děi qù kāi huì, méi kòngr gēn nǐ liáo tiānr.

I have to go to a meeting right now, and don't have time to chat with you.

B 我有事兒，得去學校。

Wǒ yǒu shìr, děi qù xuéxiào.

I have some business to attend to. I have to go to school.

The negative form of 得 *(děi)* is 不用 *(bú yòng)* (need not) or 不必 *(bú bì)* (need not), ✖ 不得.
Therefore, the correct way to say "You don't have to go to the library" is (C).

C 你不用去圖書館。 or 你不必去圖書館。

Nǐ bú yòng qù túshūguǎn. *Nǐ bú bì qù túshūguǎn.*

[✖ 你不得去圖書館。]

EXERCISES

In pairs, role-play the completed question-and-answers below by inserting 得 where appropriate.
Use exercise 1 as an example.

1 Q: 今天晚上我們去看電影，好嗎？

A: 對不起/不行，今天晚上我得看書。

2 Q: 老師，下午三點我去您的辦公室問問題，行嗎？

A: ________，______________上課。

3 Q: 白律師，明年二月你可以來我們這兒工作嗎？

A: ________，______________去英國開會。

6 Directional complements (I)

來 *(lái)* (to come) and 去 *(qù)* (to go) can serve as directional complements after such verbs as 進 *(jìn)* (to enter) and 回 *(huí)* (to return). 來 *(lái)* signifies movement toward the speaker, as in (A) and (B). 去 *(qù)* (to go) signifies movement away from the speaker, as in (C), or the speaker's own movement away from a current location, as in (D).

(You're bored in your dorm, so you ask your roommate when she's returning.)

A 你什麼時候回來？

Nǐ shénme shíhou huí lai?

When are you coming back?

(After you knock on the door, your teacher invites you into her office.)

B 進來。

Jìn lai.

Come in.

(Upon arrival at the airport, your friend drops you off and reminds you to hurry up.)

C 快進去吧!

Kuài jìn qu ba!

Just go in, quickly!

(While shopping at the mall, you text your mom to tell her when you'll be home.)

D 我六點回去。

Wǒ liù diǎn huí qu.

I'll be back at six.

More exercises

EXERCISES

Complete the sentences below by inserting the appropriate directional complements.

1 白英愛：老師，我可以進____嗎？

2 常老師：快進____。

Language Practice

F It takes two

INTERPERSONAL

Based on the information below, practice saying who does what with whom by using 跟 *(gēn)* where appropriate, e.g.:

 ◇  說中文 *(shuō Zhōngwén)*

常老師跟李友說中文。

Cháng lǎoshī gēn Lǐ Yǒu shuō Zhōngwén.

1  ◇  聊天兒 *(liáo tiānr)*

2  ◇  跳舞 *(tiào wǔ)*

3 ◇  說英文 *(shuō Yīngwén)*

4  見面吃晚飯 *(jiàn miàn chī wǎnfàn)*

Then ask your partner whom they often speak Chinese with.

G Do's and don't's

PRESENTATIONAL

Practice persuading someone to do one thing instead of another. Insert 別 *(bié)* and 得 *(děi)* where appropriate, e.g.:

⊗ 聊天兒 *liáo tiānr*

✔ 看書 *kàn shū*

你別聊天兒，你得看書。

Nǐ bié liáo tiānr, nǐ děi kàn shū.

	✗	✓
1	喝茶 *hē chá*	睡覺 *shuì jiào*
2	看電視 *kàn diànshì*	給老師打電話 *gěi lǎoshī dǎ diànhuà*
3	睡覺 *shuì jiào*	去考試 *qù kǎo shì*
4	打球 *dǎ qiú*	練習說中文 *liànxí shuō Zhōngwén*
5	去朋友家玩兒 *qù péngyou jiā wánr*	去學校工作 *qù xuéxiào gōngzuò*

Then present a list of study habits to improve your Chinese language skills to your classmates.

H Meeting up

PRESENTATIONAL

Indicate which IC characters you would or would not like to meet, using 跟 *(gēn)* and 見面 *(jiàn miàn)* where appropriate, e.g.:

我（不）想跟王朋見面。

Wǒ (bù) xiǎng gēn Wáng Péng jiàn miàn.

1 

2 

3 

4 

5 

I Day planner

INTERPERSONAL

In pairs, ask questions about your partner's schedule.

你這個星期天上午（要）做什麼？

Nǐ zhè ge xīngqītiān shàngwǔ (yào) zuò shénme?

你下個星期三下午（要）做什麼？

Nǐ xià ge xīngqīsān xiàwǔ (yào) zuò shénme?

你下個星期五晚上（要）做什麼？

Nǐ xià ge xīngqīwǔ wǎnshang (yào) zuò shénme?

J One good turn deserves another

INTERPERSONAL

Use the information and the pattern to reply to requests for help.

1 Study Chinese

2 Practice playing ball

3 Practice singing

4 Practice dancing

"If I help you . . . , you have to . . . "

要是我幫你 ____________，你得____________。

Yàoshi wǒ bāng nǐ ____________, nǐ děi ____________.

Suppose you have an oral exam tomorrow. Convince your classmate to help you study by modifying the pattern above.

What do the characters mean?

What is the common radical?

What does the radical mean?

How does the radical relate to the overall meaning of the characters?

Characterize it!

1 

2 

3 

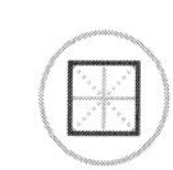

More characters

K Call me back

INTERPERSONAL

You are calling your Chinese friend to arrange a date. In pairs, role-play the conversation between the caller and the parent who answers the phone.

Caller 您好！請問李音在嗎？

Nín hǎo! Qǐng wèn Lǐ Yīn zài ma?

Parent 不在。你是哪位？

Bú zài. Nǐ shì nǎ wèi?

Caller 我是_______。

Wǒ shì _______.

Parent 你找_______有事兒嗎？

Nǐ zhǎo _______yǒu shìr ma?

Caller 我明天晚上想請她_______。

Wǒ míngtiān wǎnshang xiǎng qǐng tā _______.

Parent 她明天晚上要_______，沒空兒。

Tā míngtiān wǎnshang yào _______, méi kòngr.

Caller 那她_______有時間嗎？

Nà tā _______yǒu shíjiān ma?

Parent 她_______要_______，沒時間。

Tā _______ yào _______, méi shíjiān.

Caller 那請她回來以後_______，我等她的電話。

Nà qǐng tā huí lai yǐhòu _______, wǒ děng tā de diànhuà.

Parent 好，再見。

Hǎo, zàijiàn.

Caller 謝謝您！再見。

Xièxie nín! Zàijiàn.

You have a date tonight in Beijing's hip Gulou neighborhood and want to look your best. What would you use this product for?

GET Real WITH CHINESE

Chinese Chat

Your classmate is chatting with you on HipChat to set up a study session. How would you reply?

CULTURAL LITERACY

文化
Continue to explore

Phone etiquette

The receiver of the call usually does not self-identify immediately on answering, as is common in some other cultures. Instead, the receiver typically only says 喂 *(wéi/wèi)* and lets the caller initiate the conversation.

Cell phones

To call a cell phone, or 手機 *(shǒujī)*, neither 0 nor an area code is needed before dialing the eleven-digit cell phone number. China is now the largest cell phone market in the world. Since the early 2010s, a messaging app called WeChat, or 微信 *(Wēixìn)* (lit. micro message), has quickly become a major social media platform on cell phones and other mobile devices. Because users can call each other through the app as well as send voice messages, it is now a very popular communication tool among people in China and overseas Chinese. In English-language materials in China, the term "mobile phone" rather than "cell phone" is preferred, as in the name of the country's largest cell phone service provider, China Mobile.

Chinese

Both 中文 *(Zhōngwén)* and 漢語 *(Hànyǔ)* mean "the Chinese language." Derived from the name of one of the longest dynasties of unified China, Han 漢 *(Hàn)* refers to the predominant ethnic group in China, and 漢語 *(Hànyǔ)* literally means "the language of the Han people." Thus, many Chinese citizens of non-Han ethnic backgrounds usually refer to the Chinese language as 漢語 *(Hànyǔ)* rather than 中文 *(Zhōngwén)*, which can be understood as the language of China. Additionally, there is a subtle difference between 語 *(yǔ)* (speech) and 文 *(wén)* (writing), but for most purposes 漢語 *(Hànyǔ)* and 中文 *(Zhōngwén)* are generally considered synonymous.

The Chinese language has the most number of speakers out of any language, and is spoken in at least thirty-three countries. It is important to note that what you are currently studying is Standard Chinese, also known as Modern Standard Mandarin, or simply Mandarin. Mandarin is the standard form of the language. It is referred to as 普通話 *(Pǔtōnghuà)* ("common language") in Mainland China, 國語 *(Guóyǔ)* ("national language") in Taiwan, and 華語 *(Huáyǔ)* ("language spoken by ethnic Chinese people") in Southeast Asia.

COMPARE & CONTRAST

1 China is comparable in size to the United States, and yet there is only one time zone in the entire country: 北京時間 *(Běijīng shíjiān)* (Beijing Time). Consequently, people in the western part of the country have to make adjustments to their daily schedules. When most people in Beijing go to work at 8:00 a.m., it is hardly daybreak yet in the western city of Urumqi (烏魯木齊) *(Wūlǔmùqí)*. Based on the time zone differences, what do you think people in China are doing right now as you read this question?

2 How many time zones are there in your country? Are there other large countries that have only one time zone? Discuss the pros and cons of having one versus multiple time zones within a country.

Lesson Wrap-Up

Make It Flow!

Turn the following eight short sentences into a coherent narrative. Remember to omit repetitive elements and substitute subjects with personal pronouns where appropriate. Use the connective devices 因為 (*yīnwèi*), 所以 (*suǒyǐ*), and 可是 (*kěshì*) where appropriate.

今天是星期三。李友星期五要考試。李友想星期四下午去問常老師問題。常老師說她很忙。常老師星期三下午要開會。常老師星期四上午有課。常老師星期四下午四點以後才有空。李友說星期四下午四點半到老師的辦公室去。

Make an Appointment

Make an appointment with your teacher by email or text. Begin your message with a greeting and introduce yourself. Pick a time and find out if your teacher is free. Explain why you would like to see him/her. After you hear back from your teacher, confirm your appointment and express your thanks.

Make a Call

Call a friend who speaks Chinese. Make sure you remember how to begin a phone conversation. Ask if your friend can help you study for an upcoming Chinese exam, or would like to study together. Pick a time and find out if your friend is free. Ask if he/she would like to have Chinese food afterwards.

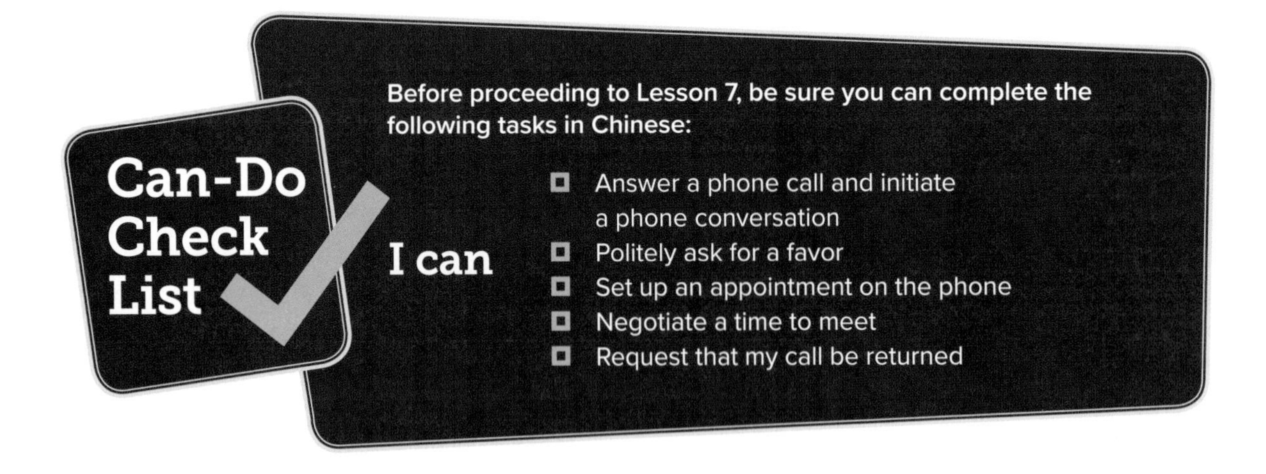

Lesson 7

第七課

Dì qī kè

學中文

Xué Zhōngwén

STUDYING CHINESE

Learning Objectives

In this lesson, you will learn to:

- Discuss your exam performance
- Comment on your character writing
- Discuss your experience learning Chinese
- Talk about your study habits
- Describe typical classroom situations

Relate & Get Ready

In your own culture/community:

- How do people talk about academic achievements?
- What are considered good study habits for learning a foreign language?

How Did You Do on the Exam?

Dialogue 1

王朋跟李友說話⋯⋯

Audio

Video

李友，你上個星期考試考得[1]怎麼樣？

因為你幫我復習，所以考得不錯。

但是我寫中國字寫得太[2]慢了！

是嗎？以後我跟你一起練習寫字，好不好[a]？

那太好了！我們現在就[3]寫，怎麼樣？

好，給我一枝筆[4]、一張紙。寫什麼字？

你教我怎麼寫"懂"字吧。

好吧。

你寫字寫得真[2]好，真快。

哪裡，哪裡[b]。你明天有中文課嗎？

我幫你預習。

明天我們學第七[5]課。第七課的語法

很容易，我都懂，可是生詞太多，

漢字也有一點兒[6]難。

沒問題，我幫你。

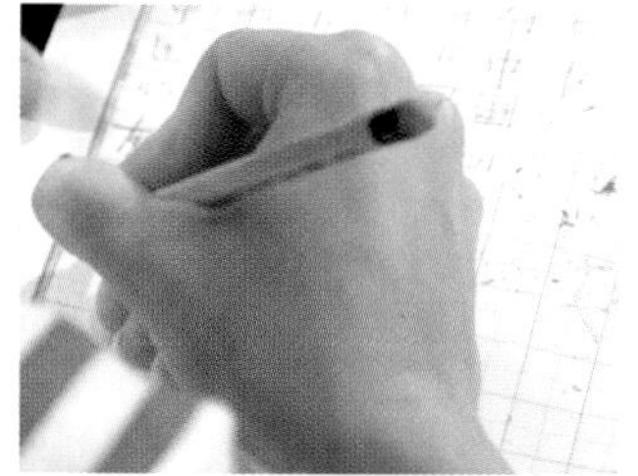

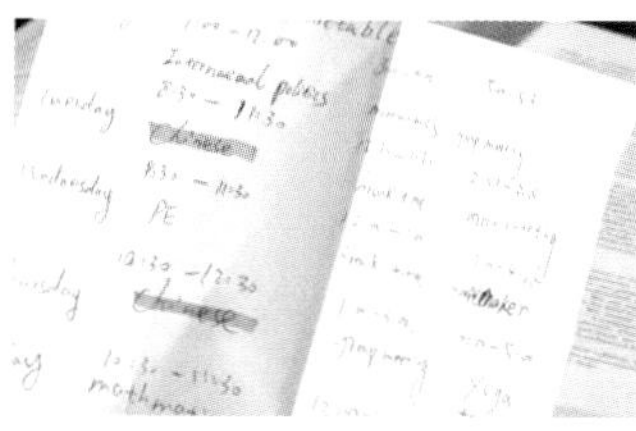

Wáng Péng gēn Lǐ Yǒu shuō huà . . .

 *Lǐ Yǒu, nǐ shàng ge xīngqī kǎo shì kǎo de*[1] *zěnmeyàng?*

 *Yīnwèi nǐ bāng wǒ fùxí, suǒyǐ kǎo de búcuò.*

Dànshì wǒ xiě Zhōngguó zì xiě de tài[2] *màn le!*

 *Shì ma? Yǐhòu wǒ gēn nǐ yìqǐ liànxí xiě zì, hǎo bu hǎo*[a]*?*

 *Nà tài hǎo le! Wǒmen xiànzài jiù*[3] *xiě, zěnmeyàng?*

 *Hǎo, gěi wǒ yì zhī bǐ*[4]*, yì zhāng zhǐ. Xiě shénme zì?*

 *Nǐ jiāo wǒ zěnme xiě "dǒng" zì ba.*

 *Hǎo ba.*

 *Nǐ xiě zì xiě de zhēn*[2] *hǎo, zhēn kuài.*

 *Nǎli, nǎli*[b]*. Nǐ míngtiān yǒu Zhōngwén kè ma? Wǒ bāng nǐ yùxí.*

 *Míngtiān wǒmen xué dì qī*[5] *kè. Dì qī kè de yǔfǎ hěn róngyì, wǒ dōu dǒng, kěshì shēngcí tài duō, Hànzì yě yǒuyìdiǎnr*[6] *nán.*

 *Méi wèntí, wǒ bāng nǐ.*

Language Notes

a 好不好 *(hǎo bu hǎo)*

Like 行嗎 *(xíng ma)* and 好嗎 *(hǎo ma)*, this expression can be used to seek someone's approval of a proposal.

b 哪裡 *(nǎli)*

This literally means "where," and is a polite reply to a compliment. In recent times, however, the phrase has become a bit old-fashioned. Many people will respond to a compliment by saying 是嗎 *(shì ma)* (is that so?). Some young people in urban areas will also acknowledge a compliment by saying 謝謝 *(xièxie)* (thanks) instead.

Vocabulary

Audio

Flashcards

No.	Word	Pinyin	Part of Speech	Definition
1	說話	*shuō huà*	vo	to talk
	話	*huà*	n	word, speech
2	上個	*shàng ge*		previous, last
3	得	*de*	p	(a structural particle) [See Grammar 1.]
4	復習	*fùxí*	v	to review
5	寫	*xiě*	v	to write
6	字	*zì*	n	character
7	慢	*màn*	adj	slow
8	枝	*zhī*	m	(measure word for long, thin, inflexible objects such as pens, pencils, etc.)
9	筆	*bǐ*	n	pen
10	張	*zhāng*	m	(measure word for flat objects such as paper, pictures, etc.)
11	紙	*zhǐ*	n	paper
12	教	*jiāo*	v	to teach
13	怎麼	*zěnme*	qpr	how, how come
14	懂	*dǒng*	v	to understand
15	真	*zhēn*	adv	really [See Grammar 2.]
16	哪裡	*nǎli*	pr	where
17	預習	*yùxí*	v	to preview
18	學	*xué*	v	to study, to learn
19	第	*dì*	prefix	(prefix for ordinal numbers) [See Grammar 5.]
20	語法	*yǔfǎ*	n	grammar

To convert a foreign driver's license in China, applicants must answer ninety out of a hundred questions correctly. If asked, could you identify this sign?

GET Real WITH CHINESE

No.	Word	Pinyin	Part of Speech	Definition
21	容易	*róngyì*	adj	easy
22	生詞	*shēngcí*	n	new words, vocabulary
23	多	*duō*	adj	many, much
24	漢字	*Hànzì*	n	Chinese characters
25	難	*nán*	adj	difficult

How About You?

我們一起練習寫字吧！
你想練習什麼字？

Wǒmen yìqǐ liànxí xiě zì ba!
Nǐ xiǎng liànxí shénme zì?

Let's practice writing characters!
What characters do you want to practice writing?

就慢教懂

我想練習寫 ______ 字。

Wǒ xiǎng liànxí xiě ______ zì.

Pick any characters you'd like to practice writing.

Grammar

1 Descriptive complements (I)

The particle 得 *(de)* can be used after a verb or an adjective. This lesson mainly deals with 得 *(de)* as it appears after a verb. The adjective, adverb, or verb phrase that follows 得 *(de)* in the construction below is called a descriptive complement. In this lesson, the descriptive complements are all adjectives that serve as comments on the actions expressed by the preceding verbs.

A 他寫字寫得很好。

Tā xiě zì xiě de hěn hǎo.

He writes characters very well.

[很好 *(hěn hǎo)* (very well) is a comment on the action 寫 *(xiě)* (to write).]

B 他昨天睡覺睡得很晚。

Tā zuótiān shuì jiào shuì de hěn wǎn.

He went to bed very late last night.

[很晚 *(hěn wǎn)* (very late) is a comment on the action 睡覺 *(shuì jiào)* (to sleep).]

C 妹妹歌唱得很好。

Mèimei gē chàng de hěn hǎo.

My younger sister sings very well.

[很好 *(hěn hǎo)* (very well) is a comment on the action 唱 *(chàng)* (to sing).]

If the complement is an adjective, it is usually preceded by 很 *(hěn)* (very), as is the case when an adjective is used as a predicate. If the verb is followed by an object, the verb has to be repeated before it can be followed by the "得 *(de)* + complement" structure, e.g., 寫字寫得 *(xiě zì xiě de)* in (A). Repeating the verb turns the "verb + object" combination preceding it into a topic and the complement that follows serves as a comment on it. [See Grammar 1, Lesson 10.] The first verb can be omitted if the meaning is clear from the context, as in (C).

EXERCISES

Complete the sentences below by using 得 to lead a complement. Use exercise 1 as an example.

1 我昨天晚上睡__________。

→ 我昨天晚上睡得不錯。

2 弟弟昨天吃晚飯吃__________。

3 王朋打球打__________。

2 The adverbs 太 *(tài)* (too), 真 *(zhēn)* (really), and 很 *(hěn)* (very)

When the adverbs 太 *(tài)* (too) and 真 *(zhēn)* (really) are used in exclamatory sentences, in most cases they convey not new factual information but the speaker's subjective judgment. If the speaker wants to make a more "objective" statement or description, other intensifiers, such as 很 *(hěn)* (very), are often used instead.

A Q: 他寫字寫得怎麼樣？

Tā xiě zì xiě de zěnmeyàng?

How well does he write characters?

One would normally answer:

A: 他寫字寫得很好。

Tā xiě zì xiě de hěn hǎo.

He writes characters very well.

Rather than:

A: 他寫字寫得真好。

Tā xiě zì xiě de zhēn hǎo.

Compare the second answer with (B).

B 小李，你寫字寫得真好！你可以教我嗎？

Xiǎo Lǐ, nǐ xiě zì xiě de zhēn hǎo! Nǐ kěyǐ jiāo wǒ ma?

Little Li, you write characters really well! Could you teach me?

太 *(tài)* can also be used in a statement, either with or without 了 *(le)* at the end. It means "excessive in degree," pertaining to a less than satisfactory thing or situation, and the stress can fall either on 太 *(tài)* or the adjective following it.

C 你和我兩個人吃飯，五個菜太多了。

Nǐ hé wǒ liǎng ge rén chī fàn, wǔ ge cài tài duō le.

It's just the two of us eating. Five dishes are too many.

D 這個電影太貴了，我不去看。

Zhè ge diànyǐng tài guì le, wǒ bú qù kàn.

It costs too much to see this movie, and I am not going to watch it.

E 我們是同學，你不要太客氣了。

Wǒmen shì tóngxué, nǐ bú yào tài kèqi le.

We are classmates. There is no need for you to be so polite.

More exercises

EXERCISES

Rewrite the declarative sentences as two exclamatory sentences, replacing 很 with 太 and 真 where appropriate. Use exercise 1 as an example.

1 那個電影很有意思。
→ 那個電影真有意思！/那個電影太有意思了！

2 第六課的語法很容易。

3 高文中的家很漂亮。

3 The adverb 就 *(jiù)* (I)

The adverb 就 *(jiù)* is used before a verb to suggest the earliness, brevity, or quickness of an action.

A 他明天七點就得上課。

Tā míngtiān qī diǎn jiù děi shàng kè.

He has to go to class early at 7:00 tomorrow.

B 我們八點看電影，他七點半就來了。

Wǒmen bā diǎn kàn diànyǐng, tā qī diǎn bàn jiù lái le.

We were supposed to see the movie at 8:00, but he came early at 7:30.

就 *(jiù)* vs. 才 *(cái)*

就 *(jiù)* suggests the perceived earliness or promptness of an action, as in (C) and (E), whereas 才 *(cái)* suggests the perceived lateness of an action, as in (D) and (F). [See also Grammar 6, Lesson 5.] When commenting on a past action, 就 *(jiù)* is always used with 了 *(le)* to indicate promptness, but 才 *(cái)* is never used with 了 *(le)*.

C 八點上課，小白七點就來了。

Bā diǎn shàng kè, Xiǎo Bái qī diǎn jiù lái le.

Class started at 8:00, but Little Bai came early at 7:00.

D 八點上課，小張八點半才來。

Bā diǎn shàng kè, Xiǎo Zhāng bā diǎn bàn cái lái.

Class starts at 8:00, but Little Zhang didn't come until 8:30.

E 我昨天五點就回家了。

Wǒ zuótiān wǔ diǎn jiù huí jiā le.

Yesterday I went home early at 5:00.

F 我昨天五點才回家。

Wǒ zuótiān wǔ diǎn cái huí jiā.

Yesterday I didn't get home until 5:00.

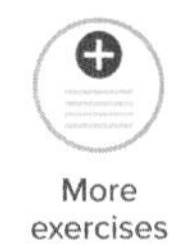

EXERCISES

Indicate the earliness or lateness of an action by inserting 就 or 才 where appropriate. Use exercise 1 as an example.

1 我明天要回家。妹妹上個星期回家了。
→ 我明天要回家，妹妹上個星期就回家了。

2 我昨天五點去打球。王朋四點去打球。

3 我們昨天晚上十一點睡覺。高文中十二點睡覺。

4 Double objects

Some verbs can take two objects. The object representing people or animate entities, usually the direct object, precedes the one representing inanimate things, usually the indirect object.

A 老師教我們生詞和語法。

Lǎoshī jiāo wǒmen shēngcí hé yǔfǎ.

The teacher teaches us vocabulary and grammar.

B 大哥給了我一瓶水。

Dà gē gěi le wǒ yì píng shuǐ.

My big brother gave me a bottle of water.

C 你教我漢字，可以嗎？

Nǐ jiāo wǒ Hànzì, kěyǐ ma?

Will you teach me Chinese characters, please?

D 我想問你一個問題。

Wǒ xiǎng wèn nǐ yí ge wèntí.

I'd like to ask you a question.

EXERCISES

Add a direct or indirect object to the sentences below. Use exercise 1 as an example.

1 老師給我＿＿＿＿＿＿。→ 老師給我一本書。

2 白英愛問＿＿＿＿＿＿一個問題。

3 王朋教李友＿＿＿＿＿＿。

5 Ordinal numbers

Ordinal numbers in Chinese are formed by placing 第 *(dì)* before cardinal numbers, e.g., 第一 *(dì yī)* (the first), 第二杯茶 *(dì èr bēi chá)* (the second cup of tea), 第三個月 *(dì sān ge yuè)* (the third month). However, 第 *(dì)* is not used directly before months, e.g., 一月, 二月, 三月 *(yīyuè, èryuè, sānyuè)* (January, February, March). Neither is it used to indicate the birth order of siblings, e.g., 大哥, 二哥, 三哥 *(dàgē, èrgē, sāngē)* (oldest brother, second oldest brother, third oldest brother); 大姐, 二姐, 三姐 *(dàjiě, èrjiě, sānjiě)* (oldest sister, second oldest sister, third oldest sister).

6 有（一）點兒 *(yǒu|yì|diǎnr)* (somewhat, rather, a little bit)

The phrase 有一點兒 *(yǒuyìdiǎnr)* precedes adjectives or verbs. It often carries a negative tone. 一 *(yī)* is optional.

A 我覺得中文有（一）點兒難。

Wǒ juéde Zhōngwén yǒu(yì)diǎnr nán.

I think Chinese is a little hard.

[⊗ 我覺得中文有（一）點兒容易。]

B 我覺得這一課生詞有（一）點兒多。

Wǒ juéde zhè yí kè shēngcí yǒu(yì)diǎnr duō.

I think there are a few too many new words in this lesson.

However, when the sentence describes a change in situation, the phrase 有（一）點兒 *(yǒu|yì|diǎnr)* can carry a positive tone.

C 我以前不喜歡他，現在有（一）點兒喜歡他了。

Wǒ yǐqián bù xǐhuan tā, xiànzài yǒu(yì)diǎnr xǐhuan tā le.

I used to dislike him, but now I rather like him. [以前 *(yǐqián)* (previously or before)] [See Lesson 8.]

Take care not to confuse 有（一）點兒 *(yǒu/yì/diǎnr)* (a little), which is an adverbial used to modify adjectives, with （一）點兒 *(/yì/diǎnr)* (a little), which usually modifies nouns. In the above sentences, 有（一）點兒 *(yǒu/yì/diǎnr)* is not interchangeable with （一）點兒 *(/yì/diǎnr)*.

D 給我（一）點兒咖啡。

Gěi wǒ (yì)diǎnr kāfēi.

Give me a little coffee.

E 給我（一）點兒時間。

Gěi wǒ (yì)diǎnr shíjiān.

Give me a little time.

F 我有（一）點兒忙。 [⊗ 我（一）點兒忙。]

Wǒ yǒu(yì)diǎnr máng.

I am kind of busy.

G 她有（一）點兒不高興。

Tā yǒu(yì)diǎnr bù gāoxìng.

She is a little unhappy.

[⊗ 她（一）點兒不高興。]

More exercises

EXERCISES

Rewrite the sentences below to reduce the intensity by inserting 有（一）點兒 where appropriate. Use exercise 1 as an example.

1 第七課很難。→ 第七課有（一）點兒難。

2 老師今天很忙。

3 王朋說中文說得很快。

Language Practice

A

How well?

PRESENTATIONAL

Describe Little Wang's traits based on the information given, inserting 得 *(de)* where appropriate. Pay attention to the structure of the verbs involved, e.g.:

考試 (VO) 好 — *kǎo shì* (VO) *hǎo*

小王常常考試考得很好。 — *Xiǎo Wáng chángcháng kǎo shì kǎo de hěn hǎo.*

1. 睡覺 (VO) 晚 — *shuì jiào* (VO) *wǎn*
2. 喝咖啡 (VO) 多 — *hē kāfēi* (VO) *duō*
3. 寫字 (VO) 快 — *xiě zì* (VO) *kuài*
4. 說中文 (VO) 好 — *shuō Zhōngwén* (VO) *hǎo*
5. 預習 (V) 不錯 — *yùxí* (V) *búcuò*
6. 工作 (V) 好 — *gōngzuò* (V) *hǎo*

B

Exclamations!

PRESENTATIONAL

Let people know how you feel by inserting the adverb 太 *(tài)* or 真 *(zhēn)* when appropriate, e.g.:

漢字◇有意思

Hànzì ◇ *yǒu yìsi*

漢字太有意思了！/ 漢字真有意思！

Hànzì tài yǒu yìsi le!/Hànzì zhēn yǒu yìsi!

1. 老師家◇漂亮 — *lǎoshī jiā* ◇ *piàoliang*
2. 考試◇容易 — *kǎo shì* ◇ *róngyì*
3. 語法◇難 — *yǔfǎ* ◇ *nán*

4 同學的中文◇好 tóngxué de Zhōngwén ◇ hǎo

5 我寫字◇慢 wǒ xiě zì ◇ màn

C Could be worse PRESENTATIONAL

Moderate your view by inserting 有（一）點兒 *(yǒu|yì|diǎnr)* where appropriate e.g.:

語法◇難 *yǔfǎ ◇ nán*

語法有（一）點兒難。 *Yǔfǎ yǒu(yì)diǎnr nán.*

1 第七課的生詞◇多 *dì qī kè de shēngcí ◇ duō*

2 我們的考試◇難 *wǒmen de kǎo shì ◇ nán*

3 中文課◇早 *(zǎo)* (early) *Zhōngwén kè ◇ zǎo* (early)

4 漢字◇難 *Hànzì ◇ nán*

5 老師說話◇快 *lǎoshī shuō huà ◇ kuài*

D Runs in the family INTERPERSONAL

In pairs, discuss how well your family members perform certain activities, e.g.:

Q: 你爸爸打球打得怎麼樣？
Nǐ bàba dǎ qiú dǎ de zěnmeyàng?

A: 我爸爸打球打得不好，我媽媽打球打得好。
Wǒ bàba dǎ qiú dǎ de bù hǎo, wǒ māma dǎ qiú dǎ de hǎo.

1 

2 

3 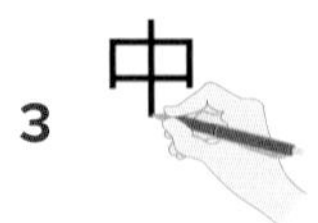

E

How's it going so far?

INTERPERSONAL

In pairs, discuss your experience learning Chinese, e.g.:

你覺得中文什麼難？生詞、語法還是漢字？

Nǐ juéde Zhōngwén shénme nán? Shēngcí, yǔfǎ háishi hànzì?

Characterize it!

What do the characters mean?
What is the common radical?
What does the radical mean?
How does the radical relate to the overall meaning of the characters?

1 快 2 慢 3 懂

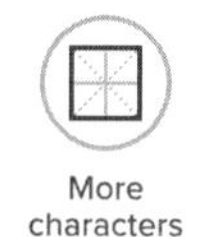

Chinese Chat

Your classmate is chatting with you on Google Hangouts about a recent test. How would you reply?

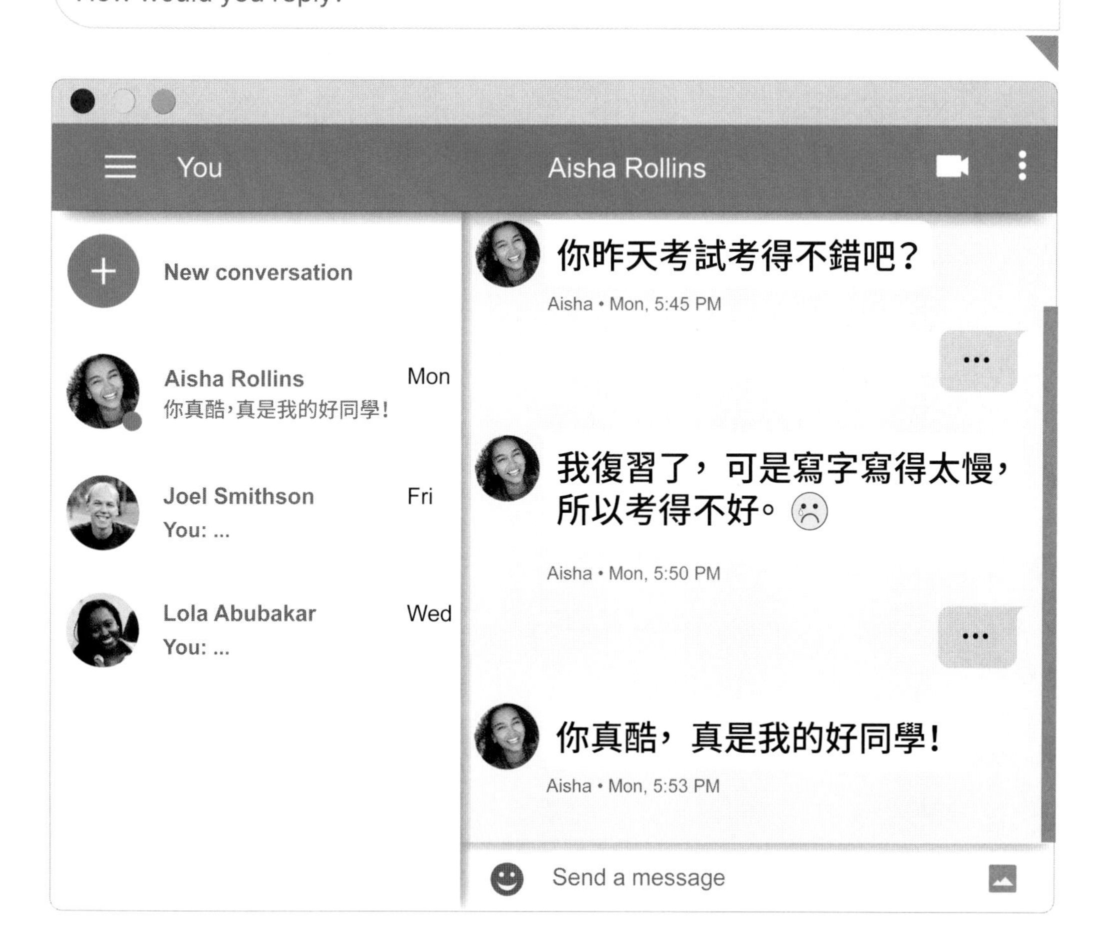

Dialogue 2

李友跟白英愛說話⋯⋯

Audio

Video

白英愛，你平常來得很早，今天怎麼[7]這麼晚？

我昨天預習中文，早上[a]四點才[3]睡覺，你也睡得很晚嗎？

我昨天十點就[3]睡了。因為王朋幫我練習中文，所以我功課做得很快。

有個中國朋友真好。

上中文課⋯⋯

大家早[b]，現在我們開始上課。第七課你們都預習了嗎？

預習了。

李友，請你念課文。⋯⋯念得很好。你昨天晚上聽錄音了吧？

我沒聽。

但是她的朋友昨天晚上幫她學習了。

你的朋友是中國人嗎？

是。

他是一個男的[8]，很帥[c]，很酷，叫王朋。[9]

Pinyin Dialogue

Lǐ Yǒu gēn Bái Yīng'ài shuō huà . . .

Bái Yīng'ài, nǐ píngcháng lái de hěn zǎo, jīntiān zěnme[7] *zhème wǎn?*

Wǒ zuótiān yùxí Zhōngwén, zǎoshang[a] *sì diǎn cái*[3] *shuì jiào, nǐ yě shuì de hěn wǎn ma?*

Wǒ zuótiān shí diǎn jiù[3] *shuì le. Yīnwèi Wáng Péng bāng wǒ liànxí Zhōngwén, suǒyǐ wǒ gōngkè zuò de hěn kuài.*

Yǒu ge Zhōngguó péngyou zhēn hǎo.

Shàng Zhōngwén kè . . .

Dàjiā zǎo[b], *xiànzài wǒmen kāishǐ shàng kè. Dì qī kè nǐmen dōu yùxí le ma?*

Yùxí le.

Lǐ Yǒu, qǐng nǐ niàn kèwén . . . Niàn de hěn hǎo. Nǐ zuótiān wǎnshang tīng lùyīn le ba?

Wǒ méi tīng.

Dànshì tā de péngyou zuótiān wǎnshang bāng tā xuéxí le.

Nǐ de péngyou shì Zhōngguó rén ma?

Shì.

Tā shì yí ge nán de[8], *hěn shuài*[c], *hěn kù, jiào Wáng Péng.*[9]

Language Notes

a 早上 *(zǎoshang)*/上午 *(shàngwǔ)*

Both words are usually translated as "morning," but the two are not interchangeable. 早上 *(zǎoshang)* refers to early morning, whereas 上午 *(shàngwǔ)* covers the entire first half of the day (until noon).

b 早 *(zǎo)*

This is a common Chinese greeting. Other morning greetings, such as 早上好 *(zǎoshang hǎo)* and 早安 *(zǎo'ān)*, still sound rather formal to many Chinese people.

c 帥 *(shuài)*

This term is usually used to describe a handsome man. 漂亮 *(piàoliang)* (pretty) is used to describe an attractive woman. The term 好看 *(hǎokàn)* (good-looking) is gender-neutral, and can be used to describe anyone.

Vocabulary

Audio

Flashcards

No.	Word	Pinyin	Part of Speech	Definition
1	平常	*píngcháng*	adv	usually
2	早	*zǎo*	adj	early
3	這麼	*zhème*	pr	so, this (late, etc.)
4	晚	*wǎn*	adj	late
5	早上	*zǎoshang*	t	morning
6	功課	*gōngkè*	n	homework, schoolwork
7	大家	*dàjiā*	pr	everybody
8	上課	*shàng kè*	vo	to go to a class, to start a class, to be in class
9	開始	*kāishǐ*	v/n	to begin, to start; beginning
10	念	*niàn*	v	to read aloud
11	課文	*kèwén*	n	text of a lesson
12	錄音	*lùyīn*	n/vo	sound recording; to record
13	學習	*xuéxí*	v	to study, to learn
14	帥	*shuài*	adj	handsome
15	酷	*kù*	adj	cool (appearance, behavior)

How About You?

你有中文書嗎？

Nǐ yǒu Zhōngwén shū ma?

Do you have Chinese books?

我有＿＿＿＿＿＿＿＿。

Wǒ yǒu ＿＿＿＿＿＿＿＿.

See index for corresponding vocabulary or research another term.

Grammar

7 **Question pronoun: 怎麼 *(zěnme)* (how, how come)**

怎麼 *(zěnme)* (how, how come) is an interrogative pronoun. It is used to ask about the manner of an action, as in (A), and sometimes the reason or the cause of an action, as in (B) and (C).

A 請你教我怎麼寫"懂"這個字。

Qǐng nǐ jiāo wǒ zěnme xiě "dǒng" zhè ge zì.

Please teach me how to write the character "懂."

B 你怎麼才來？

Nǐ zěnme cái lái?

How come you've just arrived?

C 你怎麼沒去看電影？

Nǐ zěnme méi qù kàn diànyǐng?

How come you didn't go see the movie?

Both 怎麼 *(zěnme)* (how come) and 為什麼 *(wèishénme)* (why) are used to ask about the cause of or reason for something. However, 怎麼 *(zěnme)* (how come) conveys the speaker's surprise, whereas 為什麼 *(wèishénme)* (why) does not.

EXERCISES

Join these sentences to express surprise by using 怎麼 where appropriate. Use exercise 1 as an example.

More exercises

1 我們今天考中文。你昨天晚上九點就睡了。
→ 我們今天考中文，你昨天晚上怎麼九點就睡了？

2 上個星期的考試很容易。 白英愛考得不好。

3 高小音是高文中的姐姐。 你不認識高小音。

8 The 的 *(de)* structure (I)

We have a 的 *(de)* structure when an adjective is followed by the structural particle 的 *(de)*. Grammatically, a 的 *(de)* structure is equivalent to a noun. When Bai Ying'ai says, "他是一個男的 *(Tā shì yí ge nán de)*," it is clear from the context that she means a male (one). [See also Grammar 3, Lesson 9.]

A 我寫了十個字，五個難的，五個容易的。

Wǒ xiě le shí ge zì, wǔ ge nán de, wǔ ge róngyì de.

I wrote ten characters, five difficult ones and five easy ones.

EXERCISES

Rewrite the sentences below by omitting repeated nouns and inserting the 的 structure where appropriate. Use exercise 1 as an example.

1 我練習寫了四十個漢字, 二十個難的漢字，二十個容易的漢字。
→ 我練習寫了四十個漢字，二十個難的，二十個容易的。

2 學校有三個圖書館，一個大圖書館，兩個小圖書館。

3 老師想給學生考兩個考試，一個難的考試，一個容易的考試。

9 Connecting sentences in continuous discourse

As suggested in the previous "Make It Flow!" exercises, if a noun serves as the unchanged subject in a continuous discourse, its later appearances in the ensuing clauses or sentences should generally be substituted by an appropriate pronoun or simply be omitted. The pronoun, in turn, can also be omitted after its first appearance.

A 小白很喜歡學中文。她晚上預習課文、復習語法、練習寫漢字，常常很晚才睡覺。

Xiǎo Bái hěn xǐhuan xué Zhōngwén. Tā wǎnshang yùxí kèwén, fùxí yǔfǎ, liànxí xiě Hànzì, chángcháng hěn wǎn cái shuì jiào.

Little Bai likes to study Chinese a lot. At night, she previews the text, reviews the grammar, and practices writing the characters. Often she doesn't go to bed until very late.

In (A), the subject of the second sentence remains the same as that in the beginning sentence, and therefore the proper noun 小白 *(Xiǎo Bái)* (Little Bai) is substituted by the pronoun 她 *(tā)* (she). In the subsequent clauses in the second sentence, neither the proper noun nor the pronoun is repeated. If we keep repeating the subject, as seen in (B), or the pronoun, as in (C), we will end up with a series of choppy sentences.

B 小白很喜歡學中文。小白晚上預習課文、小白復習語法、小白練習寫漢字。小白常常很晚才睡覺。

Xiǎo Bái hěn xǐhuan xué Zhōngwén. Xiǎo Bái wǎnshang yùxí kèwén, Xiǎo Bái fùxí yǔfǎ, Xiǎo Bái liànxí xiě Hànzì. Xiǎo Bái chángcháng hěn wǎn cái shuì jiào.

C 小白很喜歡學中文。她晚上預習課文，她復習語法、她練習寫漢字。她常常很晚才睡覺。

Xiǎo Bái hěn xǐhuan xué Zhōngwén. Tā wǎnshang yùxí kèwén, tā fùxí yǔfǎ, tā liànxí xiě Hànzì. Tā chángcháng hěn wǎn cái shuì jiào.

In order to form a continuous discourse, time and location expressions can be used as transitional elements.

D 昨天晚上，王朋和李友去高文中家玩兒。在高文中家他们認識了高文中的姐姐。她叫高小音，在學校圖書館工作。他們一起聊天兒、看電視。十二點大家才說再見。

Zuótiān wǎnshang, Wáng Péng hé Lǐ Yǒu qù Gāo Wénzhōng jiā wánr. Zài Gāo Wénzhōng jiā tāmen rènshi le Gāo Wénzhōng de jiějie. Tā jiào Gāo Xiǎoyīn, zài xuéxiào túshūguǎn gōngzuò. Tāmen yìqǐ liáo tiānr, kàn diànshì. Shí'èr diǎn dàjiā cái shuō zàijiàn.

Yesterday evening, Wang Peng and Li You went to Gao Wenzhong's place for a visit. There they met Gao Wenzhong's older sister. Her name is Gao Xiaoyin, and she works in the school library. They talked and watched TV together, and didn't say their goodbyes until midnight.

In (D), the discourse would not be cohesive without the time and location expressions marked in blue.

This quotation by Chairman Mao (毛主席) (Máo Zhǔxí) appears on posters, signs; even everyday items like this pencil case. What does its popularity say about Chinese values? How do you think it's being used here?

F Having an off day

INTERPERSONAL

In pairs, use the prompts below to contrast how someone behaved today with his/her usual habits. Insert 怎麼 *(zěnme)* and 這麼 *(zhème)* where appropriate, e.g.:

來學校◇早 vs. 晚

lái xuéxiào ◇ *zǎo* vs. *wǎn*

你平常來學校來得很早，今天怎麼來得這麼晚？

Nǐ píngcháng lái xuéxiào lái de hěn zǎo, jīntiān zěnme lái de zhème wǎn?

1 預習生詞◇好 vs. 不好 — *yùxí shēngcí* ◇ *hǎo* vs. *bù hǎo*

2 念課文◇快 vs. 慢 — *niàn kèwén* ◇ *kuài* vs. *màn*

3 考試◇不錯 vs. 不好 — *kǎoshì* ◇ *búcuò* vs. *bù hǎo*

4 寫字◇漂亮 vs. 難看 *(nánkàn)* (ugly) — *xiě zì* ◇ *piàoliang* vs. *nánkàn*

There are further signs your friend is having an off day. Complete the questions to show your bewilderment.

5 今天是你媽媽的生日，你怎麼不/沒……

Jīntiān shì nǐ māma de shēngrì, nǐ zěnme bù/méi . . .

6 明天你有考試，你怎麼不……

Míngtiān nǐ yǒu kǎoshì, nǐ zěnme bù . . .

G Change in schedule

INTERPERSONAL

Below is Gao Wenzhong's usual schedule contrasted with what he actually did yesterday. In pairs, form a question-and-answer by using 就 *(jiù)* or 才 *(cái)* where appropriate, e.g.:

Q: 高文中平常幾點開始學習中文？

Gāo Wénzhōng píngcháng jǐdiǎn kāishǐ xuéxí Zhōngwén?

A: 他平常上午九點開始學習中文。

可是他昨天上午八點三刻就開始學習中文了。

Tā píngcháng shàngwǔ jiǔ diǎn kāishǐ xuéxí Zhōngwén.

Kěshì tā zuótiān shàngwǔ bā diǎn sān kè jiù kāishǐ xuéxí Zhōngwén le.

His Usual Schedule		What Happened Yesterday	
9:00 a.m.	study Chinese	8:30 a.m.	studied Chinese
10:00 a.m.	listen to the audio	9:30 a.m.	listened to the audio
10:45 a.m.	go to school	10:15 a.m.	went to school
12:00 p.m.	go home	12:30 p.m.	returned home
1:00 p.m.	have lunch	2:00 p.m.	had lunch

H Learning curve

PRESENTATIONAL

Describe your reasons for not performing as well as expected when learning a foreign language by using 得 *(de)* where appropriate, e.g.:

生詞　多　學　慢

shēngcí　duō　xué　màn

生詞太多，我（學生詞）學得很慢。

Shēngcí tài duō, wǒ (xué shēngcí) xué de hěn màn.

1 功課　多 做　慢

gōngkè　duō　zuò　màn

2 語法　難 復習　不好

yǔfǎ　nán　fùxí　bù hǎo

3 漢字 多 寫 慢

Hànzì *duō* *xiě* *màn*

4 考試 (n) 難 考試 (VO) 不好

kǎoshì *nán* *kǎo shì* *bù hǎo*

I Learning tips

PRESENTATIONAL

How do you best learn a foreign language? What suggestions can you give based on your experience? For example, discuss what works for you before a new lesson, in class, and after class. List your advice or write a blog post.

Chinese Chat

Wang Peng just replied to a Weibo (微博) (*Wēibó*) post by Li You. What do you think Wang Peng is like as a friend?

王朋

7-6 10:36 AM 來自iPhone 7

明天有中文課嗎？我幫你預習吧!//@李友：王朋真酷，常常幫我練習中文，有個中國朋友真好！

轉發 | 評論 | 讚

Characterize it!

How do you pronounce the characters?

What is the common component?

How do you pronounce the common component?

How does the component relate to the pronunciation of the characters?

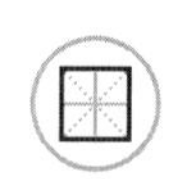

More characters

Simplified vs traditional

In the 1950s, as part of its campaign to raise the nation's literacy rate, the Chinese government set out to simplify some of the more complex characters, or 漢字 *(Hànzì)*. This accounts for the bifurcation between 簡體字 *(jiǎntǐzì)* (simplified characters) and 繁體字 *(fántǐzì)* (traditional characters, lit. complex characters).* Currently, simplified characters are used in Mainland China, Singapore, and Malaysia, while people in Taiwan, Hong Kong, and many overseas Chinese communities still write traditional characters. Many of the simplified characters were not actually new inventions. They had been used at different times in China's long history, and a few have an even longer history than their *fantizi* counterparts. The additional burden on Chinese learners caused by this bifurcation is actually not as onerous as it may seem. After all, many of the characters were not affected and remain the same in both systems. For those characters that do have two different forms, what is affected is often a familiar component, in many cases the radical.

COMPARE & CONTRAST

1 Have writing systems and practices within your culture changed over time?

2 An anadrome is a word or sentence that forms another when read backwards. Here is an anecdote to illustrate the often amusing ambiguity that can result from reading a Chinese store sign. As the story goes, a father took his five-year-old son to a restaurant called 友朋小吃 *(Yǒupéng Xiǎochī)* for a good meal, only to have the son cry loudly at the door and adamantly refuse to enter. Why do you think the little boy refused to enter? Can you think of an example of an English anadrome?

* The English term "traditional characters" was brought into common usage by Cheng & Tsui in the 1990s.

Writing Conventions

Traditionally, Chinese was written from top to bottom and from right to left. Store signs and placards, however, were often inscribed horizontally, typically from right to left. Since a 1955 government mandate, left-to-right writing has become standard in Mainland China. However, the traditional way of writing is still kept alive in calligraphy, and occasionally it is still possible to see a store sign that reads from right to left.

For many centuries, the Chinese wrote with a 毛筆 *(máobǐ)*, or "writing brush." But people have switched to more convenient Western-style writing instruments such as 鉛筆 *(qiānbǐ)* (pencils), 鋼筆 *(gāngbǐ)* (fountain pens), and 圓珠筆 *(yuánzhūbǐ)* (ballpoint pens), which are also known as 原子筆 *(yuánzǐbǐ)* in Taiwan. The traditional 毛筆 *(máobǐ)* is now used almost only for calligraphy. Moreover, in the digital era, typing and texting have significantly eroded the importance of handwriting in general.

Four treasures

The term 文房四寶 *(wénfáng sì bǎo)* ("Four Treasures of the Study") is often used to refer to traditional Chinese stationery, which usually includes 筆 *(bǐ)* (writing brush), 墨 *(mò)* (ink stick), 紙 *(zhǐ)* (paper), and 硯 *(yàn)* (inkstone). The traditional paper for writing and painting is known as 宣紙 *(xuānzhǐ)*, named after its most famous place of production, 宣城 *(Xuānchéng)* in Anhui Province. Ink is made by grinding an ink stick on an inkstone with water. Many inkstones are carved. Two of the most famous kinds are 端硯 *(duānyàn)* and 歙硯 *(shèyàn)*, from Guangdong and Anhui, respectively. Ink sticks are typically made from burnt pinewood with a binding agent and an aromatic substance. Antique ink sticks and inkstones are highly prized as collectibles.

Lesson Wrap-Up

Make It Flow!

Rearrange the following sentences into a logical sequence. Then combine them into a coherent narrative. Remember to omit repetitive elements and substitute subjects with personal pronouns where appropriate. Use connective devices such as 因為 (*yīnwèi*) and 所以 (*suǒyǐ*).

__1__ 王朋昨天幫李友練習中文了。
_____ 李友昨天晚上功課做得很快。
_____ 李友昨天晚上十點就睡了。
_____ 李友今天有中文課。
_____ 李友念得很好。
_____ 老師請李友念課文。

Study Buddy

Pre-interview: Assess your strengths and weaknesses.

你常常聽錄音嗎？
你的發音好嗎？
你覺得生詞難嗎？
第六課的語法你懂了嗎？
你寫漢字寫得怎麼樣？
你中文考試考得怎麼樣？

Interview: What are your classmates' strengths? Interview three classmates.

你覺得中文語法容易嗎？
你覺得漢字怎麼樣，難嗎？
你想和同學一起學習中文嗎？
你什麼時候有時間？

Can you think of any other questions that would help you find a good study partner?

Skit

Prepare a skit based on the prompts, then perform it in front of the class.

Student A Your friend has been acting strangely. Usually, he/she is never late to class. You want to find out why.

Student B You've been very busy and going to bed very late. You've been having difficulty with your Chinese class. The grammar is very difficult. There is a lot of homework and new vocabulary. And there are many tests!

Student A Can you relate to your friend? What can you do to help?

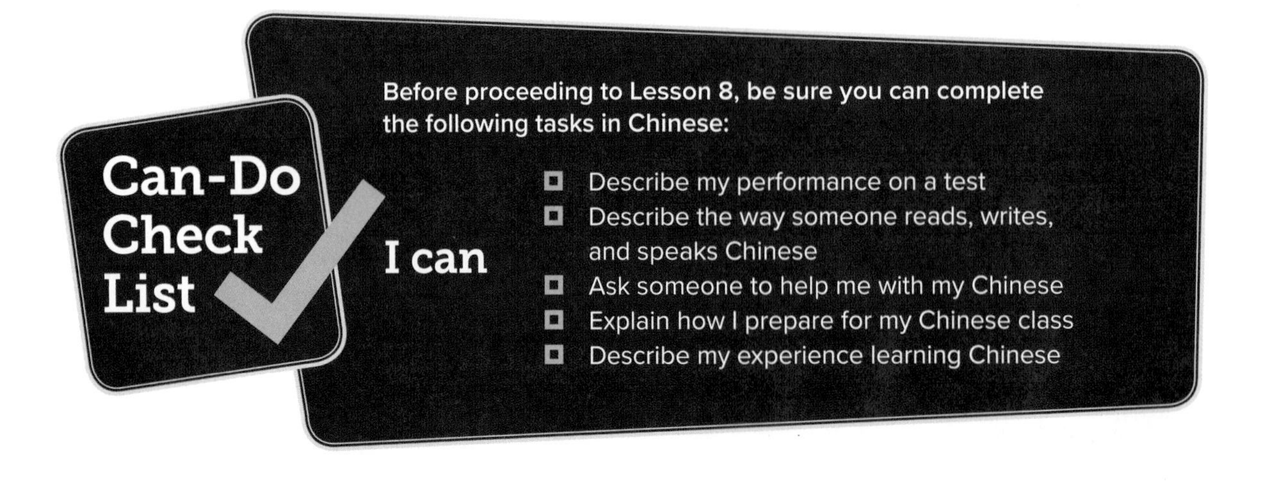

Lesson 8

第八課

Dì bā kè

學校生活

Xuéxiào shēnghuó

SCHOOL LIFE

Learning Objectives

In this lesson, you will learn to:

- Describe a student's daily routine
- Write a simple diary entry or blog post
- Write a brief letter or formal email applying appropriate conventions
- Update a friend on recent activities
- Express hope that a friend will accept your invitation

Relate & Get Ready

In your own culture/community:

- How do people connect with friends?
- How has technology affected letter-writing conventions?
- How do you think people will communicate about their daily lives and connect with others in the future?

A Typical School Day

Diary Entry

Audio

Video

李友的一篇日記

十一月三日 星期二

今天我很忙，很累。早上七點半起床[1]，洗了澡以後就[2]吃早飯。我一邊吃飯，一邊[3]聽錄音。九點到教室去上課[4]。

第一節課是中文，老師教我們發音、生詞和語法，也教我們寫字，還給了[5]我們一篇新課文[6]，這篇課文很有意思。第二節是電腦[a]課，很難。

中午我和同學們一起到餐廳去吃午飯。我們一邊吃，一邊練習說中文。下午我到圖書館去上網。四點王朋來找我打球。五點三刻吃晚飯。七點半我去白英愛的宿舍跟她聊天（兒）。到那兒的時候，她正在[7]做功課。我八點半回家。睡覺以前，高文中給我打了一個電話，告訴我明天要考試，我說我已經知道了。

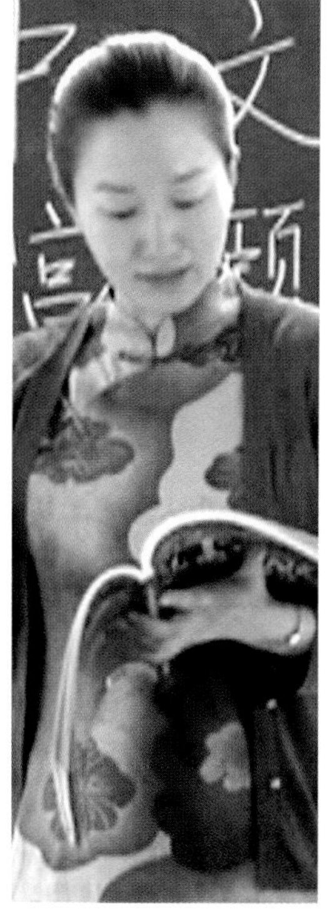

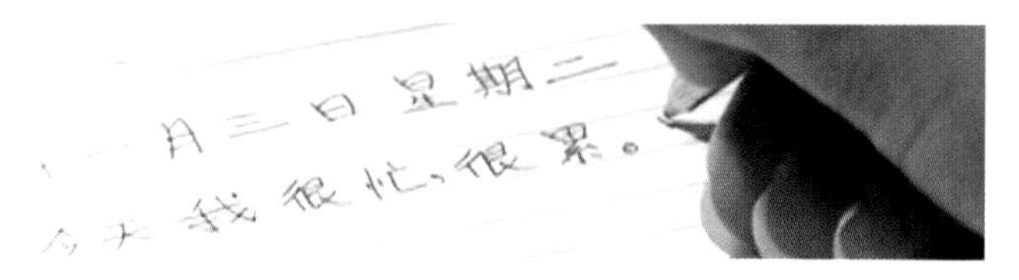

Lǐ Yǒu de yì piān rìjì

Shíyī yuè sān rì xīngqī'èr

Jīntiān wǒ hěn máng, hěn lèi. Zǎoshang qī diǎn bàn qǐ chuáng[1]*, xǐ le zǎo yǐhòu jiù*[2] *chī zǎofàn. Wǒ yìbiān chī fàn, yìbiān*[3] *tīng lùyīn. Jiǔ diǎn dào jiàoshì qù shàng kè*[4]*.*

Dì yī jié kè shì Zhōngwén, lǎoshī jiāo wǒmen fāyīn, shēngcí hé yǔfǎ, yě jiāo wǒmen xiě zì, hái gěi le[5] *wǒmen yì piān xīn kèwén*[6]*, zhè piān kèwén hěn yǒu yìsi. Dì èr jié shì diànnǎo*[a] *kè, hěn nán.*

Zhōngwǔ wǒ hé tóngxuémen yìqǐ dào cāntīng qù chī wǔfàn. Wǒmen yìbiān chī, yìbiān liànxí shuō Zhōngwén. Xiàwǔ wǒ dào túshūguǎn qù shàng wǎng. Sì diǎn Wáng Péng lái zhǎo wǒ dǎ qiú. Wǔ diǎn sān kè chī wǎnfàn. Qī diǎn bàn wǒ qù Bái Yīng'ài de sùshè gēn tā liáo tiān(r). Dào nàr de shíhou, tā zhèngzài[7] *zuò gōngkè. Wǒ bā diǎn bàn huí jiā. Shuì jiào yǐqián, Gāo Wénzhōng gěi wǒ dǎ le yí ge diànhuà, gàosu wǒ míngtiān yào kǎoshì, wǒ shuō wǒ yǐjīng zhīdao le.*

Language Note

a 電腦 *(diànnǎo)*

The usual colloquial term for a computer is 電腦 *(diànnǎo)*, literally "electric brain." A more formal term, especially in Mainland China, is 電子計算機 *(diànzǐ jìsuànjī)* (electronic computing machine) or simply 計算機 *(jìsuànjī)*. But in Taiwan, 計算機 *(jìsuànjī)* means a calculator. In Mainland China, a calculator is called 計算器 *(jìsuànqì)*.

Vocabulary

Audio

Flashcards

No.	Word	Pinyin	Part of Speech	Definition
1	篇	*piān*	m	(measure word for essays, articles, etc.)
2	日記	*rìjì*	n	diary
3	累	*lèi*	adj	tired
4	起床	*qǐ chuáng*	vo	to get up
	床	*chuáng*	n	bed
5	洗澡	*xǐ zǎo*	vo	to take a bath/shower
6	早飯	*zǎofàn*	n	breakfast
7	一邊	*yìbiān*	adv	simultaneously, at the same time [See Grammar 3.]
8	教室	*jiàoshì*	n	classroom
9	發音	*fāyīn*	n	pronunciation
10	新	*xīn*	adj	new
11	電腦	*diànnǎo*	n	computer
	腦	*nǎo*	n	brain
12	中午	*zhōngwǔ*	t	noon
13	餐廳	*cāntīng*	n	dining room, cafeteria
14	午飯	*wǔfàn*	n	lunch, midday meal
15	上網	*shàng wǎng*	vo	to go online, to surf the internet
16	宿舍	*sùshè*	n	dormitory
17	那兒	*nàr*	pr	there
18	正在	*zhèngzài*	adv	in the middle of (doing something) [See Grammar 7.]

Street food in China ranges from steamed buns to scallion pancakes. Based on the character with the smiley face, determine whether this food truck serves breakfast, lunch, or dinner.

GET Real WITH CHINESE

No.	Word	Pinyin	Part of Speech	Definition
19	以前	*yǐqián*	t	before
20	告訴	*gàosu*	v	to tell
21	已經	*yǐjīng*	adv	already
22	知道	*zhīdao*	v	to know

你和朋友在哪兒見面？

Nǐ hé péngyou zài nǎr jiànmiàn?

Where do you meet your friends?

How About You?

我們在 ____________ 見面。

Wǒmen zài ____________ jiànmiàn.

See index for corresponding vocabulary or research another term.

Grammar

1 The position of time-when expressions

Time-when expressions come before the verb. They often appear after the subject, but sometimes precede the subject under certain conditions. In this lesson, we focus on practicing time-when expressions positioned after the subject.

A 我們十點上課。

Wǒmen shí diǎn shàng kè.

We start class at ten.

B 我們幾點去？

Wǒmen jǐ diǎn qù?

What time are we going?

C 你什麼時候睡覺？

Nǐ shénme shíhou shuì jiào?

When do you go to bed?

D 他明天上午八點來。

Tā míngtiān shàngwǔ bā diǎn lái.

He will come at eight tomorrow morning.

More exercises

EXERCISES

Form two new sentences by inserting time-when expressions where appropriate. Use exercise 1 as an example.

1 王朋去學校看書。 昨天晚上七點

→ 王朋昨天晚上七點去學校看書了。

2 李友去高文中家玩兒。 上個星期六

3 常老師要去中國開會。 下個月

2 The adverb 就 (*jiù*) (II)

The adverb 就 (*jiù*) connects two verbs or verb phrases to indicate that the second action happens as soon as the first one is completed. [See also Grammar 3, Lesson 7.]

A 他今天早上起床以後就聽中文錄音了。

Tā jīntiān zǎoshang qǐ chuáng yǐhòu jiù tīng Zhōngwén lùyīn le.

He listened to the Chinese audio right after he got up this morning.

B 王朋看了電視以後就去睡覺了。

Wáng Péng kàn le diànshì yǐhòu jiù qù shuì jiào le.

Wang Peng went to bed right after watching TV.

C 我做了功課以後就去朋友家玩兒。

Wǒ zuò le gōngkè yǐhòu jiù qù péngyou jiā wánr.

I will go to my friend's place right after I finish my homework.

EXERCISES

Link the two actions to form a sentence, inserting 就 where appropriate. Use exercise 1 as an example.

1. 常老師起床以後　　去洗澡
   → 常老師起床以後就去洗澡。
2. 李友吃了晚飯　　去找人打球
3. 小王給他弟弟打了電話　　去學校上課

3 Describing simultaneity using 一邊… 一邊… (*yìbiān . . . yìbiān . . .*)

This structure describes two simultaneous actions. Typically, the first action is the principal one, which begins before the second, accompanying action.

A 我們一邊吃晚飯，一邊練習說中文。

Wǒmen yìbiān chī wǎnfàn, yìbiān liànxí shuō Zhōngwén.

We practiced speaking Chinese while having dinner.

B 他常常一邊吃飯一邊看電視。

Tā chángcháng yìbiān chī fàn yìbiān kàn diànshì.

He often eats and watches TV at the same time.

C 我一邊洗澡一邊唱歌。

Wǒ yìbiān xǐ zǎo, yìbiān chàng gē.

I sang while I was showering.

D 我妹妹喜歡一邊看書一邊聽音樂。

Wǒ mèimei xǐhuan yìbiān kàn shū, yìbiān tīng yīnyuè.

My younger sister likes to listen to music while she reads.

More exercises

EXERCISES

Form sentences to indicate the simultaneity of the two actions by inserting 一邊…一邊… where appropriate. Use exercise 1 as an example.

1 高小音 看書 聽音樂

→ 高小音一邊看書，一邊聽音樂。

2 王朋和朋友 看球 聊天兒

3 白老師 看電影 喝可樂

4 Series of verbs/verb phrases

Some verbs and verb phrases can be used in succession to represent a series of actions. Their sequential order usually coincides with the temporal order of the actions.

A 他常常去高小音家吃飯。

Tā chángcháng qù Gāo Xiǎoyīn jiā chī fàn.

He often goes to eat at Gao Xiaoyin's place.

B 下午我要到圖書館去看書。

Xiàwǔ wǒ yào dào túshūguǎn qù kàn shū.

This afternoon, I will go to the library to read.

C 我明天想找同學去打球。

Wǒ míngtiān xiǎng zhǎo tóngxué qù dǎ qiú.

I'd like to find some classmates to play ball with tomorrow.

D 你明天來我家吃晚飯吧。

Nǐ míngtiān lái wǒ jiā chī wǎnfàn ba.

Come and have dinner at my house tomorrow.

EXERCISES

Answer the questions by adding another verb phrase where appropriate. Use exercise 1 as an example.

More exercises

1 Q: 小王今天去哪兒吃晚飯？ 去朋友家

→ A: 他今天去朋友家吃晚飯。

2 Q: 週末我們去哪兒打球？ 去學校

3 Q: 小白在哪兒上網？ 在家

5 The particle 了 *(le)* (II)

If a statement enumerates a series of realized actions or events, 了 *(le)* usually appears at the end of the series rather than after each verb. [See also Grammar 5, Lesson 5, and Grammar 2, Lesson 1, Volume 2.]

A 昨天第一節課是中文。老師教我們發音、生詞和語法，也教我們寫字，還給了我們一篇新課文。那篇課文很有意思。

Zuótiān dì yī jié kè shì Zhōngwén. Lǎoshī jiāo wǒmen fāyīn, shēngcí hé yǔfǎ, yě jiāo wǒmen xiě zì, hái gěi le wǒmen yì piān xīn kèwén. Nà piān kèwén hěn yǒu yìsi.

Yesterday, the first class was Chinese. Our teacher taught us pronunciation, vocabulary, and grammar. She also taught us how to write characters and gave us a new text. That text was very interesting.

6 The particle 的 *(de)* (III)

When a disyllabic or polysyllabic adjective modifies a noun, the particle 的 *(de)* is usually inserted between the adjective and the noun.

A

漂亮的學校	容易的漢字	有意思的電影
piàoliang de xuéxiào	*róngyì de Hànzì*	*yǒu yìsi de diànyǐng*
beautiful school	easy character	interesting movie

However, with monosyllabic adjectives, 的 *(de)* is generally not required.

B

新課文	新電腦	大教室	好老師
xīn kèwén	*xīn diànnǎo*	*dà jiàoshì*	*hǎo lǎoshī*
new text	new computer	big classroom	good teacher

If the adjective is preceded by 很 *(hěn)*, however, 的 *(de)* cannot be dropped, e. g., 很大的教室 *(hěn dà de jiàoshì)* (very big classroom), 很好的老師 *(hěn hǎo de lǎoshī)* (very good teacher).

7 The 正在 (*zhèngzài*) v structure (be doing . . .)

The 正在 (*zhèngzài*) v structure (be doing . . .) denotes an ongoing or progressive action at a certain point of time. It is more emphatic than 在 (*zài*), which can serve the same function.

A Q: 李友，你在做什么？

Lǐ Yǒu, nǐ zài zuò shénme?

Li You, what are you doing?

A: 我在練習寫漢字。

Wǒ zài liànxí xiě Hànzì.

I'm practicing writing Chinese characters.

B 我們現在正在上課，你別打電話。

Wǒmen xiànzài zhèngzài shàng kè, nǐ bié dǎ diànhuà.

We are in class right now. Don't make phone calls.

C 我昨天到他宿舍的時候，他正在練習發音。

Wǒ zuótiān dào tā sùshè de shíhou, tā zhèngzài liànxí fāyīn.

When I got to his dorm yesterday, he was in the middle of practicing pronunciation.

D Q: 你知道不知道王老師在哪兒？

Nǐ zhīdao bù zhīdào Wáng lǎoshī zài nǎr?

Do you know where Teacher Wang is?

A: 他正在辦公室開會。

Tā zhèngzài bàngōngshì kāi huì.

He is having a meeting in his office.

EXERCISES

Join the two sentences by inserting the "…的時候，…正在…" construction where appropriate. Use exercise 1 as an example.

More exercises

1 王朋給我打電話。 我做功課。
→ 王朋給我打電話的時候，我正在做功課。

2 我打電話回家。 爸爸媽媽吃晚飯。

3 我到她宿舍。 她上網。

Language Practice

A What a day! PRESENTATIONAL

Describe Little Gao's schedule using appropriate time expressions, e.g.:

小高早上八點起床。

Xiǎo Gāo zǎoshang bā diǎn qǐ chuáng.

MON	TUE	WED	THU	FRI	SAT	SUN
29	30	31	01	02	03	04
05	06	07	08	09	10	11
12	13	14	15	16	17	18
19	20	21	22	23	24	25

- 8.00 AM
- 8.30 AM (SCHOOL)
- 9.15 AM
- 12.00 PM (LIBRARY)

B Multitasking INTERPERSONAL

Using the images below, practice how to describe two simultaneous actions by inserting 一邊⋯ 一邊⋯ (*yìbiān ... yìbiān ...*) where appropriate. Then ask if your partner multitasks, e.g.:

他們一邊喝茶，一邊聊天兒。

Tāmen yìbiān hē chá, yìbiān liáo tiānr.

你也常常和朋友一邊喝茶，一邊聊天嗎？

Nǐ yě chángcháng hé péngyou yìbiān hē chá, yìbiān liáo tiānr ma?

1 

2 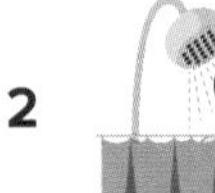

3 

4 

C Putting things in order

INTERPRETIVE

Determine the logical sequence of the actions and fill in the blanks with appropriate locations or personal names. Then rearrange the phrases into complete sentences, e.g.:

王朋　去玩（兒）　到______家

Wáng Péng　qù wán (r)　dào______jiā

王朋到高小音家去玩（兒）。

Wáng Péng dào Gāo Xiǎoyīn jiā qù wán(r).

1	到______去 *dào ______qù*	高文中 *Gāo Wénzhōng*	問老師問題 *wèn lǎoshī wèntí*
2	打球 *dǎ qiú*	王朋 *Wáng Péng*	找______ *zhǎo ______*
3	找同學聊天 *zhǎo tóngxué liáo tiān*	去______ *qù ______*	小白 *Xiǎo Bái*
4	教她怎麼寫漢字 *jiāo tā zěnme xiě Hànzì*	李友 *Lǐ Yǒu*	請______ *qǐng ______*

D Lesson plans

PRESENTATIONAL

Based on your class schedule, tell the class how you would organize classes on pronunciation, vocabulary, grammar, Chinese characters, and the lesson texts if you were the teacher, e.g.:

我星期一教大家生詞，星期二教大家語法，……

Wǒ xīngqīyī jiāo dàjiā shēngcí, xīngqīèr jiāo dàjiā yǔfǎ, . . .

Which topics do students have the most questions about?

學生常常問老師發音的問題。

Xuésheng chángcháng wèn lǎoshī fāyīn de wèntí.

E Keeping tabs

INTERPERSONAL

In pairs, form a question-and-answer about what people are doing based on the images below. Use 正在 (*zhèngzài*), e.g.:

Q: 他正在做什麼？

Tā zhèngzài zuò shénme?

A: 他正在睡覺。

Tā zhèngzài shuì jiào.

1 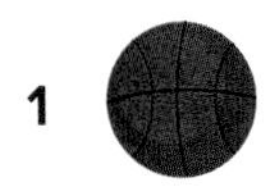

2 

3 

4 

F Business as usual

INTERPERSONAL

In pairs, form a question-and-answer about your partner's daily routines, e.g.:

Q: 你平常幾點起床？ *Nǐ píngcháng jǐ diǎn qǐ chuáng?*

A: 我平常八點起床。 *Wǒ píngcháng bā diǎn qǐchuáng.*

你平常幾點吃早飯/去上课/吃午飯/吃晚飯？

Nǐ píngcháng jǐ diǎn chī zǎofàn/qù shàng kè/chī wǔfàn/chī wǎnfàn?

你平常什麼時候洗澡？

Nǐ píngcháng shénme shíhou xǐ zǎo?

你（是）起床以後還是睡覺以前洗澡？

Nǐ (shì) qǐ chuáng yǐhòu háishi shuì jiào yǐqián xǐ zǎo?

G Character development

INTERPRETIVE PRESENTATIONAL

Present a day in the life of a fictional character from a screenplay or novel you'd like to write, e.g.:

王文早上九點起床，吃了早飯以後就去上課，……
下午兩點去找同學打球，……

Wáng Wén zǎoshang jiǔ diǎn qǐ chuáng, chī le zǎofàn yǐhòu jiù qù shàng kè, . . .

Xiàwǔ liǎng diǎn qù zhǎo tóngxué dǎ qiú, . . .

Then quiz the class about your character's day, e.g.:

王文吃了午飯以後做什麼？

Wáng Wén chī le wǔfàn yǐhòu zuò shénme?

王文練習了中文以後做什麼？

Wáng Wén liànxí le Zhōngwén yǐhòu zuò shénme?

王文跟朋友打了球以後做什麼？

Wáng Wén gēn péngyou dǎ le qiú yǐhòu zuò shénme?

Characterize it!

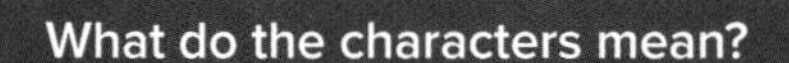

What do the characters mean?

What is the common radical?

What does the radical mean?

How does the radical relate to the overall meaning of the characters?

1 洗

2 澡

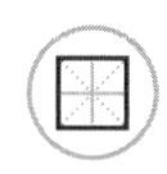

More characters

Chinese Chat

Your friend is texting you through Facebook Messenger about when to hang out. How would you reply?

Writing to a Friend

Letter

Audio

Video

一封信

這是李友給高小音的一封信。

小音：

你好！好久不見，最近怎麼樣？

這個學期我很忙，除了專業課以外，還[8]得學中文。我們的中文課很有意思。因為我們的中文老師只會[9]說中文，不會說英文，所以上課的時候我們只說中文，不說英文。開始我覺得很難，後來[a]，王朋常常幫我練習中文，就[10]覺得不難了[b]。

你喜歡聽音樂嗎？下個星期六，我們學校有一個音樂會，希望你能[9]來。我用中文寫信寫得很不好，請別笑我。祝

好!

你的朋友

李友

十一月十八日

Yì fēng xìn

Zhè shì Lǐ Yǒu gěi Gāo Xiǎoyīn de yì fēng xìn.

Xiǎoyīn:

Nǐ hǎo! Hǎo jiǔ bú jiàn, zuìjìn zěnmeyàng?

Zhè ge xuéqī wǒ hěn máng, chúle zhuānyè kè yǐwài, hái[8] *děi xué Zhōngwén. Wǒmen de Zhōngwén kè hěn yǒu yìsi. Yīnwèi wǒmen de Zhōngwén lǎoshī zhǐ huì*[9] *shuō Zhōngwén, bú huì shuō Yīngwén, suǒyǐ shàng kè de shíhou wǒmen zhǐ shuō Zhōngwén, bù shuō Yīngwén. Kāishǐ wǒ juéde hěn nán, hòulái*[a]*, Wáng Péng chángcháng bāng wǒ liànxí Zhōngwén, jiù*[10] *juéde bù nán le*[b]*.*

Nǐ xǐhuan tīng yīnyuè ma? Xià ge xīngqīliù, wǒmen xuéxiào yǒu yí ge yīnyuèhuì, xīwàng nǐ néng[9] *lái. Wǒ yòng Zhōngwén xiě xìn xiě de hěn bù hǎo, qǐng bié xiào wǒ. Zhù*

Hǎo!

Nǐ de péngyou

Lǐ Yǒu

Shíyīyuè shíbā rì

Language Notes

a 後來 *(hòulái)*

This is usually translated as "later," but it pertains only to actions and situations in the unspecified past.

b 了 *(le)*

This sentence-final particle usually indicates a change in status or the realization of a new situation. [See also Grammar 2, Lesson 1, Volume 2.]

Vocabulary

Audio

Flashcards

No.	Word	Pinyin	Part of Speech	Definition
1	封	*fēng*	m	(measure word for letters)
2	信	*xìn*	n	letter (correspondence)
3	最近	*zuìjìn*	t	recently
	最	*zuì*	adv	(of superlative degree, most, -est)
	近	*jìn*	adj	close, near
4	學期	*xuéqī*	n	school term, semester, quarter
5	除了…以外	*chúle . . . yǐwài*	conj	in addition to, besides [See Grammar 8.]
6	專業	*zhuānyè*	n	major (in college), specialty
7	會	*huì*	mv	can, know how to [See Grammar 9.]
8	後來	*hòulái*	t	later
9	音樂會	*yīnyuèhuì*	n	concert
10	希望	*xīwàng*	v/n	to hope; hope [See Grammar 9.]
11	能	*néng*	mv	can, to be able to [See Grammar 9.]
12	用	*yòng*	v	to use
13	笑	*xiào*	v	to laugh at, to laugh, to smile
14	祝	*zhù*	v	to wish (well)

你的專業是什麼？

Nǐ de zhuānyè shì shénme?

What's your major?

How About You?

我的專業是＿＿＿＿＿＿。

Wǒ de zhuānyè shì ＿＿＿＿＿＿.

See index for corresponding vocabulary or research another term.

Grammar

8 Indicating inclusiveness: 除了…以外，還/也… (*chúle . . . yǐwài, hái/ yě . . .*) (in addition to, also)

除了… 以外 (*chúle . . . yǐwài*) means "apart from" or "in addition to." When followed by 還… (*hái . . .*) (also, too, as well) or 也 (*yě*) (too, also), it indicates inclusiveness of the content inserted between 除了 (*chúle*) and 以外 (*yǐwài*).

A 我除了學專業課以外，還學中文。

Wǒ chúle xué zhuānyè kè yǐwài, hái xué Zhōngwén.

Besides the courses in my major, I also take Chinese.

B 上個週末我們除了看電影以外，還聽音樂了。

Shàng ge zhōumò wǒmen chúle kàn diànyǐng yǐwài, hái tīng yīnyuè le.

Last weekend, besides seeing a movie, we also listened to music.

C 他除了喜歡聽音樂以外，還喜歡打球。

Tā chúle xǐhuan tīng yīnyuè yǐwài, hái xǐhuan dǎ qiú.

In addition to listening to music, he also likes to play ball.

The activities in (A), (B), and (C) are performed by the same subject. If activities are done by different subjects, the adverb 也 has to be used. In these cases, the first subject follows 除了, and the second subject precedes 也, as in (D).

D 除了小王以外，小李也喜歡唱歌、跳舞。

Chúle Xiǎo Wáng yǐwài, Xiǎo Lǐ yě xǐhuan chàng gē, tiào wǔ.

Like Little Wang, Little Li also enjoys singing and dancing.

EXERCISES

Join the two sentences to indicate inclusiveness by inserting 除了… 以外，還/也… where appropriate. Use exercise 1 as an example.

More exercises

1 她這個學期學中文。她這個學期學日文。

→ 她這個學期除了學中文以外，還學日文。

2 王朋今天晚上想看球。王朋今天晚上想上網。

3 李友週末想看電影。白英愛週末想看電影。

9 Comparing 能 (*néng*) and 會 (*huì*) (I)

Both 能 (*néng*) and 會 (*huì*) have several meanings. The basic meaning of 能 (*néng*) is "to be capable of (doing something)," as in (A). It can also indicate the viability of an action, as in (B) and (C). Additional meanings will be introduced in later lessons. 會 (*huì*), as used in (D), (E), and (F), means having acquired the skill to do something through learning.

A 我能喝十杯咖啡。

Wǒ néng hē shí bēi kāfēi.

I can drink ten cups of coffee.

B 今天下午我要開會，不能去聽音樂會。

Jīntiān xiàwǔ wǒ yào kāi huì, bù néng qù tīng yīnyuèhuì.

I have a meeting this afternoon. I cannot go to the concert.

C 我們不能在圖書館聊天兒。

Wǒmen bù néng zài túshūguǎn liáo tiānr.

We cannot chat in the library.

D 李友會說中文。

Lǐ Yǒu huì shuō Zhōngwén.

Li You can speak Chinese.

E 小白會唱很多美國歌。

Xiǎo Bái huì chàng hěn duō Měiguó gē.

Little Bai can sing many American songs.

F 我不會打球，請你教我。

Wǒ bú huì dǎ qiú, qǐng nǐ jiāo wǒ.

I don't know how to play ball. Please teach me how.

EXERCISES

In pairs, ask about your partner's capabilities or availability by inserting 會 or 能 when appropriate.

1 Q: 你_______用中文寫信嗎？ A: 我_______。

2 Q: 明天考試，今天晚上你_______去看電影嗎？

A: 我_______。

10 The conjunctions 要是 (*yàoshi*) and 因為 (*yīnwèi*) and the adverb 就 (*jiù*) (III)

In this structure, the first clause conveys a condition or reason while the second clause denotes the result or conclusion. The adverb 就 (*jiù*) indicates the close relationship between the two. The relationship is often causal, as in (A) and (B), or conditional, as in (C) and (D).

A （因為）小高喜歡吃中國菜，（所以）我們就吃中國菜。

(Yīnwèi) Xiǎo Gāo xǐhuan chī Zhōngguó cài, (suǒyǐ) wǒmen jiù chī Zhōngguó cài.

Little Gao prefers Chinese food, so we went for Chinese food.

B （因為）小王的專業是中文，（所以）我就請他教我怎麼說中文。

(Yīnwèi) Xiǎo Wáng de zhuānyè shì Zhōngwén, (suǒyǐ) wǒ jiù qǐng tā jiāo wǒ zěnme shuō Zhōngwén.

Little Wang's major is Chinese, so I asked him to teach me how to speak Chinese.

C 要是同學幫我復習，我考試就考得很好。

Yàoshi tóngxué bāng wǒ fùxí, wǒ kǎoshì jiù kǎo de hěn hǎo.

If my classmates help me review, I do very well on my tests.

D 要是你不能來，我就去你那兒。

Yàoshi nǐ bù néng lái, wǒ jiù qù nǐ nàr.

If you can't come over, I will go to your place.

E 寫漢字，開始覺得很難，（要是）常常練習，就覺得容易了。

Xiě Hànzì, kāishǐ juéde hěn nán, (yàoshi) chángcháng liànxí, jiù juéde róngyì le.

Learning to write Chinese characters might be very difficult at first. It becomes easier with practice.

More exercises

EXERCISES

Join the sentences to indicate the close relationship between two actions or situations. Use exercise 1 as an example.

1 你喜歡看美國電影。我們看美國電影。
→ 你喜歡看美國電影，我們就看美國電影。

2 你不喜歡吃中國菜。我們不吃中國菜。

3 你不會用中文跟他聊天。你用英文跟他聊天。

Upon enrollment, Chinese university students are given a basic ID card (學生卡) (xuéshēngkǎ) and a more detailed ID book (學生證) (xuéshēngzhèng). Based on her ID book, describe this student as best you can.

Language Practice

H In addition

INTERPERSONAL

In pairs, ask each other these questions using 除了…以外，還… (*chúle . . . yǐwài, hái . . .*):

1 你今天除了上中文課以外，還上什麼課？

Nǐ jīntiān chúle shàng Zhōngwén kè yǐwài, hái shàng shénme kè?

2 你們上中文課除了練習語法以外，還做什麼？

Nǐmen shàng Zhōngwén kè chúle liànxí yǔfǎ yǐwài, hái zuò shénme?

3 你除了會說中文以外，還會說什麼話？

Nǐ chúle huì shuō Zhōngwén yǐwài, hái huì shuō shénme huà?

I Ends and means

INTERPERSONAL

In pairs, form a question-and-answer about what tools people use to perform certain actions. Use 用 (*yòng*), e.g.:

上網 ◇ 電腦

shàng wǎng ◇ *diànnǎo*

Q: 你用什麼上網？
Nǐ yòng shénme shàng wǎng?

A: 我用電腦上網。
Wǒ yòng diànnǎo shàng wǎng.

1 做功課 ◇ 筆

zuò gōngkè ◇ *bǐ*

2 練習發音 ◇ 電腦

liànxí fāyīn ◇ *diànnǎo*

3 喝茶 ◇ 咖啡杯

hē chá ◇ kāfēi bēi

4 寫日記 ◇ 中文

xiě rìjì ◇ Zhōngwén

5 看電影 ◇ 電腦

kàn diànyǐng ◇ diànnǎo

J Get personal

INTERPERSONAL

Survey your classmates about how they write letters and diary entries.

你寫信嗎?

Nǐ xiě xìn ma?

你常常給誰寫信?

Nǐ chángcháng gěi shéi xiě xìn?

你會用電腦寫信嗎?

Nǐ huì yòng diànnǎo xiě xìn ma?

你寫日記嗎?

Nǐ xiě rìjì ma?

你用中文寫日記還是用英文寫日記?

Nǐ yòng Zhōngwén xiě rìjì háishi Yòng yīngwén xiě rìjì?

Characterize it!

What do the characters mean?

What is the common radical?

What does the radical mean?

How does the radical relate to the overall meaning of the characters?

❶ 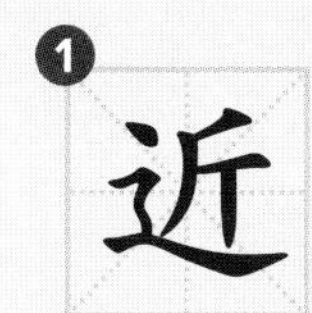

❷ 

❸ 

More characters

Chinese Chat

Li You just published a post on Qzone (**QQ空間**) *(QQ kōngjiān)*, a Chinese social networking site. What comment would you leave?

Continue to explore

Semesters

Colleges and universities in both Mainland China and Taiwan are on the semester system. Typically, the fall semester starts in late August or early September, and ends in mid-January. The winter break lasts about a month. Since the Chinese New Year usually falls in late January or early February, college students can take advantage of the break to go home and celebrate the most important holiday of the year with their families. The spring semester starts around mid-February and lasts until early July. A semester at a Chinese college is about three weeks longer than a typical American college semester.

COMPARE & CONTRAST

Applicants to Chinese universities and colleges are required to take the National Higher Education Entrance Examination, also known as *Gaokao* (高考) (*gāo kǎo*). In 2015, more than nine million people took the test. The admission rate was about 75%. Although the majority of applicants make it into college, only those with the highest scores are admitted into a 一本大學 (*yī běn dàxué*) (first-tier university). Others go to a 二本大學 (*èr běn dàxué*) (second-tier university), 三本大學 (*sān běn dàxué*) (third-tier university), or higher vocational college. Compare *Gaokao* and the equivalent standardized test in your own country, and discuss the advantages and disadvantages of different college admission processes.

Yours truly

The traditional way to end a formal letter is to use the closing 祝好 (zhù hǎo) (I wish you well), with the character 祝 (zhù) (to wish) following the final sentence of the letter and the character 好 (hǎo) at the very beginning of the next line.

However, it is now more common to keep the two characters 祝好 (zhù hǎo) unseparated. With the advent of new technology like social media, formal writing conventions (including salutations and sign-offs) are changing rapidly.

Lesson Wrap-Up

Make It Flow!

Rearrange the following sentences into chronological order. Then combine them into a coherent narrative. Remember to avoid repeating the same nouns by replacing them with pronouns where appropriate. Use 一邊⋯ 一邊⋯ (*yìbiān . . . yìbiān . . .*), 除了⋯以外, 還⋯ (*chúle . . . yǐwài, hái . . .*) where appropriate.

____李友早上7點起床。

____李友吃早飯的時候聽錄音。

____李友上午有中文課。

__1__李友今天很忙。

____李友下午3點去圖書館上網。

____李友晚上8點半和王朋一起練習說中文。

____李友11點半才睡覺。

____李友7點半吃早飯。

____李友5點半吃晚飯。

____李友上午有三節課。

____李友4點去打球。

____李友上午還有電腦課。

Blog

Using the diary format, post a blog entry describing your day.

Email

Write an email describing your Chinese teacher and outlining why he/she should be nominated for a teaching award. Use formal letter-writing conventions.

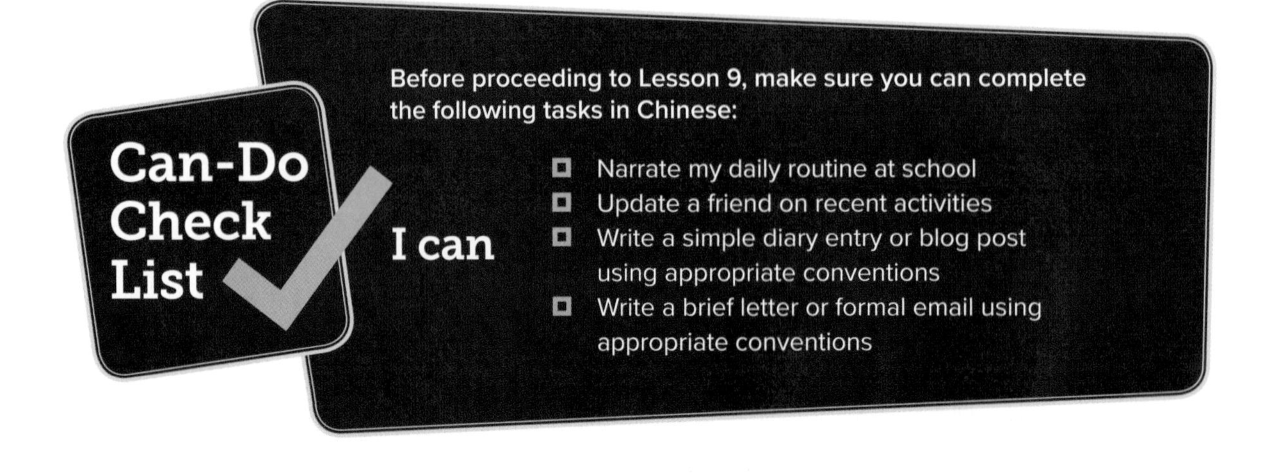

Lesson 9

第九課

Dì jiǔ kè

買東西

Mǎi dōngxi

SHOPPING

Learning Objectives

In this lesson, you will learn to:

- Describe the color, size, and price of a purchase
- Recognize Chinese currency
- Pay in cash or with a credit card
- Determine the proper change you should receive
- Ask for merchandise in a different size or color
- Exchange merchandise

Relate & Get Ready

In your own culture/community:

- Do people haggle over prices in stores?
- Can merchandise be returned or exchanged?
- Do people typically pay for their purchases with cash?

Shopping for Clothes

Dialogue 1

李友在商店買東西，售貨員問她……

Audio

Video

小姐，您要[1]買什麼衣服？

我想買一件[2]襯衫。

您喜歡什麼顏色的[3]，黃的還是紅的？

我喜歡穿[a]紅的。我還想買一條[2]褲子[b]。

多[4]大的？大號的、中號的、還是小號的？

中號的。不要太貴的，也不要太便宜[c]的。

這條褲子怎麼樣？

顏色很好。如果長短合適的話，我就買。

您試一下。

Li You checks the size on the label and measures the pants against her legs.

不用試。可以。

這件襯衫呢？

也不錯。一共多少錢？

襯衫二十一塊五，褲子三十二塊九毛九，一共是五十四塊四毛九分[5]。

好，這是一百塊錢。

找您四十五塊五毛一。

謝謝。

Lǐ Yǒu zài shāngdiàn mǎi dōngxi, shòuhuòyuán wèn tā . . .

Xiǎojiě, nín yào[1] *mǎi shénme yīfu?*

Wǒ xiǎng mǎi yí jiàn[2] *chènshān.*

Nín xǐhuan shénme yánsè de[3]*, huáng de háishi hóng de?*

Wǒ xǐhuan chuān[a] *hóng de. Wǒ hái xiǎng mǎi yì tiáo*[2] *kùzi*[b]*.*

Duō[4] *dà de? Dà hào de, zhōng hào de, háishi xiǎo hào de?*

Zhōng hào de. Bú yào tài guì de, yě bú yào tài piányi[c] *de.*

Zhè tiáo kùzi zěnmeyàng?

Yánsè hěn hǎo, rúguǒ chángduǎn héshì de huà, wǒ jiù mǎi.

Nín shì yí xia.

Li You checks the size on the label and measures the pants against her legs.

Búyòng shì, kěyǐ.

Zhè jiàn chènshān ne?

Yě búcuò. Yígòng duōshao qián?

Chènshān èrshíyī kuài wǔ, kùzi sānshí'èr kuài jiǔ máo jiǔ, yígòng shì wǔshísì kuài sì máo jiǔ fēn[5]*.*

Hǎo, zhè shì yìbǎi kuài qián.

Zhǎo nín sìshíwǔ kuài wǔ máo yī.

Xièxie.

Language Notes

a 穿 *(chuān)*

Note that this verb can mean both "to wear" and "to put on." However, for most accessories, 戴 *(dài)* (to wear, to put on) is used instead.

b 一條褲子 *(yì tiáo kùzi)*

In Chinese, a pair of pants is considered a single piece of clothing. Hence, it is 一條褲子 *(yì tiáo kùzi)* (lit. a trouser) instead of ⊗ 一雙褲子 *(yì shuāng kùzi)* (lit. a pair of trousers).

c 便宜 *(piányi)*

The first character of 便宜 *(piányi)* (inexpensive) is pronounced "*pián*." But in 方便 *(fāngbiàn)* (convenient), the same character is pronounced "*biàn*." Sometimes the same character can have different pronunciations that carry different meanings. Other examples include 樂 (*yuè* or *lè*) and 覺 (*jué* or *jiào*): 音樂 *(yīnyuè)* (music), 可樂 *(kělè)* (cola), 覺得 *(juéde)* (to feel), and 睡覺 *(shuì jiào)* (to sleep).

Vocabulary

Audio

Flashcards

No.	Word	Pinyin	Part of Speech	Definition
1	商店	*shāngdiàn*	n	store, shop
2	買	*mǎi*	v	to buy
3	東西	*dōngxi*	n	things, objects
4	售貨員	*shòuhuòyuán*	n	shop assistant, salesclerk
5	衣服	*yīfu*	n	clothes
6	件	*jiàn*	m	(measure word for shirts, dresses, jackets, coats, etc.)
7	襯衫	*chènshān*	n	shirt
8	顏色	*yánsè*	n	color
9	黃	*huáng*	adj	yellow
10	紅	*hóng*	adj	red
11	穿	*chuān*	v	to wear, to put on
12	褲子	*kùzi*	n	pants
13	號	*hào*	n	size
14	中	*zhōng*	adj	medium, middle
15	便宜	*piányi*	adj	cheap, inexpensive
16	如果	*rúguǒ*	conj	if
	的話	*de huà*		
17	長短	*chángduǎn*	n	length
	長	*cháng*	adj	long
	短	*duǎn*	adj	short
18	合適	*héshì*	adj	suitable
19	試	*shì*	v	to try
20	不用	*búyòng*		need not
21	一共	*yígòng*	adv	altogether
22	多少	*duōshao*	qpr	how much/many

You are wandering the Shilin Night Market in Taipei and come across this vendor selling imagawayaki (車輪餅) (*chēlúnbǐng*). *How many can you buy with 100 yuan?*

GET Real WITH CHINESE

No.	Word	Pinyin	Part of Speech	Definition
23	錢	*qián*	n	money
24	塊	*kuài*	m	(measure word for the basic Chinese monetary unit [equivalent of a dollar])
25	毛	*máo*	m	(measure word for 1/10 of a kuai [equivalent of a dime])
26	分	*fēn*	m	(measure word for 1/100 of a kuai [equivalent of a cent])
27	百	*bǎi*	nu	hundred
28	找（錢）	*zhǎo (qián)*	v(o)	to give change

How About You?

您要買什麼衣服？

Nín yào mǎi shénme yīfu?

What would you like to buy?

我想買＿＿＿＿＿＿＿。

Wǒ xiǎng mǎi ＿＿＿＿＿＿＿.

See index for corresponding vocabulary or research another term.

Grammar

1 The modal verb 要 *(yào)* (want to do) (II)

要 *(yào)* can also mean "to desire to do something." [See also Grammar 2, Lesson 6.]

A 明天是週末，你要做什麼？

Míngtiān shì zhōumò, nǐ yào zuò shénme?

Tomorrow is the weekend. What do you want to do?

B 我要去圖書館看書，你去不去？

Wǒ yào qù túshūguǎn kàn shū, nǐ qù bu qù?

I want to go to the library to read. Do you want to come?

C 我要喝可樂，他要喝茶。

Wǒ yào hē kělè, tā yào hē chá.

I want to drink cola. He wants to drink tea.

To negate it, use 不想 *(bù xiǎng)*.

D 我不想去圖書館。

Wǒ bù xiǎng qù túshūguǎn.

I don't want to go to the library.

E 今天我不想做功課。

Jīntiān wǒ bù xiǎng zuò gōngkè.

I don't want to do my homework today.

Both of the modal verbs 想 *(xiǎng)* and 要 *(yào)* can express a desire or an intention, but 要 *(yào)* carries a stronger tone.

EXERCISES

Answer the following questions using 要 where appropriate.

More exercises

1 李友要去商店買什麼？

2 你這個週末要做什麼？

2 Measure words (II)

These are useful "measure word + noun" combinations. [See also Grammar 2, Lesson 2.]

Word	Pinyin	Definition
一個人	*yí ge rén*	a person
一位先生	*yí wèi xiānsheng*	a gentleman
一杯茶	*yì bēi chá*	a cup of tea
一瓶可樂	*yì píng kělè*	a bottle of cola
一枝筆	*yì zhī bǐ*	a pen
一張紙	*yì zhāng zhǐ*	a piece of paper
一節課	*yì jié kè*	a class period
一篇課文	*yì piān kèwén*	the text of a lesson
一件襯衫	*yí jiàn chènshān*	a shirt
一條褲子	*yì tiáo kùzi*	a pair of pants
一雙鞋	*yì shuāng xié*	a pair of shoes [See Dialogue 2.]
一塊錢	*yí kuài qián*	one yuan
一毛錢	*yì máo qián*	one mao (1/10 of a yuan)
一分錢	*yì fēn qián*	one fen (1/100 of a yuan)
一本書	*yì běn shū*	a book
一隻鞋	*yì zhī xié*	a shoe (one of a pair) [See also "a pair of shoes," above.]

EXERCISES

Fill in the blanks with the proper measure words.

1 兩______咖啡

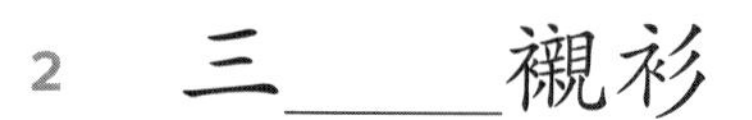
2 三______襯衫

3 The 的 (de) structure (II)

We have a 的 (*de*) structure when a noun, a pronoun, an adjective, or a verb is followed by the structural particle 的 (*de*). Grammatically, a 的 (*de*) structure is equivalent to a noun, e.g., 老師的 (*lǎoshī de*) (the teacher's), 我的 (*wǒ de*) (mine), 大的 (*dà de*) (the big one), 吃的 (*chī de*) (things to eat). [See also Grammar 8, Lesson 7.]

More exercises

EXERCISES

Answer the following questions using the 的 structure where appropriate.

1 你的襯衫是大號的、中號的還是小號的？

2 你爸爸喜歡穿什麼顏色的褲子？

4 Using 多 (duō) interrogatively

The adverb 多 (*duō*) is often used in questions asking about degree or extent. The adjectives that follow 多 (*duō*) typically suggest an expansive quality, such as 大 (*dà*) (big), as in (A) and (B), and 高 (*gāo*) (tall, high), as in (C). Note that words that denote a diminutive quality, such as 小 (*xiǎo*) (small, little) and 矮 (*ǎi*) (short), are not used in this construction.

A 你今年多大？ [See Lesson 3.]

Nǐ jīnnián duō dà?

How old are you this year?

B 你穿多大的衣服？

Nǐ chuān duō dà de yīfu?

What size clothes do you wear?

C 你弟弟多高？

Nǐ dìdi duō gāo?

How tall is your younger brother?

More exercises

EXERCISES

Form questions asking about degree or extent by inserting 多 where appropriate.

1 高文中　高

2 你弟弟　大

Denominations of currency

The denominations of Chinese currency are as follows.

Usage	Unit of Currency	1/10 of a Unit	1/100 of a Unit
Standard[a]	元 *(yuán)*	角 *(jiǎo)*	分 *(fēn)*
Colloquial	塊 *(kuài)*	毛 *(máo)*	分 *(fēn)*

[a]Store prices are typically listed in 元 *(yuán)* and 角 *(jiǎo)*.

In colloquial speech, ¥5.99 is 五塊九毛九分錢 *(wǔ kuài jiǔ máo jiǔ fēn qián)*. In conversation, abbreviated forms are also used, e.g., 五塊九毛九分 (omitting 錢 *[qián]* [money]) and 五塊九毛九 (omitting 錢 *[qián]* and the last unit). If 錢*(qián)* is included, the preceding measure (e.g., 分 *[fēn]*) must also be included. ✖ 五塊九毛九錢.

One or more zeroes occurring internally in a complex number are read as 〇 *(líng)* (zero). To avoid ambiguity, 毛 *(máo)* and 分 *(fēn)* must be retained, as in (D) or (E).

A 八塊五毛五（分）（錢）
bā kuài wǔ máo wǔ (fēn) (qián)
¥8.55

B 十五塊三（毛）（錢）
shíwǔ kuài sān (máo) (qián)
¥15.30

C 一百〇三塊（錢）
yìbǎi líng sān kuài (qián)
¥103

D 一百塊〇三毛（錢）
yìbǎi kuài líng sān máo (qián)
¥100.30

E 一百塊〇三分（錢）
yìbǎi kuài líng sān fēn (qián)
¥100.03

EXERCISES

Say the following amounts of money in Chinese.

More exercises

1 ¥9.99

2 ¥135.20

3 ¥86.04

Language Practice

A I'll check my calendar

INTERPERSONAL

In pairs, form a question-and-answer about what Little Wang wants to do next week based on the following calendar. [See also Grammar 2, Lesson 6.] Insert 要 *(yào)* where appropriate, e.g.:

星期一 *(xīngqīyī)*

Q: 小王下個星期一要做什麼？

Xiǎo Wáng xià ge xīngqīyī yào zuò shénme?

A: 小王下個星期一要去上課。

Xiǎo Wáng xià ge xīngqīyī yào qù shàng kè.

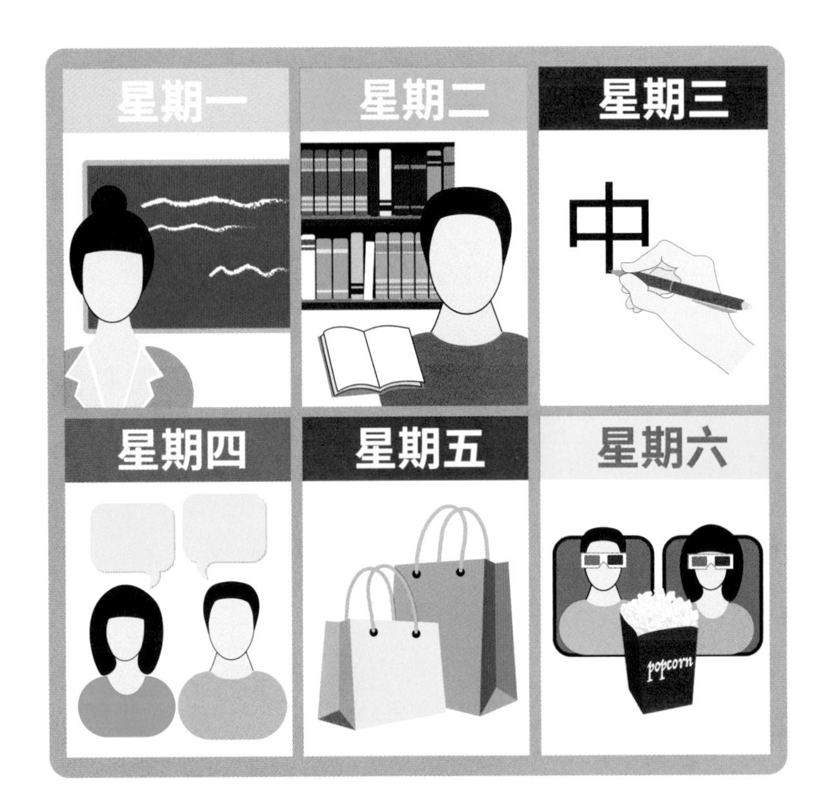

Then discuss your partner's plans for next week, e.g.:

Q: 你呢？你下個星期要做什麼？

Nǐ ne? Nǐ xià ge xīngqī yào zuò shénme?

A: 我下個星期一…… 星期二……

Wǒ xià ge xīngqīyī . . . xīngqīèr . . .

B Online shopping spree

PRESENTATIONAL

Little Li is an avid online shopper. Recap what's in her shopping cart based on the images below, using 想 *(xiǎng)* where appropriate, e.g.:

小李想買一件新衣服。

Xiǎo Lǐ xiǎng mǎi yí jiàn xīn yīfu.

1 

2

3

4

Then share what's on your online wish list with the class and explain why you want the items, e.g.:

我喜歡白色/我沒有白色的褲子，
所以我想買一條白色的褲子。

Wǒ xǐhuān báisè/Wǒ méiyǒu báisè de kùzi, suǒyǐ wǒ xiǎng mǎi yì tiáo báisè de kùzi.

C Lost and found

INTERPERSONAL

In pairs, identify to whom the objects belong. Use 的 *(de)*, e.g.:

Q: 這瓶可樂是誰的？

Zhè píng kělè shì shéi de?

A: 這瓶可樂是高文中的。

Zhè píng kělè shì Gāo Wénzhōng de.

1 

2 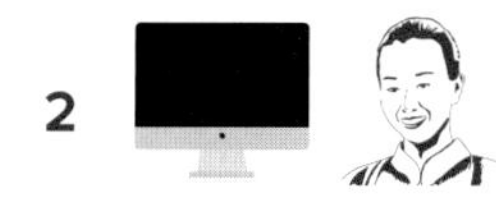

3 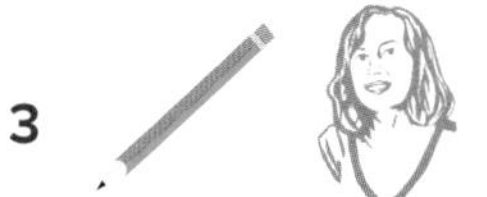

Then identify the colors of Little Wang's belongings, using 的 *(de)*, e.g.:

Q: 小王的筆是什麼顏色的？

Xiǎo Wáng de bǐ shì shénme yánsè de?

A: 小王的筆是黃色的。

Xiǎo Wáng de bǐ shì huángsè de.

1 

2 

3 

D Questions, questions, questions!

INTERPERSONAL

In pairs, ask questions about your friend's sibling's age, the price of your friend's pants, etc., by using 多 *(duō)*.

E Shopping poll

INTERPERSONAL

Poll your classmates on their shopping habits for the student newspaper, e.g.:

你喜歡買東西嗎？

Nǐ xǐhuan mǎi dōngxi ma?

你喜歡買什麼東西？

Nǐ xǐhuan mǎi shénme dōngxi?

你常常去買東西嗎？

Nǐ chángcháng qù mǎi dōngxi ma?

你喜歡買衣服嗎？

Nǐ xǐhuan mǎi yīfu ma?

你常常去哪兒買東西？

Nǐ chángcháng qù nǎr mǎi dōngxi?

你常常跟誰一起去買東西？

Nǐ chángcháng gēn shéi yìqǐ qù mǎi dōngxi?

你有幾件襯衫？

Nǐ yǒu jǐ jiàn chènshān?

你有幾條褲子？

Nǐ yǒu jǐ tiáo kùzi?

F Fashion blogger

INTERPERSONAL PRESENTATIONAL

Present a popular fashion blogger to the class, then start a dialogue about his/her sense of style, e.g.:

(Fashion blogger's name) 喜歡什麼顏色？

(Fashion blogger's name) *xǐhuan shénme yánsè?*

她/他喜歡穿什麼顏色的衣服？

Tā xǐhuan chuān shénme yánsè de yīfu?

她/他今天的衣服是什麼顏色的？

Tā jīntiān de yīfu shì shénme yánsè de?

你覺得她/他今天的衣服長短合適不合適？

Nǐ juéde tā jīntiān de yīfu chángduǎn héshì bù héshì?

她/他的衣服多嗎？

Tā de yīfu duō ma?

Characterize it!

What do the characters mean?
What is the common radical?
What does the radical mean?
How does the radical relate to the overall meaning of the characters?

❶ 襯

❷ 

❸ 

More characters

Chinese Chat

Your friend is messaging you on LINE while shopping. How would you reply?

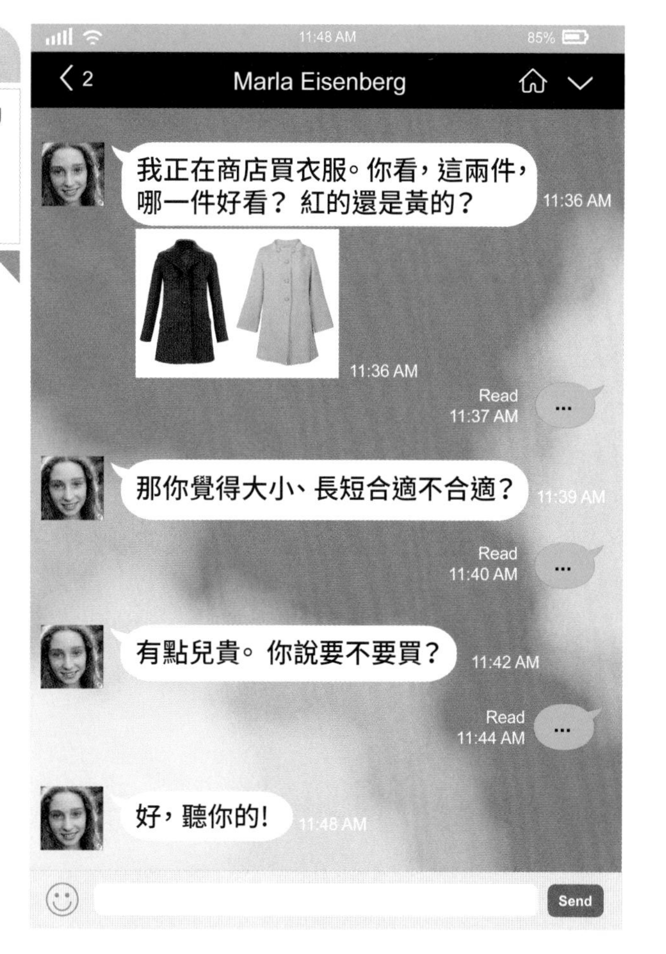

Exchanging Shoes

Dialogue 2

王朋想換一雙鞋，他問售貨員……

Audio

Video

對不起，這雙鞋太小了。
能不能換一雙？

沒問題。您看，這雙怎麼樣？

也不行，這雙跟那雙一樣[6]大。

那這雙黑的呢？

這雙鞋雖然大小合適，可是[7]顏色不好。
有沒有咖啡色的？

對不起，這種鞋只有黑的。

這雙鞋樣子挺好的[a]，就是它吧[b]。
你們這兒可以刷卡嗎?

對不起，我們不收信用卡。
不過，這雙的錢跟那雙一樣，
您不用再付錢了。

Pinyin Dialogue

Wáng Péng xiǎng huàn yì shuāng xié, tā wèn shòuhuòyuán . . .

 *Duìbuqǐ, zhè shuāng xié tài xiǎo le. Néng bu néng huàn yì shuāng?*

 *Méi wèntí. Nín kàn, zhè shuāng zěnmeyàng?*

 *Yě bù xíng, zhè shuāng gēn nà shuāng yíyàng*[6] *dà.*

 *Nà zhè shuāng hēi de ne?*

 *Zhè shuāng xié suīrán dàxiǎo héshì, kěshì*[7] *yánsè bù hǎo. Yǒu méiyǒu kāfēisè de?*

 *Duìbuqǐ, zhè zhǒng xié zhǐ yǒu hēi de.*

 *Zhè shuāng xié yàngzi tíng hǎo de*[a]*, jiù shì tā ba*[b]*. Nǐmen zhèr kěyǐ shuā kǎ ma?*

 *Duìbuqǐ, wǒmen bù shōu xìnyòngkǎ. Búguò, zhè shuāng de qián gēn nà shuāng yíyàng, nín búyòng zài fù qián le.*

Language Notes

a 挺 *(tǐng)*

The construction 挺 + adj + 的 *(tǐng + adj + de)* means "it's rather + adj." 的 *(de)* is optional.

b 就是它吧 *(jiù shì tā ba)*

This expression is often used to indicate the completion of a selection. It means "I'll take this one." [See Keeping It Casual (L5–L10).]

Vocabulary

Audio

Flashcards

No.	Word	Pinyin	Part of Speech	English
1	雙	*shuāng*	m	(measure word for a pair)
2	鞋	*xié*	n	shoes
3	換	*huàn*	v	to exchange, to change
4	一樣	*yíyàng*	adj	same, alike [See Grammar 6.]
5	雖然	*suīrán*	conj	although [See Grammar 7.]
6	大小	*dàxiǎo*	n	size
7	咖啡色	*kāfēisè*	n	brown, coffee color
8	種	*zhǒng*	m	(measure word for kinds, sorts, types)
9	黑	*hēi*	adj	black
10	樣子	*yàngzi*	n	style
11	挺	*tǐng*	adv	very, rather
12	它	*tā*	pr	it
13	這兒	*zhèr*	pr	here
14	刷卡	*shuā kǎ*	vo	to pay with a credit card
	刷	*shuā*	v	to brush, to swipe
	卡	*kǎ*	n	card
15	收	*shōu*	v	to receive, to accept
16	信用卡	*xìnyòngkǎ*	n	credit card
17	不過	*búguò*	conj	however, but
18	再	*zài*	adv	again
19	付錢	*fù qián*	vo	to pay money
	付	*fù*	v	to pay

In many countries, there is heated debate over who should appear on currency. In China, many figures used to appear but, since 1999, all have been replaced with Chairman Mao. What are the denominations of these fourth edition bills (on the right)? Research the names of the ethnic groups depicted.

GET Real WITH CHINESE

你喜歡什麼顏色?

Nǐ xǐhuan shénme yánsè?

What color do you like?

How About You?

我喜歡＿＿＿＿＿。

Wǒ xǐhuan ＿＿＿＿＿.

See index for corresponding vocabulary or research another term.

Characterize it!

- What do the characters mean?
- What is the common radical?
- What does the radical mean?
- How does the radical relate to the overall meaning of the characters?

1.  果
2.  床
3.  杯
4.  末

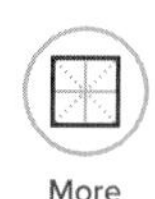
More characters

Grammar

6 Comparing using 跟/和⋯(不)一樣 (*gēn/hé...[bù] yíyàng*) ([not] the same as . . .)

To express similarity or dissimilarity between objects, people, or actions, use the structure 跟/和⋯(不)一樣 (*gēn/hé . . . [bù] yíyàng*) ([not] the same as . . .). Following 一樣 (*yíyàng*) (same, alike) an adjective can be used, as in (C), (D), and (E).

A 你的襯衫跟我的一樣。

Nǐ de chènshān gēn wǒ de yíyàng.

Your shirt is the same as mine.

B 貴的衣服和便宜的衣服不一樣。

Guì de yīfu hé piányi de yīfu bù yíyàng.

Expensive clothes are different from cheap ones.

C 弟弟跟哥哥一樣高。

Dìdi gēn gēge yíyàng gāo.

The younger brother is as tall as the older one.

D 這個電腦跟那個電腦一樣新。

Zhè ge diànnǎo gēn nà ge diànnǎo yíyàng xīn.

This computer is as new as that one.

E 常老師寫漢字寫得跟王老師(寫漢字寫得)一樣漂亮。

Cháng lǎoshī xiě Hànzì xiě de gēn Wáng lǎoshī (xiě Hànzì xiě de) yíyàng piàoliang.

Teacher Chang writes Chinese characters as beautifully as Teacher Wang does.

More exercises

EXERCISES

Form sentences by combining these words and inserting the A 跟/和 B 一樣 structure where appropriate. Use exercise 1 as an example.

1 妹妹　　姐姐　　高

→ 妹妹和/跟姐姐一樣高。

2 這件襯衫　那件襯衫　漂亮

3 你的電腦　我的電腦　貴

7 The conjunctions 雖然…，可是/但是… (*suīrán . . . , kěshì/dànshì . . .*) (although . . . yet . . .)

This pair of conjunctions links two clauses to form a complex sentence. Note, however, that 雖然 (*suīrán*) (although) is often optional.

A 雖然這雙鞋很便宜，可是大小不合適。

Suīrán zhè shuāng xié hěn piányi, kěshì dàxiǎo bù héshì.

Although this pair of shoes is very inexpensive, they're not the right size.

B 這件襯衫大小很合適，可是太貴了。

Zhè jiàn chènshān dàxiǎo hěn héshì, kěshì tài guì le.

This shirt is the right size, but it's too expensive.

C 學中文不容易，但是很有意思。

Xué Zhōngwén bù róngyì, dànshì hěn yǒu yìsi.

Learning Chinese is not easy, but it's very interesting.

Whether or not 雖然 (*suīrán*) is used in the first clause, 可是/但是 (*kěshì/dànshì*) (but) cannot be omitted in the second.

[⊗ 雖然學中文不容易，很有意思。]

EXERCISES

Join these sentences by using the 雖然…，可是/但是… structure and deleting identical nouns and pronouns where appropriate. Use exercise 1 as an example.

1. 這個電腦很快。　這個電腦很貴。
   → 雖然這個電腦很快，可是（這個電腦）很貴。
2. 這條褲子大小很合適。　這條褲子顏色不好。
3. 這個商店的東西很便宜。這個商店不收信用卡。

Language Practice

G Just the same

PRESENTATIONAL

Form sentences by combining these words and inserting the A 跟/和 *(gēn/hé)* B 一樣 *(yíyàng)* structure in the ◇, e.g.:

這件衣服 ◇ 那件衣服 ◇ 漂亮

zhè jiàn yīfu ◇ nà jiàn yīfu ◇ piàoliang

這件衣服跟那件衣服一樣漂亮。

Zhè jiàn yīfu gēn nà jiàn yīfu yíyàng piàoliang.

1. 這枝筆 ◇ 那枝筆 ◇ 便宜 — *zhè zhī bǐ ◇ nà zhī bǐ ◇ piányi*
2. 這條褲子 ◇ 那條褲子 ◇ 貴 — *zhè tiáo kùzi ◇ nà tiáo kùzi ◇ guì*
3. 這雙鞋 ◇ 那雙鞋 ◇ 合適 — *zhè shuāng xié ◇ nà shuāng xié ◇ héshì*
4. 這件襯衫 ◇ 那件襯衫 ◇ 大 — *zhè jiàn chènshān ◇ nà jiàn chènshān ◇ dà*
5. 第九課的語法 ◇ 第八課的語法 ◇ 難 — *dì jiǔ kè de yǔfǎ ◇ dì bā kè de yǔfǎ ◇ nán*

H All shopped out

PRESENTATIONAL

Form sentences expressing shopping frustrations by using the 雖然 *(suīrán)* … ，可是/但是 *(kěshì/dànshì)* … structure where appropriate, e.g.:

雖然這個商店的鞋都很漂亮，可是她都不喜歡。

Suīrán zhè ge shāngdiàn de xié dōu hěn piàoliang, kěshi tā dōu bù xǐhuan.

1. 他的新衣服很多 ◇ 他都不穿 — *tā de xīn yīfu hěn duō ◇ tā dōu bù chuān*
2. 這條褲子很便宜 ◇ 長短不合適 — *zhè tiáo kùzi hěn piányi ◇ chángduǎn bù héshì*
3. 這件襯衫的顏色很好看 ◇ — *zhè jiàn chènshān de yánsè hěn hǎokàn ◇*

有一點兒小 *yǒu yìdiǎnr xiǎo*

4 這雙鞋樣子挺不錯的 ◇ *zhè shuāng xié yàngzi tǐng búcuò de* ◇

太貴了 *tài guì le*

5 這個商店不小 ◇ *zhè ge shāngdiàn bù xiǎo* ◇

不能刷卡 *bù néng shuā kǎ*

I Double trouble PRESENTATIONAL

Here's some information about two sisters who are identical twins. Describe what they have in common, using 跟/和 *(gēn/hé)* …一樣 *(yíyàng)* where appropriate, e.g.:

王文京跟王文英一樣大。 *Wáng Wénjīng gēn Wáng Wényīng yíyàng dà.*

1 Height: 5'5" 5'5"

2 Shirts: size 6 size 6

3 Pants: red red

J INTERPERSONAL Taking stock INTERPRETIVE

You're starting your own fashion line. To determine your business strategy, survey your classmates about their color preferences and sizes. Then jot down your findings.

鞋/襯衫/褲子 *xié/chènshān/kùzi*

你喜歡穿什麼顏色的？ *Nǐ xǐhuan chuān shénme yánsè de?*

你穿多大的？ *Nǐ chuān duō dà de?*

Chinese Chat

Li You just updated her status on Facebook, and Wang Peng left a comment. What do you think Wang Peng is hinting at?

文化

Continue to explore

Traditional Clothes

Contemporary Chinese fashion is largely similar to that of the West. On formal occasions, Chinese men wear suits and ties and women wear Western-style dresses. When dressing casually, many young people wear jeans and T-shirts. However, more traditional clothing from the early tewntieth century can still be seen around China.

One of the most enduring examples of traditional Chinese fashion is 旗袍 *(qípáo)*, a close-fitting woman's dress with a high collar and a slit skirt. It was extremely popular among urban women until 1949 in Mainland China and into the 1960s and 70s in Taiwan. Today, you can still see women in *qipao* at weddings and formal parties. Specialized stores offer *qipao* designs in both modernized and traditional versions. They are popular among foreign tourists, and several fashion brands in Europe and North America have introduced *qipao*-influenced designs.

For Chinese men in the early twentieth century, the traditional formal attire was a long robe called 長袍 *(chángpáo)* (lit. long gown) and a short jacket called 馬褂 *(mǎguà)* (Mandarin jacket). Today they have disappeared from city streets, but remain an important part of Chinese visual culture. Characters in popular period dramas and films, as well as performers of 相聲 *(xiàngsheng)* (cross-talk), a type of traditional stand-up comedy involving two comics, and storytelling arts such as 評彈 *(píngtán)* (Suzhou-style ballad singing), are frequently seen in 長袍 *(chángpáo)*. Until the 1990s, almost every Chinese man wore the 中山裝 *(Zhōngshānzhuāng)* ("Sun Yat-sen suit"), better known in the West as the "Mao suit." Even today, Chinese leaders wear the high-collared jacket in place of a Western-style suit jacket on some formal occasions, and padded versions can still be seen in rural China in winter.

Prices

In Mainland China, prices are usually non-negotiable in supermarkets and large department stores, but bargaining is routine at street-side stalls and small shops. It is also not customary to tip at a restaurant, although upscale restaurants often charge a service fee.

COMPARE & CONTRAST

E-commerce is becoming prevalent in China. For many people, online shopping, 網上購物 (*wǎngshang gòuwù*) or 網購 (*wǎng gòu*), is the preferred way to find the best deal. Two of the most popular sites, 天貓 (*Tiānmāo*: www.tmall.com) and 淘寶 (*Táobǎo*: www.taobao.com), are owned by Alibaba. Alibaba's sales dwarf those of Amazon and eBay combined.

Search for an item on one of these sites, put it in the shopping cart, and describe how the experience compares with your usual online shopping.

Forms of Address

In Mainland China, a salesperson in a department store is usually addressed as 售貨員 (*shòuhuòyuán*), and a server in a restaurant is usually called 服務員 (*fúwùyuán*) (service person). Both male and female taxi drivers and bus drivers are commonly addressed as 師傅 (*shīfu*) (an old term of respect for a master craftsman or skilled worker). However, these forms of address vary according to the age and preference of the speaker as well as the status or function of the person spoken to, and usage has very much been in flux. Students should carefully observe actual usage and follow suit. In Taiwan, 小姐 (*xiǎojiě*) (Miss) and 先生 (*xiānsheng*) (Mr.) are the preferred terms in all these contexts. Most recently, 老師 (*lǎoshī*) (teacher) has come to be used as a respectful form of address for people in the arts (such as writers, painters, and actors) on both sides of the Taiwan Strait, regardless of whether they teach professionally.

Lesson Wrap-Up

Make It Flow!

Rearrange the following sentences into a logical sequence. Then combine them into a coherent narrative. Remember to omit repetitive elements and substitute subjects with personal pronouns where appropriate. Time expressions and place words can also serve as useful connective devices.

____售貨員找給李友四十五塊五毛一。

____李友買的襯衫是中號的。

____李友買了一件襯衫。

__1__李友在商店買衣服。

____李友買的襯衫是紅的。

____李友還買了一條褲子。

____李友一共得付五十四塊四毛九。

____李友給了售貨員一百塊錢。

Role-Play

It's your younger brother's birthday next week. You want to get him a shirt. His favorite color is blue and his size is medium. You want to buy something that's stylish yet not too expensive, but the salesperson tries to get you to buy the most expensive shirt in the store. Create a short skit with your partner, and perform it in class or make a video and post it on social media.

Social Media

On social media, post three items of clothing you are considering buying. Tell your friends what you like about them (style, color, etc.). See which item gets the most likes.

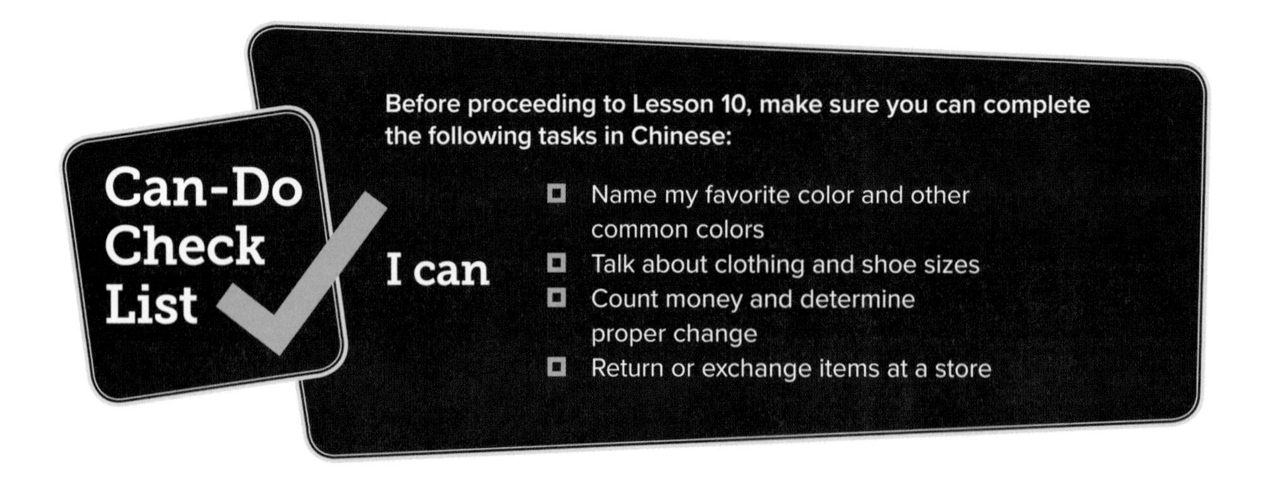

Lesson 10

第十課

Dì shí kè

交通

Jiāotōng

TRANSPORTATION

Learning Objectives

In this lesson, you will learn to:

- Discuss different means of transportation
- Explain how to transfer from one subway or bus line to another
- Navigate public transit
- Express gratitude after receiving a favor
- Offer New Year wishes

Relate & Get Ready

In your own culture/community:

- How often do people use public transportation?
- Do people hail taxis or do they order rides on their phone?
- How do people express gratitude?
- What do people say to each other on New Year's Day?

Going Home for Winter Vacation

Dialogue

李友跟王朋說話……

李友，寒假你回家嗎？

對，我要回家。

飛機票你買了嗎[1]？

已經買了。是二十一號的。

飛機是幾點的？

晚上八點的。

你怎麼去[a]機場？

我想坐公共汽車或者[2]坐地鐵。你知道怎麼走[a]嗎？

你先坐一路汽車，坐三站下車，然後換地鐵。先坐紅線，再[3]換綠線，最後換藍線。

不行，不行，太麻煩了。我還是[4]打車[b]吧。

出租汽車太貴，我開車送你去吧。

謝謝你。

不用客氣。

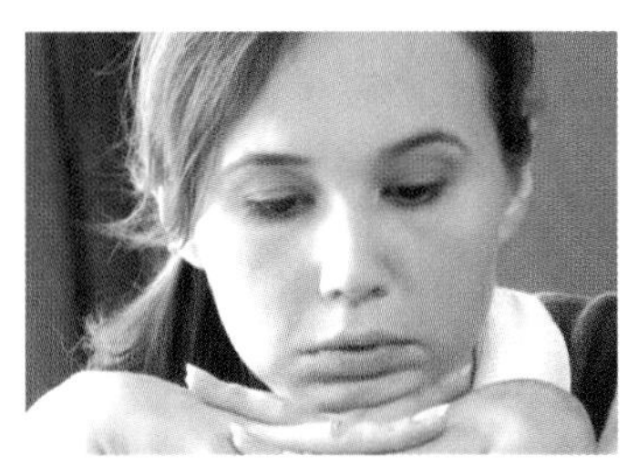
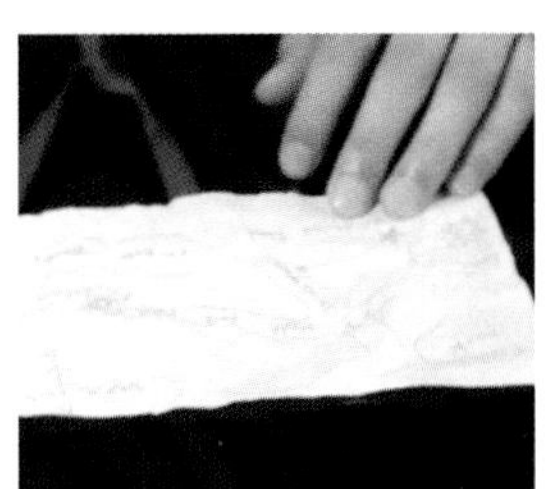

Lǐ Yǒu gēn Wáng Péng shuō huà . . .

 *Lǐ Yǒu, hánjià nǐ huí jiā ma?*

 *Duì, wǒ yào huí jiā.*

 *Fēijī piào nǐ mǎi le ma*[1]*?*

 *Yǐjīng mǎi le. Shì èrshíyī hào de.*

 *Fēijī shì jǐ diǎn de?*

 *Wǎnshang bā diǎn de.*

 *Nǐ zěnme qù*[a] *jīchǎng?*

 *Wǒ xiǎng zuò gōnggòng qìchē huòzhě*[2] *zuò dìtiě. Nǐ zhīdao zěnme zǒu*[a] *ma?*

 *Nǐ xiān zuò yī lù qìchē, zuò sān zhàn xià chē, ránhòu huàn dìtiě. Xiān zuò hóng xiàn, zài*[3] *huàn lǜ xiàn, zuìhòu huàn lán xiàn.*

 *Bù xíng, bù xíng, tài máfan le. Wǒ háishi*[4] *dǎ chē*[b] *ba.*

 *Chūzū qìchē tài guì, wǒ kāi chē sòng nǐ qù ba.*

 *Xièxie nǐ.*

 *Búyòng kèqi.*

Language Notes

a 怎麼去 *(zěnme qù)* and 怎麼走 *(zěnme zǒu)*

怎麼去 *(zěnme qù)* is used to ask about the means of transportation, whereas 怎麼走 *(zěnme zǒu)* is used to ask for directions.

b 打車 *(dǎ chē)*

This means "to take a taxi." A common variant is 打的 *(dǎ dī)*. Taxis are 出租（汽）車 *(chūzū [qì]chē)* in Mainland China, but 計程車 *(jìchéng chē)* (metered cars) in Taiwan.

Vocabulary

Audio

Flashcards

No.	Word	Pinyin	Part of Speech	Definition
1	寒假	*hánjià*	n	winter vacation
2	飛機	*fēijī*	n	airplane
	飛	*fēi*	v	to fly
	機	*jī*	n	machine
3	票	*piào*	n	ticket
4	（飛）機場	*(fēi)jīchǎng*	n	airport
5	坐	*zuò*	v	to travel by
6	公共汽車	*gōnggòng qìchē*	n	bus
	公共	*gōnggòng*	adj	public
	汽車	*qìchē*	n	automobile
	車	*chē*	n	vehicle, car
7	或者	*huòzhě*	conj	or [See Grammar 2.]
8	地鐵	*dìtiě*	n	subway
9	走	*zǒu*	v	to go by way of, to walk
10	先	*xiān*	adv	first [See Grammar 3.]
11	路	*lù*	n	route, road
12	站	*zhàn*	m	(measure word for bus stops, train stops, etc.)
13	下車	*xià chē*	vo	to get off (a bus, train, etc.)
14	然後	*ránhòu*	adv	then
15	綠	*lǜ*	adj	green
16	線	*xiàn*	n	line
17	最後	*zuìhòu*		final, last
18	藍	*lán*	adj	blue
19	麻煩	*máfan*	adj	troublesome

You've just arrived in Beijing and downloaded some apps your friend recommended. Which would you use to get a ride? Can you identify the other apps?

GET Real WITH CHINESE

No.	Word	Pinyin	Part of Speech	Definition
20	打車	*dǎ chē*	vo	to take a taxi
21	出租汽車	*chūzū qìchē*	n	taxi
	出租	*chūzū*	v	to rent out, to let
	租	*zū*	v	to rent
22	開車	*kāi chē*	vo	to drive a car
	開	*kāi*	v	to drive, to operate
23	送	*sòng*	v	to see off or out, to take (someone somewhere)

How About You?

你怎麼回家？

Nǐ zěnme huí jiā?

How do you get home?

我 ______________。

Wǒ ______________.

See index for corresponding vocabulary or research another term.

Grammar

1 Topic-comment sentences

In a topic-comment sentence, the previously established noun, noun phrase, or object of the verb becomes the topic, and moves to the beginning of the sentence. The rest of the sentence serves as the comment.

A **Student A** 我昨天買了一枝筆。

Wǒ zuótiān mǎi le yì zhī bǐ.

I bought a pen yesterday.

Student B 那枝筆你用了嗎？

Nà zhī bǐ nǐ yòng le ma?

Have you used it?

B Q: 你知道我的襯衫在哪兒嗎？

Nǐ zhīdao wǒ de chènshān zài nǎr ma?

Do you know where my shirt is?

A: 你的襯衫我給你媽媽了。

Nǐ de chènshān wǒ gěi nǐ māma le.

I gave your shirt to your mother.

C Q: 你有朋友嗎？

Nǐ yǒu péngyou ma?

Do you have any friends?

A: 朋友我有很多，可是都不在這兒。

Péngyou wǒ yǒu hěn duō, kěshì dōu bú zài zhèr.

I have many friends, but none of them are here.

D 她不想去紐約，可是飛機票她媽媽已經幫她買了。

Tā bù xiǎng qù Niǔyuē, kěshì fēijī piào tā māma yǐjīng bāng tā mǎi le.

She does not want to go to New York, but her mother has already bought her a plane ticket.

EXERCISES

Join these sentences to form a topic-comment sentence. Use exercise 1 as an example.

More exercises

1 我昨天買了一件襯衫。
我很喜歡那件襯衫。
→ 我昨天買了一件襯衫。那件襯衫我很喜歡。

2 學校有一個商店。
我常常去那個商店。

3 Q: 李友買飛機票了嗎？
A: 李友已經買飛機票了。

2 Indicating alternatives: 或者 (*huòzhě*) (or) and 還是 (*háishi*) (or)

Both 或者 (*huòzhě*) (or) and 還是 (*háishi*) (or) connect words or phrases to indicate alternatives. The former usually appears in statements, the latter in questions.

A Q: 你今天晚上做什麼？

Nǐ jīntiān wǎnshang zuò shénme?

What are you going to do tonight?

A: 聽音樂或者看電影。

Tīng yīnyuè huòzhě kàn diànyǐng.

Listen to music or watch a movie.

B Q: 你週末想看電影還是跳舞？

Nǐ zhōumò xiǎng kàn diànyǐng háishi tiào wǔ?

Would you like to see a movie or go dancing this weekend?

A: 看電影或者跳舞都行。

Kàn diànyǐng huòzhě tiào wǔ dōu xíng.

Either seeing a movie or going dancing would be fine with me.

C Q: 你喜歡什麼顏色的鞋？黑色的還是咖啡色的？

Nǐ xǐhuan shénme yánsè de xié? Hēisè de háishi kāfēisè de?

What color shoes do you like? Black or brown?

A: 黑色的或者咖啡色的我都不喜歡，我喜歡白的。

Hēisè de huòzhě kāfēisè de wǒ dōu bù xǐhuan, wǒ xǐhuan bái de.

I don't like either black or brown; I like white ones.

D 明天你去開會或者小高去開會都可以。

Míngtiān nǐ qù kāi huì huòzhě Xiǎo Gāo qù kāi huì dōu kěyǐ.

Either you or Little Gao may attend tomorrow's meeting.

More exercises

EXERCISES

Connect these words to form a question or a statement by inserting either 或者 or 還是 as appropriate. Use exercise 1 as an example.

1 今天晚上我們　去跳舞　去打球
→ 今天晚上我們去跳舞或者去打球。

2 白醫生想　坐地鐵　坐公共汽車　去機場

3 高文中　星期五　星期六　請客

3 Indicating sequence: 先⋯再⋯ (*xiān . . . zài . . .*) (first . . . , then . . .)

In this structure, 再 (*zài*) (then) indicates a sequence of actions rather than repetition.

A 我想先打球再去圖書館。

Wǒ xiǎng xiān dǎ qiú zài qù túshūguǎn.

I'd like to play ball and then go to the library.

B 弟弟常常先做功課再上網聊天兒。

Dìdi chángcháng xiān zuò gōngkè zài shàng wǎng liáo tiānr.

My little brother often does his homework first and then chats online.

C Q: 你什麼時候給媽媽打電話?

Nǐ shénme shíhou gěi māma dǎ diànhuà?

When are you going to call Mom?

A: 下課以後再打。

Xià kè yǐhòu zài dǎ.

I'll call her after class.

As adverbs, 先 (*xiān*) and 再 (*zài*) must come before a verb. They should not be placed in front of the subject.

D 小王先買東西再吃晚飯。

Xiǎo Wáng xiān mǎi dōngxi zài chī wǎnfàn.

Little Wang will shop first before having dinner.

[⊗ 先小王買東西再吃晚飯。]

EXERCISES

Combine these words to indicate sequence by inserting 先⋯再⋯ where appropriate.

Use exercise 1 as an example.

1 小王 坐公共汽車 坐地鐵 去學校上課

→ 小王先坐公共汽車，再坐地鐵去學校上課。

2 王朋常常 看電視 做功課

3 張律師今天 吃晚飯 開車 去機場

4 Pondering alternatives: 還是⋯（吧） (*háishi . . . [ba]*) (had better)

The structure 還是⋯（吧） (*háishi . . . [ba]*) (had better) can be used to suggest an alternative.

A Q: 我們星期五去看電影，好不好？

Wǒmen xīngqīwǔ qù kàn diànyǐng, hǎo bù hǎo?

Let's go to a movie on Friday. How's that?

A: 還是星期六去吧。

Háishi xīngqīliù qù ba.

Let's go on Saturday instead.

B **Student A** 我們今天晚上去聽音樂會吧。

Wǒmen jīntiān wǎnshang qù tīng yīnyuèhuì ba.

How about we go to a concert tonight?

Student B 可是我明天考試。

Kěshì wǒ míngtiān kǎo shì.

But I have a test tomorrow.

Student A 那別去聽音樂會了。你還是在家復習功課吧。

Nà bié qù tīng yīnyuèhuì le. Nǐ háishi zài jiā fùxí gōngkè ba.

Let's not go to the concert then. You'd better stay home and review.

EXERCISES

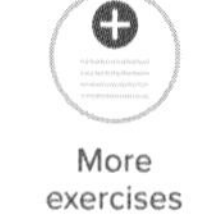

In pairs, use these words to discuss alternatives by inserting 還是…吧 where appropriate. Use exercise 1 as an example.

1 打球　有點兒累　明天

Student A 我想打球，可是有點兒累。

Student B 你有點兒累，還是明天打吧。

2 打車去學校　打車太貴　坐公共汽車

3 看球　明天考中文　復習生詞語法

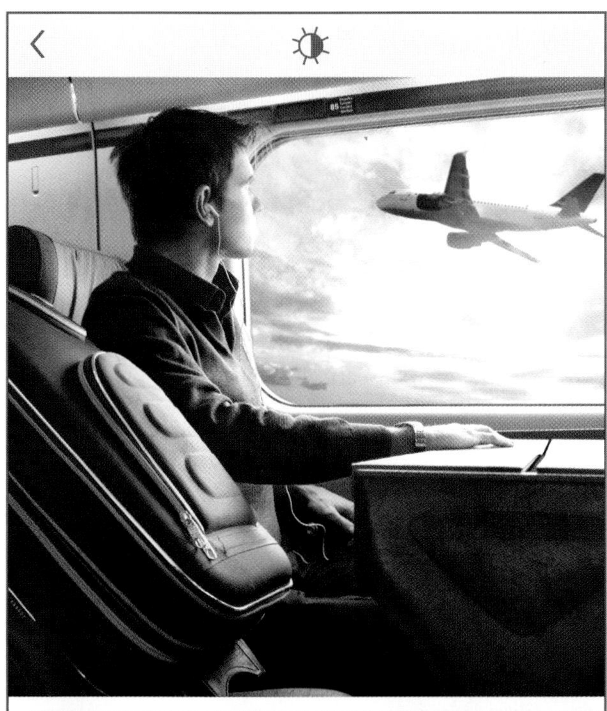

Chinese Chat

You're about to post this picture of your trip on Instagram. What caption would you write? Use the hashtag #寒假.

Language Practice

A On topic

INTERPERSONAL

In pairs, answer the questions in the affirmative or negative using the topic-comment structure, e.g.:

Q: 你喜歡我這件衣服嗎？
Nǐ xǐhuan wǒ zhè jiàn yīfu ma?

A: 這件衣服我不喜歡。
Zhè jiàn yīfu wǒ bù xǐhuan.

1 你會不會打球？
Nǐ huì bu huì dǎ qiú?

2 你復習課文了嗎？
Nǐ fùxí kèwén le ma?

3 你現在想不想喝咖啡？
Nǐ xiànzài xiǎng bu xiǎng hē kāfēi?

4 你認識白英愛嗎？
Nǐ rènshi Bái Yīng'ài ma?

B Fine either way

INTERPERSONAL

In pairs, suggest and accept alternatives, inserting 或者 *(huòzhě)* or 還是 *(háishi)* where appropriate, e.g.:

今天晚上做什麼 ◇ 聽音樂/看電視
jīntiān wǎnshang zuò shénme ◇ *tīng yīnyuè/kàn diànshì*

Q: 我們今天晚上做什麼？聽音樂還是看電視？
Wǒmen jīntiān wǎnshang zuò shénme? Tīng yīnyuè háishi kàn diànshì?

A: 聽音樂或者看電視都行。
Tīng yīnyuè huòzhě kàn diànshì dōu xíng.

1 明天下午做什麼 ◇ 去打球/去跳舞
míngtiān xiàwǔ zuò shénme ◇ *qù dǎ qiú/qù tiào wǔ*

2 明天晚上做什麼 ◇ 去商店買東西/去朋友家聊天兒
míngtiān wǎnshang zuò shénme ◇ *qù shāngdiàn mǎi dōngxi/qù péngyou jiā liáo tiānr*

3 這個週末怎麼去機場◇坐地鐵/打車

zhège zhōumò zěnme qù jīchǎng ◇ zuò dìtiě/dǎ chē

4 喝什麼茶◇中國茶/英國茶

hē shénme chá ◇ Zhōngguó chá/Yīngguó chá

5 買什麼顏色的車◇藍的/黑的

mǎi shénme yánsè de chē ◇ lán de/hēi de

C First things first

PRESENTATIONAL

Based on the images, sequence these actions using 先 *(xiān)*⋯再 *(zài)*⋯ where appropriate, e.g.:

他先吃早飯，再去圖書館學習。

Tā xiān chī zǎofàn, zài qù túshūguǎn xuéxí.

1 

2 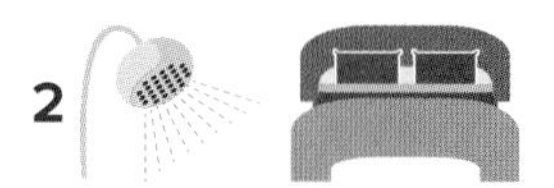

3 

4 

5 

Characterize it!

What do the characters mean?

What is the common radical?

What does the radical mean?

How does the radical relate to the overall meaning of the characters?

1  地

2 場

3  坐

4  在

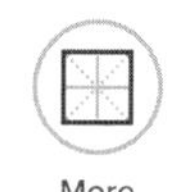

More characters

D Plan B

INTERPERSONAL

Use 還是…吧 (*háishi . . . ba*) and the information below to form question-and-answers. The answers should propose alternatives to the original suggestions, e.g.:

聽音樂 ◇ 看電視

tīng yīnyuè ◇ *kàn diànshì*

Q: 我們聽音樂，好嗎？
Wǒmen tīng yīnyuè, hǎo ma?

A: 我們還是看電視吧。
Wǒmen háishi kàn diànshì ba.

1 坐地鐵去機場 ◇ 開車
zuò dìtiě qù jīchǎng ◇ *kāi chē*

2 坐公共汽車去買東西 ◇ 打車
zuò gōnggòng qìchē qù mǎi dōngxi ◇ *dǎ chē*

3 買黑色的襯衫 ◇ 買紅色的
mǎi hēisè de chènshān ◇ *mǎi hóngsè de*

4 學中文專業 ◇ 學電腦專業
xué Zhōngwén zhuānyè ◇ *xué diànnǎo zhuānyè*

E En route

INTERPERSONAL

In pairs, take turns asking and giving directions to the following destinations by using 先 (*xiān*) ··· 再 (*zài*) ··· where appropriate.

1 Dr. Wang's office: Take the subway–the Red Line. Get off after five stops.

2 Sofia's house: Take Bus #5. Get off after four stops. Then change to the subway. Take the Green Line first and then switch to the Red Line. Get off after six stops.

3 Mark's school: Take Bus #29. Get off after six stops. Then switch to the subway. Take the Red Line first and then switch to the Blue Line. Get off after three stops.

F Exchange student

PRESENTATIONAL

You will be studying Chinese at Peking University next summer. How will you get to Tian'anmen Square from campus? After researching transportation options, share your plan with your partner. Use expressions such as 先 *(xiān)* ···, 再 *(zài)* ···, and 然後 *(ránhòu)*···.

Chinese Chat

Your friend is sending you WeChat messages from the subway. How would you reply?

Thanks for the Ride

Email

Audio

Video

李友給王朋寫電子郵件[a]：

Date: 12月20日

From: 李友

To: 王朋

Subject: 謝謝!

王朋：

謝謝你那天開車送我到機場。不過，讓你花那麼多時間，真不好意思。我這幾天每天都[5]開車出去看老朋友。這個城市的人開車開得特別快。我在高速公路上開車，真有點兒緊張。可是這兒沒有公共汽車，也沒有地鐵，只能自己開車，很不方便。

有空兒的話打我的手機或者給我發短信，我想跟你聊天兒。

新年快要到了[6]，祝你新年快樂！

李友

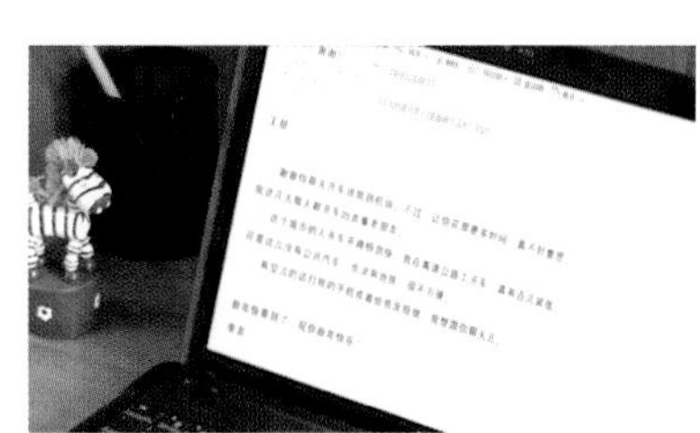

Lǐ Yǒu gěi Wáng Péng xiě diànzǐ yóujiàn[a]*:*

Date: *12 yuè 20 rì*

From: *Lǐ Yǒu*

To: *Wáng Péng*

Subject: *Xièxie!*

Wáng Péng:

Xièxie nǐ nà tiān kāi chē sòng wǒ dào jīchǎng. Búguò, ràng nǐ huā nàme duō shíjiān, zhēn bù hǎoyìsi. Wǒ zhè jǐ tiān měi tiān dōu[5] *kāi chē chūqu kàn lǎo péngyou. Zhè ge chéngshì de rén kāi chē kāi de tèbié kuài. Wǒ zài gāosù gōnglù shang kāi chē, zhēn yǒudiǎn(r) jǐnzhāng. Kěshì zhèr méiyǒu gōnggòng qìchē, yě méiyǒu dìtiě, zhǐ néng zìjǐ kāi chē, hěn bù fāngbiàn.*

Yǒu kòngr de huà dǎ wǒ de shǒujī huòzhě gěi wǒ fā duǎnxìn, wǒ xiǎng gēn nǐ liáo tiānr.

Xīnnián kuài yào dào le[6]*, zhù nǐ xīnnián kuàilè!*

Lǐ Yǒu

Language Note

a 電子郵件 *(diànzǐ yóujiàn)*

As in English, the Chinese word for electronic mail, 電子郵件 *(diànzǐ yóujiàn)*, is often abbreviated as 電郵 *(diàn yóu)* (email).

Vocabulary

Audio

Flashcards

No.	Word	Pinyin	Part of Speech	Definition
1	電子郵件	*diànzǐ yóujiàn*	n	email/electronic mail
	電子	*diànzǐ*	n	electron
2	讓	*ràng*	v	to allow or cause (somebody to do something)
3	花	*huā*	v	to spend
4	不好意思	*bù hǎoyìsi*		to feel embarrassed
5	出去	*chū qu*	vc	to go out
6	每	*měi*	pr	every, each [See Grammar 5.]
7	城市	*chéngshì*	n	city
8	特別	*tèbié*	adv	especially
9	高速公路	*gāosù gōnglù*	n	highway
	高速	*gāosù*	adj	high speed
	公路	*gōnglù*	n	highway, public road
	路	*lù*	n	road, path
10	緊張	*jǐnzhāng*	adj	nervous, anxious
11	自己	*zìjǐ*	pr	oneself
12	手機	*shǒujī*	n	cell phone
13	發短信	*fā duǎnxìn*	vo	to send a text message (lit. to send a short message)
14	新年	*xīnnián*	n	new year
15	快樂	*kuàilè*	adj	happy

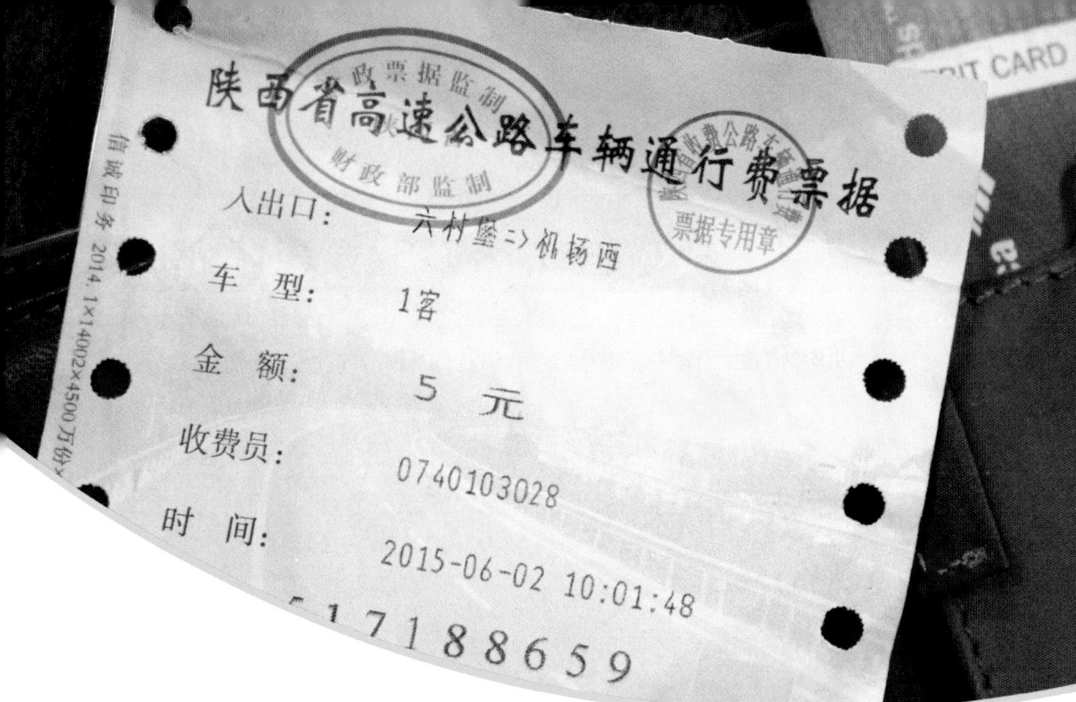

Your friend made a payment in Shaanxi Province. How much did she pay, and why? What other information can you identify from this receipt?

GET Real WITH CHINESE

Characterize it!

What do the characters mean?
What is the common radical?
What does the radical mean?
How does the radical relate to the overall meaning of the characters?

1 跳

2 

3 

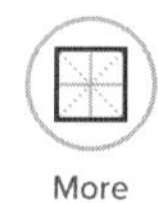

More characters

你怎麼去機場？

Nǐ zěnme qù jīchǎng?

How do you get to the airport?

How About You?

我＿＿＿＿＿＿＿＿。

Wǒ ＿＿＿＿＿＿＿＿.

See index for corresponding vocabulary or research another term.

Grammar

5 Indicating totality: 每…都… (*měi . . . dōu . . .*) (every)

In sentences that contains the term 每 (*měi*) (every), the adverb 都 (*dōu*) (both, all) is usually inserted before the verb.

A 他每天晚上都預習課文。

Tā měi tiān wǎnshang dōu yùxí kèwén.

He studies the lessons in advance every night.

B 我每節課都來。

Wǒ měi jié kè dōu lái.

I come to every class.

C 這兒每個人我都認識。

Zhèr měi gè rén wǒ dōu rènshi.

I know everyone here.

D 常老師的字每個都好看。

Cháng lǎoshī de zì měi ge dōu hǎokàn.

Every one of Teacher Chang's characters looks good.

More exercises

EXERCISES

Translate the English phrase by using 每 and add it to the sentence, inserting 都 where appropriate. Use exercise 1 as an example.

1 我在高速公路上開車。 Every day

→ 我每天都在高速公路上開車。

2 王律師坐飛機去紐約。 Every month

3 白英愛的鞋很漂亮。 Each pair

6 Indicating imminence: 要⋯了 *(yào . . . le)* (soon)

The 要⋯了 *(yào . . . le)* (soon) structure indicates the imminence of an anticipated action or situation. It also appears in the form of 快要⋯了 *(kuài yào . . . le)*.

A 新年快要到了，我們給爸爸媽媽打一個電話吧。

Xīnnián kuài yào dào le, wǒmen gěi bàba māma dǎ yí ge diànhuà ba.

New Year is around the corner. Let's call Mom and Dad.

B 寒假要到了，你要做什麼？

Hánjià yào dào le, nǐ yào zuò shénme?

It'll be winter break soon. What do you want to do?

C 電影快要開始了，你買票了嗎？

Diànyǐng kuài yào kāishǐ le, nǐ mǎi piào le ma?

The movie is going to start soon. Did you get the tickets?

D 快要考試了，我們大家得準備一下。

Kuài yào kǎo shì le, wǒmen dàjiā děi zhǔnbèi yí xià.

The exam is coming. We have to prepare.

EXERCISES

Form a new sentence to indicate the imminence of an action or situation by inserting (快) 要⋯了 where appropriate. Use exercise 1 as an example.

More exercises

1 新年到 → 新年快要到了。

2 我們考中文

3 我們上課

Language Practice

G Creature of habit

INTERPERSONAL

Use 每⋯都⋯ (*měi . . . dōu . . .*) and the words below to form a sentence describing Little Bai's lifestyle, e.g.:

晚上◇復習生詞語法

wǎnshang ◇ fùxí shēngcí yǔfǎ

小白每天晚上都復習生詞語法。

Xiǎo Bái měi tiān wǎnshang dōu fùxí shēngcí yǔfǎ.

1 早上◇洗澡 *zǎoshang ◇ xǐ zǎo*

2 襯衫◇是白色的 *chènshān ◇ shì báisè de*

3 褲子◇是三十二號的 *kùzi ◇ shì sānshíèr hào de*

4 週末◇去商店買東西 *zhōumò ◇ qù shāngdiàn mǎi dōngxi*

5 寒假◇坐飛機回家 *hánjià ◇ zuò fēijī huí jiā*

Then take turns finding out if your partner also follows a routine.

1 你每天都吃早飯嗎？

Nǐ měi tiān dōu chī zǎofàn ma?

2 你每天都給同學發短信嗎？

Nǐ měi tiān dōu gěi tóngxué fā duǎnxìn ma?

3 你每個星期都上網跟朋友聊天兒嗎？

Nǐ měi ge xīngqī dōu shàng wǎng gēn péngyǒu liáotiānr ma?

4 你每年都換手機嗎？

Nǐ měi nián dōu huàn shǒujī ma?

H INTERPERSONAL **Behind the wheel** PRESENTATIONAL

Use the following questions to survey your classmates about their driving habits, then present the results to the class.

你會開車嗎？

Nǐ huì kāi chē ma?

你每天都開車嗎？

Nǐ měitiān dōu kāi chē ma?

你開車開得快不快？

Nǐ kāi chē kāi de kuài bu kuài?

在高速公路上開車讓你緊張嗎？

Zài gāosù gōnglù shang kāi chē ràng nǐ jǐnzhāng ma?

Chinese Chat

Li You just published a post on Renren Network 人人網 *(Rénrénwǎng)*, a Chinese social networking service, and Wang Peng left a comment with questions. Why do you think he's asking these questions?

Continue to explore

HIGH-SPEED RAIL

For many decades before the early 1990s, the railroad system was the principal means of travel and transport in China. However, both the highway system and air travel infrastructure grew rapidly around the turn of the century. China now has seventy thousand miles of highway, the most of any country in the world, and is second only to the United States in total number of air passengers per year. In the 1990s, passenger train service rapidly lost market share to airlines and highway travel, but it soon made an astonishing comeback with the construction of an expansive high-speed railroad network, referred to as 高速鐵路 *(gāosù tiělù)* or 高鐵 *(gāotiě)*. As of December 2014, the system had more track in service than the rest of the world combined. Now, about two and a half million people take *gaotie* every day. Traveling by train between Beijing and Shanghai, which took as long as seventeen hours in 1980, now takes only five hours.

TAXI DRIVERS

Taxi drivers in China, especially those in Beijing, are known for being very outgoing. If you visit China and your taxi driver happens to be chatty, you might find yourself with a good opportunity to learn about ordinary Chinese people's lives and their opinions on current affairs.

COMPARE & CONTRAST

To get a sense of the scale of human movement over the Chinese New Year, look up 春運 *(chūnyùn)* on Google Images. What is the busiest travel day in your country? How do most people travel? Discuss holiday travel with a Chinese friend or a Chinese student on campus. Your conversation can include such questions as: How do you get around? Do you like driving? Is it easy for you to buy plane or train tickets online? How do you get to the airport or train station?

NEW YEAR TRAFFIC

Chinese New Year, also known as 春節 *(Chūnjié)* (Spring Festival), is the most important annual holiday in Chinese communities. The date is determined by the lunar calendar and usually falls in late January or early February. However, nowadays, the international New Year on January 1 is also recognized. The most common New Year greetings are 新年好 *(xīnnián hǎo)* and 新年快樂 *(xīnnián kuàilè)*, which can be used for both New Years. However, many people still prefer the traditional Chinese New Year greeting 恭喜發財 *(gōngxǐ fācái)*. This phrase, which literally means "Congratulations and may you make a fortune," can be translated as "May you be happy and prosperous!"

The largest human migration on earth is known as 春運 *(chūnyùn)* (Spring Festival traffic) in Chinese. Over a forty-day period around the time of the Chinese New Year, millions of Chinese people return home by train or long-distance bus to reunite with their families and then make their way back to their places of work. In 2015, the total number of trips taken was estimated to be around 3.7 billion; migrant laborers from inland provinces accounted for a significant portion of this figure.

Lesson Wrap-Up

Make It Flow!

Rearrange the following sentences into a logical sequence. Then combine them into a coherent narrative. If the subject remains the same, replace it with a personal pronoun. Remember to avoid unnecessary repetitions of identical elements. Add 但是 *(dànshì)*, 再 *(zài)*, or 最後 *(zuìhòu)* where appropriate.

____李友得先坐三站汽車，然後換地鐵。

____李友坐綠線地鐵以後得換藍線地鐵。

__1__李友寒假要回家。

____李友買了二十一號晚上8點的機票。

____李友想坐公共汽車和地鐵去機場。

____李友坐紅線地鐵以後得換綠線地鐵。

____王朋說他可以開車送李友去。

____李友得先坐紅線地鐵。

____李友覺得太麻煩。

____王朋說打車太貴。

____李友想打車。

Research

You work for a travel company catering to Chinese tourists. They've asked you to provide directions for taking public transportation from Boston's Logan Airport to Harvard Square. Research the information online, summarize it in Chinese, and post it on social media. 從洛根 *(Luògēn)* (Logan) 機場到哈佛廣場 *(Hāfó Guǎngchǎng)* (Harvard Square) 怎麼走？

Presentation

In your opinion, which city in your country has the best transportation system? Consider:

這個城市大嗎？
這個城市有沒有地鐵？
這個城市地鐵有幾條線？
這個城市有幾個機場？機場大嗎？
在這個城市裡開車容易嗎？為什麼？
在這個城市沒有車方便嗎？為什麼?

Present your case to the class using a slideshow. After everyone finishes, have a vote.

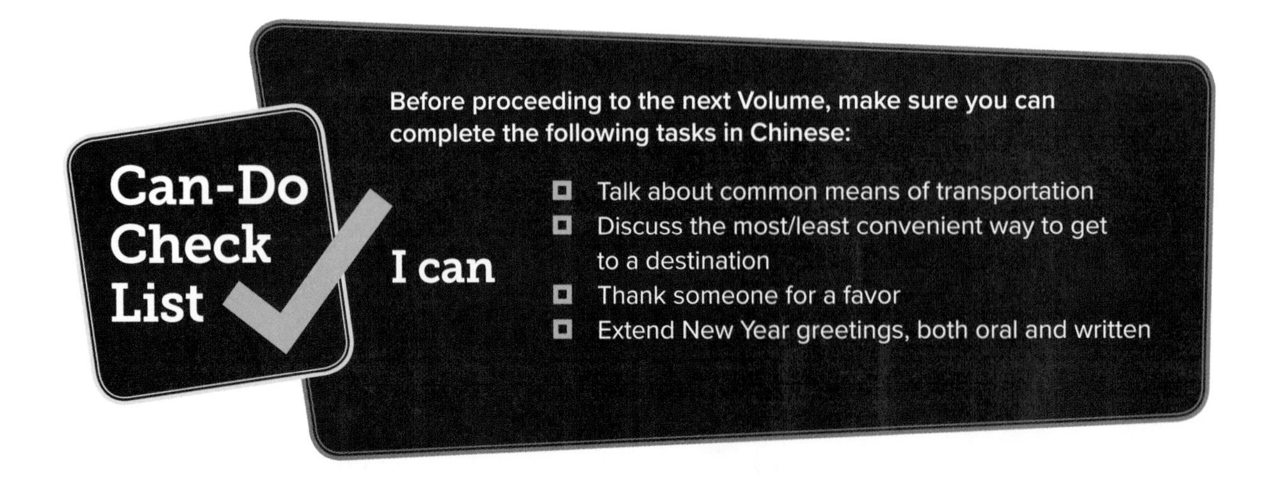

Keeping It Casual (L6–L10)

Before you progress to the next volume, we'll review how some of the functional expressions from Lessons 6–10 are used in casual Chinese. After you complete the review, note any other casual expressions you would like to learn, then share the list with your teacher.

1 喂 *(wéi)* (hello [on the phone])

Say this to start a phone conversation. [See Lesson 6.]

A

Li You's Roommate 喂，你好，請問哪位？
Wéi, nǐ hǎo, qǐng wèn nǎ wèi?
Hello! May I ask who's calling?

Wang Peng 你好，我是王朋。請問，李友在嗎？
Nǐ hǎo, wǒ shì Wáng Péng. Qǐng wèn, Lǐ Yǒu zài ma?
Hello! This is Wang Peng. Is Li You there, please?

Li You's Roommate 在，你等等，我去叫她。
Zài, nǐ děngdeng, wǒ qù jiào tā.
Yes. Wait a minute. I'll go get her.

B

Little Li 喂，你找誰？
Wéi, nǐ zhǎo shéi?
Hello! Who would you like to speak to?

Teacher Chang 我找小李。
Wǒ zhǎo Xiǎo Lǐ.
I'd like to speak to Little Li.

Little Li 我就是。你是哪位？
Wǒ jiù shì. Nǐ shì nǎ wèi?
This is she. Who's speaking?

Teacher Chang 我是常老師。
Wǒ shì Cháng lǎoshī.
This is Teacher Chang.

C

Little Li 喂，請問小王在嗎？

Wéi, qǐng wèn Xiǎo Wáng zài ma?

Hello! Is Little Wang there, please?

Old Wang 在，你是哪位？

Zài, nǐ shì nǎ wèi?

Yes, he is. Who is this, please?

Little Li 我是小李。

Wǒ shì Xiǎo Lǐ.

This is Little Li.

Old Wang 好，請等一下。

Hǎo, qǐng děng yí xià.

OK. Please wait a minute.

2 沒問題 *(méi wèntí)* **(no problem)**

Say this to put someone at ease that you will agree to do something, or to assure someone that there is no need to worry. [See Lesson 6.]

A

Li You 王朋，你今天晚上幫我練習中文，好嗎？

Wáng Péng, nǐ jīntiān wǎnshang bāng wǒ liànxí Zhōngwén, hǎo ma?

Wang Peng, would you help me practice Chinese this evening?

Wang Peng 沒問題。晚上見。

Méi wèntí. Wǎnshang jiàn.

No problem. See you this evening.

B

Little Li 英愛，坐地鐵太麻煩了。
你開車送我去機場，好嗎？

Yīng'ài, zuò dìtiě tài máfan le.

Nǐ kāi chē sòng wǒ qù jīchǎng, hǎo ma?

Ying'ai, it's too much trouble to take the subway.

Would you drive me to the airport instead?

Bai Ying'ai 沒問題。

Méi wèntí.

Sure thing.

C

Li You 你下午有空兒幫我準備考試嗎？要是你没時間，就算了。

Nǐ xiàwǔ yǒu kòngr bāng wǒ zhǔnbèi kǎoshì ma?

Yàoshi nǐ méi shíjiān, jiù suàn le.

Do you have time this afternoon to help me prepare for my test?

Never mind if you're too busy.

Wang Peng 没問題，我有空兒。

Méi wèntí, wǒ yǒu kòngr.

Don't worry, I have time.

3 Expressions of gratitude

Say these phrases to express and acknowledge gratitude.

A

Wang Peng 小李，這是你的手機嗎？

Xiǎo Lǐ, zhèshì nǐ de shǒujī ma?

Little Li, is this cell phone yours?

Little Li 謝謝！

Xièxie!

Thanks!

Wang Peng 不客氣。

Bú kèqi.

You're welcome.

B

Little Bai 小高，請喝茶。

Xiǎo Gāo, qǐng hē chá.

Please have some tea, Little Gao.

Little Gao 多謝！

Duō xiè.

Thanks a lot.

Little Bai 不謝。

Bú xiè.

No thanks needed.

C

Waitress 王小姐，這是你的咖啡。

Wáng xiǎojiě, zhè shì nǐ de kāfēi.

Miss Wang, here's your coffee.

Miss Wang 謝謝！

Xièxie!

Thanks!

Waitress 没事兒。

Méi shìr.

No problem.

D

Dr. Wang 白醫生，你的書。

Bái Yīshēng, nǐ de shū.

Dr. Bai, your book.

Dr. Bai 謝了。

Xiè le.

Thanks.

Dr. Wang 不用謝。

Búyòng xiè.

No thanks needed.

4 哪裡，哪裡 *(nǎli, nǎli)* **(I'm flattered)** or 是嗎 *(shì ma)* **(is that so?)**

When receiving a compliment, Chinese people often express modesty by saying 哪裡 *(nǎli)* or 是嗎 *(shì ma)*. Nowadays, however, some people say 謝謝 *(xièxie)* instead. [See Lesson 7.]

A

Student A 你今天很漂亮。

Nǐ jīntiān hěn piàoliang.

You look very pretty today.

Student B 哪裡，哪裡。

Nǎli, nǎli.

I'm flattered.

B

Student A 你寫漢字寫得很漂亮。

Nǐ xiě Hànzì xiě de hěn piàoliang.

You write Chinese characters beautifully.

Student B 哪裡，寫得不好。

Nǎli, xiě de bù hǎo.

I wish that were true. My writing isn't good.

C

Student A 你說中文說得真好！

Nǐ shuō Zhōngwén shuō de zhēn hǎo!

You speak Chinese really well!

Student B 是嗎？我覺得我說得不好。

Shì ma? Wǒ juéde wǒ shuō de bù hǎo.

You think so? I don't think I speak very well.

5 就是它吧 *(jiù shì tā ba)* **(let's go with that)** or 就是他/她了 *(jiù shì tā le)* **(we'll go with him/her)**

Say these when you've made a decision. [See Lesson 9.]

A

Salesperson 先生，你知道要哪一雙了嗎？

Xiānsheng, nǐ zhīdao yào nǎ yì shuāng le ma?

Sir, do you know which pair you'd like?

Mr. Gao 就是它吧。

Jiù shì tā ba.

I'll take that one.

B

Li You 王老師，小李打球打得不太好，
你找別人跟你一起練習吧。

Wáng lǎoshī, Xiǎo Lǐ dǎ qiú dǎ de bú tài hǎo,

nǐ zhǎo bié rén gēn nǐ yìqǐ liànxí ba.

Teacher Wang, Little Li is not a very good ball player.

Why don't you find someone else to practice with?

Teacher Wang 就是他了。別人都沒空兒。

Jiù shì tā le. Biérén dōu méi kòngr.

I'll have to go with him. Everyone else is busy.

6 祝 *(zhù)* (I wish . . .)

To express good wishes, say the verb 祝 *(zhù)* at the beginning of a sentence. [See Lesson 10.]

A

祝你新年快樂！

Zhù nǐ xīnnián kuàilè!

Happy New Year!

B

祝你生日快樂！

Zhù nǐ shēngrì kuàilè!

Happy birthday!

C

祝你考試考得好！

Zhù nǐ kǎo shì kǎo de hǎo!

I hope you do well on the exam!

D

祝寒假快樂！

Zhù hánjià kuàilè!

Have a pleasant winter break!

E

祝感恩節快樂！

Zhù Gǎn'ēnjié kuàilè!

Happy Thanksgiving!

F

祝春節快樂！

Zhù Chūnjié kuàilè!

Happy Chinese New Year!

G

祝一路平安！

Zhù yí lù píng'ān!

Have a safe trip!

H

祝旅途愉快！

Zhù lǚtú yúkuài!

Bon voyage!

Vocabulary Index (Chinese-English)

The Chinese-English index is alphabetized according to *pinyin*. Words containing the same Chinese characters are grouped together first. Homonyms appear in the order of their tonal pronunciation (i.e., first tones first, second tones second, third tones third, fourth tones fourth, and neutral tones last).

Traditional	Simplified	Pinyin	Part of Speech	Definition	Lesson
		A			
啊		*a*	p	(a sentence-final particle of exclamation, interrogation, etc.)	6
		B			
爸爸		*bàba*	n	father, dad	2
吧		*ba*	p	(a sentence-final particle)	5
白英愛	白英爱	*Bái Yīng'ài*	pn	(a personal name)	2
百		*bǎi*	nu	hundred	9
半		*bàn*	nu	half, half an hour	3
辦公室	办公室	*bàngōngshì*	n	office	6
幫	帮	*bāng*	v	to help	6
杯		*bēi*	m	(measure word for things contained in a cup or glass)	5
北京		*Běijīng*	pn	Beijing	1
筆	笔	*bǐ*	n	pen	7
別	别	*bié*	adv	don't	6
別人	别人	*biérén*	n	other people, another person	4
不		*bù*	adv	not, no	1
不錯	不错	*búcuò*	adj	pretty good	4
不過	不过	*búguò*	conj	however, but	9
不好意思		*bù hǎoyìsi*		to feel embarrassed	10
不用		*bú yòng*		need not	9

Traditional	Simplified	Pinyin	Part of Speech	Definition	Lesson
C					
才		*cái*	adv	not until, only then	5
菜	菜	*cài*	n	dish, cuisine	3
餐廳	餐厅	*cāntīng*	n	dining room, cafeteria	8
茶	茶	*chá*	n	tea	5
常常		*chángcháng*	adv	often	4
常老師	常老师	*Cháng lǎoshī*	pn	Teacher Chang	6
長短	长短	*chángduǎn*	n	length	9
唱歌（兒）	唱歌（儿）	*chàng gē(r)*	vo	to sing (a song)	4
襯衫	衬衫	*chènshān*	n	shirt	9
城市		*chéngshì*	n	city	10
吃		*chī*	v	to eat	3
除了…以外		*chúle . . . yǐwài*	conj	in addition to, besides	8
出去		*chūqu*	vc	to go out	10
出租汽車	出租汽车	*chūzū qìchē*	n	taxi	10
穿		*chuān*	v	to wear, to put on	9
D					
打車	打车	*dǎ chē*	vo	to take a taxi	10
打電話	打电话	*dǎ diànhuà*	vo	to make a phone call	6
打球		*dǎ qiú*	vo	to play ball	4
大		*dà*	adj	big, old	3
大哥		*dàgē*	n	eldest/oldest brother	2
大家		*dàjiā*	pr	everybody	7
大姐		*dàjiě*	n	eldest/oldest sister	2

Traditional	Simplified	Pinyin	Part of Speech	Definition	Lesson
大小		dàxiǎo	n	size	9
大學生	大学生	dàxuéshēng	n	college student	2
但是		dànshì	conj	but	6
到		dào	v	to go to, to arrive	6
的		de	p	(a possessive or descriptive particle)	2
得		de	p	(a structural particle)	7
得		děi	av	must, to have to	6
等		děng	v	to wait, to wait for	6
第		dì	prefix	(prefix for ordinal numbers)	7
弟弟		dìdi	n	younger brother	2
地鐵	地铁	dìtiě	n	subway	10
點	点	diǎn	m	o'clock (lit. dot, point, thus "points on the clock")	3
點（兒）	点（儿）	diǎn(r)	m	a little, a bit, some	5
電腦	电脑	diànnǎo	n	computer	8
電視	电视	diànshì	n	television	4
電影	电影	diànyǐng	n	movie	4
電子郵件	电子邮件	diànzǐ yóujiàn	n	email/electronic mail	10
東西	东西	dōngxi	n	things, objects	9
懂	懂	dǒng	v	to understand	7
都		dōu	adv	both, all	2
對	对	duì	adj	right, correct	4
對不起	对不起	duìbuqǐ	v	sorry	5
多		duō	adv	how many/much, to what extent	3

Traditional	Simplified	Pinyin	Part of Speech	Definition	Lesson
多		*duō*	adj	many, much	7
多少		*duōshao*	qpr	how much/how many	9
			E		
兒子	儿子	*érzi*	n	son	2
二姐		*èrjiě*	n	second oldest sister	2
			F		
發短信	发短信	*fā duǎnxìn*	vo	to send a text message (lit. to send a short message)	10
發音	发音	*fāyīn*	n	pronunciation	8
飯	饭	*fàn*	n	meal, (cooked) rice	3
方便		*fāngbiàn*	adj	convenient	6
飛機	飞机	*fēijī*	n	airplane	10
（飛）機場	（飞）机场	*(fēi)jīchǎng*	n	airport	10
分		*fēn*	m	(measure word for 1/100 of a kuai [equivalent of a cent])	9
封		*fēng*	m	(measure word for letters)	8
付錢	付钱	*fù qián*	vo	to pay money	9
復習	复习	*fùxí*	v	to review	7
			G		
高速公路		*gāosù gōnglù*	n	highway	10
高文中		*Gāo Wénzhōng*	pn	(a personal name)	2
高小音		*Gāo Xiǎoyīn*	pn	(a personal name)	5
高興	高兴	*gāoxìng*	adj	happy, pleased	5
告訴	告诉	*gàosu*	v	to tell	8
哥哥		*gēge*	n	older brother	2
個	个	*gè/ge*	m	(measure word for many common everyday objects)	2

Traditional	Simplified	Pinyin	Part of Speech	Definition	Lesson
給	给	*gěi*	v	to give	5
給	给	*gěi*	prep	to, for	6
跟		*gēn*	prep	with	6
公共汽車	公共汽车	*gōnggòng qìchē*	n	bus	10
功課	功课	*gōngkè*	n	homework, schoolwork	7
工作		*gōngzuò*	n/v	job; to work	2
貴	贵	*guì*	adj	honorable, expensive	1
		H			
還	还	*hái*	adv	also, too, as well	3
還是	还是	*háishi*	conj	or	3
孩子		*háizi*	n	child	2
寒假		*hánjià*	n	winter vacation	10
漢字	汉字	*Hànzì*	n	Chinese characters	7
好		*hǎo*	adj	fine, good, nice, OK, it's settled	1
好久		*hǎojiǔ*		a long time	4
號	号	*hào*	m	(measure word for a position in a numerical series, day of the month)	3
號	号	*hào*	n	size	9
喝		*hē*	v	to drink	5
和		*hé*	conj	and	2
合適	合适	*héshì*	adj	suitable	9
黑		*hēi*	adj	black	9
很		*hěn*	adv	very	3
紅	红	*hóng*	adj	red	9

Traditional	Simplified	Pinyin	Part of Speech	Definition	Lesson
後來	后来	*hòulái*	t	later	8
花	花	*huā*	v	to spend	10
換	换	*huàn*	v	to exchange, to change	9
黃	黄	*huáng*	adj	yellow	9
回家		*huí jiā*	vo	to go home	5
回來	回来	*huí lai*	vc	to come back	6
會	会	*huì*	mv	can, know how to	8
或者		*huòzhě*	conj	or	10
			J		
幾	几	*jǐ*	nu	how many, some, a few	2
家		*jiā*	n	family, home	2
件		*jiàn*	m	(measure word for shirts, dresses, jackets, coats, etc.)	9
見	见	*jiàn*	v	to see	3
見面	见面	*jiàn miàn*	vo	to meet up, to meet with	6
教		*jiāo*	v	to teach	7
教室		*jiàoshì*	n	classroom	8
叫		*jiào*	v	to be called, to call	1
節	节	*jié*	m	(measure word for class periods)	6
姐姐		*jiějie*	n	older sister	2
介紹	介绍	*jièshào*	v	to introduce	5
今年		*jīnnián*	t	this year	3
今天		*jīntiān*	t	today	3
緊張	紧张	*jǐnzhāng*	adj	nervous, anxious	10
進	进	*jìn*	v	to enter	5

Traditional	Simplified	Pinyin	Part of Speech	Definition	Lesson
進來	进来	*jìn lai*	vc	to come in	5
九月		*jiǔyuè*	n	September	3
就		*jiù*	adv	precisely, exactly	6
覺得	觉得	*juéde*	v	to feel, to think	4
		K			
咖啡		*kāfēi*	n	coffee	5
咖啡色		*kāfēisè*	n	brown, coffee color	9
開車	开车	*kāi chē*	vo	to drive a car	10
開會	开会	*kāi huì*	vo	to have a meeting	6
開始	开始	*kāishǐ*	v/n	to begin, to start; beginning	7
看		*kàn*	v	to watch, to look, to read	4
考試	考试	*kǎo shì*	vo/n	to give or take a test; test	6
可樂	可乐	*kělè*	n	cola	5
可是		*kěshì*	conj	but	3
可以		*kěyǐ*	mv	can, may	5
刻		*kè*	m	quarter (of an hour)	3
課	课	*kè*	n	class, course, lesson	6
課文	课文	*kèwén*	n	text of a lesson	7
客氣	客气	*kèqi*	adj	polite	6
空（兒）	空（儿）	*kòng(r)*	n	free time	6
口		*kǒu*	m	(measure word for number of family members)	2
酷		*kù*	adj	cool (appearance, behavior)	7
褲子	裤子	*kùzi*	n	pants	9
快		*kuài*	adj/adv	fast, quick; quickly	5

Traditional	Simplified	Pinyin	Part of Speech	Definition	Lesson
快樂	快乐	*kuàilè*	adj	happy	10
塊	块	*kuài*	m	(measure word for the basic Chinese monetary unit [equivalent of a dollar])	9
			L		
來	来	*lái*	v	to come	5
藍	蓝	*lán*	adj	blue	10
老師	老师	*lǎoshī*	n	teacher	1
了		*le*	p	(a dynamic particle)	5
累		*lèi*	adj	tired	8
李友		*Lǐ Yǒu*	pn	(a personal name)	1
練習	练习	*liànxí*	v	to practice	6
兩	两	*liǎng*	nu	two, a couple of	2
聊天（兒）	聊天（儿）	*liáo tiān(r)*	vo	to chat	5
路		*lù*	n	route, road	10
錄音	录音	*lùyīn*	n/vo	sound recording; to record	7
綠	绿	*lǜ*	adj	green	10
律師	律师	*lǜshī*	n	lawyer	2
			M		
媽媽	妈妈	*māma*	n	mother, mom	2
嗎	吗	*ma*	qp	(question particle)	1
麻煩	麻烦	*máfan*	adj	troublesome	10
買	买	*mǎi*	v	to buy	9
慢		*màn*	adj	slow	7
忙		*máng*	adj	busy	3
毛		*máo*	m	(measure word for 1/10 of a kuai [equivalent of a dime])	9

Traditional	Simplified	Pinyin	Part of Speech	Definition	Lesson
沒	没	*méi*	adv	not	2
每		*měi*	pr	every, each	10
美國	美国	*Měiguó*	pn	America	1
妹妹		*mèimei*	n	younger sister	2
明天		*míngtiān*	t	tomorrow	3
名字		*míngzi*	n	name	1
N					
哪		*nǎ/něi*	qpr	which	6
哪裡	哪里	*nǎli*	pr	where	7
哪兒	哪儿	*nǎr*	qpr	where	5
那		*nà*	pr	that	2
那		*nà*	conj	in that case, then	4
那兒	那儿	*nàr*	pr	there	8
男		*nán*	adj	male	2
難	难	*nán*	adj	difficult	7
呢		*ne*	qp	(question particle)	1
能		*néng*	mv	can, to be able to	8
你		*nǐ*	pr	you	1
年級	年级	*niánjí*	n	grade in school	6
念		*niàn*	v	to read aloud	7
您		*nín*	pr	you (honorific for 你)	6
紐約	纽约	*Niǔyuē*	pn	New York	1
女		*nǚ*	adj	female	2
女兒	女儿	*nǚ'ér*	n	daughter	2

Traditional	Simplified	Pinyin	Part of Speech	Definition	Lesson
		P			
朋友		*péngyou*	n	friend	3
篇		*piān*	m	(measure word for essays, articles, etc.)	8
便宜		*piányi*	adj	cheap, inexpensive	9
票		*piào*	n	ticket	10
漂亮	漂亮	*piàoliang*	adj	pretty	5
瓶		*píng*	m/n	(measure word for bottled liquid, etc.)	5
平常		*píngcháng*	adv	usually	7
		Q			
起床	起床	*qǐ chuáng*	vo	to get up	8
錢	钱	*qián*	n	money	9
請	请	*qǐng*	v	please (polite form of request), to treat or to invite (somebody)	1
請客	请客	*qǐng kè*	vo	to invite someone (to dinner, coffee, etc.), to play the host	4
去		*qù*	v	to go	4
		R			
然後	然后	*ránhòu*	adv	then	10
讓	让	*ràng*	v	to allow or cause (somebody to do something)	10
人		*rén*	n	people, person	1
認識	认识	*rènshi*	v	to be acquainted with, to recognize	3
日記	日记	*rìjì*	n	diary	8
容易		*róngyì*	adj	easy	7
如果…的話	如果…的话	*rúguǒ . . . de huà*	conj	if	9

Traditional	Simplified	Pinyin	Part of Speech	Definition	Lesson
S					
商店		*shāngdiàn*	n	store, shop	9
上個	上个	*shàng ge*		previous, last	7
上課	上课	*shàng kè*	vo	to go to a class, to start a class, to be in class	7
上網	上网	*shàng wǎng*	vo	to go online, to surf the internet	8
上午		*shàngwǔ*	t	morning	6
誰	谁	*shéi*	qpr	who, whom	2
什麼	什么	*shénme*	qpr	what	1
生詞	生词	*shēngcí*	n	new words, vocabulary	7
生日		*shēngrì*	n	birthday	3
十八		*shíbā*	nu	eighteen	3
十二		*shí'èr*	nu	twelve	3
時候	时候	*shíhou*	n	(a point in) time, moment, (a duration of) time	4
時間	时间	*shíjiān*	n	time	6
試	试	*shì*	v	to try	9
事（兒）	事（儿）	*shì(r)*	n	matter, affair, event	3
是		*shì*	v	to be	1
收		*shōu*	v	to receive, to accept	9
手機	手机	*shǒujī*	n	cell phone	10
售貨員	售货员	*shòuhuòyuán*	n	shop assistant, salesclerk	9
書	书	*shū*	n	book	4
刷卡		*shuā kǎ*	vo	to pay with a credit card	9
帥	帅	*shuài*	adj	handsome	7

Traditional	Simplified	Pinyin	Part of Speech	Definition	Lesson
雙	双	*shuāng*	m	(measure word for a pair)	9
水		*shuǐ*	n	water	5
睡覺	睡觉	*shuì jiào*	vo	to sleep	4
說	说	*shuō*	v	to say, to speak	6
說話	说话	*shuō huà*	vo	to talk	7
送		*sòng*	v	to see off or out, to take (someone somewhere)	10
宿舍		*sùshè*	n	dormitory	8
算了		*suàn le*		forget it, never mind	4
雖然	虽然	*suīrán*	conj	although	9
歲	岁	*suì*	n	year (of age)	3
所以		*suǒyǐ*	conj	so	4
T					
他		*tā*	pr	he, him	2
她		*tā*	pr	she, her	2
它		*tā*	pr	it	9
太…了		*tài . . . le*		too, extremely	3
特別	特别	*tèbié*	adv	especially	10
天		*tiān*	n	day	3
條	条	*tiáo*	m	(measure word for pants and long, thin objects)	9
跳舞		*tiào wǔ*	vo	to dance	4
聽	听	*tīng*	v	to listen	4
挺		*tǐng*	adv	very, rather	9
同學	同学	*tóngxué*	n	classmate	3
圖書館	图书馆	*túshūguǎn*	n	library	5

Traditional	Simplified	Pinyin	Part of Speech	Definition	Lesson
W					
外國	外国	*wàiguó*	n	foreign country	4
玩（兒）	玩（儿）	*wán(r)*	v	to have fun, to play	5
晚		*wǎn*	adj	late	7
晚飯	晚饭	*wǎnfàn*	n	dinner, supper	3
晚上		*wǎnshang*	t	evening, night	3
王朋		*Wáng Péng*	pn	(a personal name)	1
喂		*wéi/wèi*	interj	(on the phone) Hello!, Hey!	6
位		*wèi*	m	(polite measure word for people)	6
為什麼	为什么	*wèishénme*	qpr	why	3
問	问	*wèn*	v	to ask (a question)	1
問題	问题	*wèntí*	n	question, problem	6
我		*wǒ*	pr	I, me	1
我們	我们	*wǒmen*	pr	we, us	3
午飯	午饭	*wǔfàn*	n	lunch, midday meal	8
X					
希望	希望	*xīwàng*	v/n	to hope; hope	8
喜歡	喜欢	*xǐhuan*	v	to like	3
洗澡		*xǐ zǎo*	vo	to take a bath/shower	8
下車	下车	*xià chē*	vo	to get off (a bus, train, etc.)	10
下個	下个	*xià ge*		next	6
下午		*xiàwǔ*	t	afternoon	6
先		*xiān*	adv	first	10
先生		*xiānsheng*	n	Mr., husband, teacher	1
線	线	*xiàn*	n	line	10

Traditional	Simplified	Pinyin	Part of Speech	Definition	Lesson
現在	现在	*xiànzài*	t	now	3
想		*xiǎng*	av	to want to, would like to	4
小		*xiǎo*	adj	small, little	4
小姐		*xiǎojiě*	n	Miss, young lady	1
笑		*xiào*	v	to laugh at, to laugh, to smile	8
鞋		*xié*	n	shoes	9
寫	写	*xiě*	v	to write	7
謝謝	谢谢	*xièxie*	v	to thank	3
新		*xīn*	adj	new	8
新年		*xīnnián*	n	new year	10
信		*xìn*	n	letter (correspondence)	8
信用卡		*xìnyòngkǎ*	n	credit card	9
星期		*xīngqī*	n	week	3
星期四		*xīngqīsì*	n	Thursday	3
行		*xíng*	v	all right, OK	6
姓		*xìng*	v/n	(one's) family name is . . . ; family name	1
學	学	*xué*	v	to study, to learn	7
學期	学期	*xuéqī*	n	school term, semester, quarter	8
學生	学生	*xuésheng*	n	student	1
學習	学习	*xuéxí*	v	to study, to learn	7
學校	学校	*xuéxiào*	n	school	5
		Y			
呀		*ya*	p	(interjectory particle used to soften a question)	5
顏色	颜色	*yánsè*	n	color	9
樣子	样子	*yàngzi*	n	style	9

Traditional	Simplified	Pinyin	Part of Speech	Definition	Lesson
要		*yào*	v	to want	5
要		*yào*	mv	will, to be going to; to want to, to have a desire to	6
要是		*yàoshi*	conj	if	6
也		*yě*	adv	too, also	1
一邊	一边	*yìbiān*	adv	simultaneously, at the same time	8
一共		*yígòng*	adv	altogether	9
一起	一起	*yìqǐ*	adv	together	5
一下		*yí xià*	n+m	once, a bit	5
一樣	一样	*yíyàng*	adj	same, alike	9
衣服		*yīfu*	n	clothes	9
醫生	医生	*yīshēng*	n	doctor, physician	2
以後	以后	*yǐhòu*	t	after, from now on, later on	6
以前		*yǐqián*	t	before	8
已經	已经	*yǐjīng*	adv	already	8
因為	因为	*yīnwèi*	conj	because	3
音樂	音乐	*yīnyuè*	n	music	4
音樂會	音乐会	*yīnyuèhuì*	n	concert	8
英國	英国	*Yīngguó*	pn	Britain	3
英文	英文	*Yīngwén*	n	the English language	2
用		*yòng*	v	to use	8
有		*yǒu*	v	to have, to exist	2
有的		*yǒude*	pr	some	4
有意思		*yǒu yìsi*	adj	interesting	4
語法	语法	*yǔfǎ*	n	grammar	7

Traditional	Simplified	Pinyin	Part of Speech	Definition	Lesson
預習	预习	*yùxí*	v	to preview	7
月		*yuè*	n	month	3
		Z			
在		*zài*	prep	at, in, on	5
在		*zài*	v	to be present, to be at (a place)	6
再		*zài*	adv	again	9
再見	再见	*zàijiàn*	v	goodbye, see you again	3
早		*zǎo*	adj	early	7
早飯	早饭	*zǎofàn*	n	breakfast	8
早上		*zǎoshang*	t	morning	7
怎麼	怎么	*zěnme*	qpr	how, how come	7
怎麼樣	怎么样	*zěnmeyàng*	qpr	Is it OK? How is that? How does that sound?	3
站		*zhàn*	m	(measure word for bus stops, train stops, etc.)	10
張	张	*zhāng*	m	(measure word for flat objects such as paper, pictures, etc.)	7
找		*zhǎo*	v	to look for	4
找（錢）	找（钱）	*zhǎo (qián)*	v(o)	to give change	9
照片		*zhàopiàn*	n	picture, photo	2
這	这	*zhè*	pr	this	2
這麼	这么	*zhème*	pr	so, this (late, etc.)	7
這兒	这儿	*zhèr*	pr	here	9
真		*zhēn*	adv	really	7
正在		*zhèngzài*	adv	in the middle of (doing something)	8
枝		*zhī*	m	(measure word for long, thin, inflexible objects such as pens, pencils, etc.)	7

Traditional	Simplified	Pinyin	Part of Speech	Definition	Lesson
知道		*zhīdao*	v	to know	8
只		*zhǐ*	adv	only	4
紙	纸	*zhǐ*	n	paper	7
中		*zhōng*	adj	medium, middle	9
中國	中国	*Zhōngguó*	pn	China	1
中文		*Zhōngwén*	n	the Chinese language	6
中午		*zhōngwǔ*	t	noon	8
種	种	*zhǒng*	m	(measure word for kinds, sorts, types)	9
週末	周末	*zhōumò*	n	weekend	4
祝		*zhù*	v	to wish (well)	8
專業	专业	*zhuānyè*	n	major (in college), specialty	8
準備	准备	*zhǔnbèi*	v	to prepare	6
字		*zì*	n	character	7
自己		*zìjǐ*	pr	oneself	10
走		*zǒu*	v	to go by way of, to walk	10
最後	最后	*zuìhòu*		final, last	10
最近		*zuìjìn*	t	recently	8
昨天		*zuótiān*	t	yesterday	4
做		*zuò*	v	to do	2
坐		*zuò*	v	to sit	5
坐		*zuò*	v	to travel by	10

Vocabulary Index (English-Chinese)

The English-Chinese index is organized based on the alphabetical order of the English definitions. For ease of reference, indefinite articles and definite articles are omitted when they are at the beginning of a phrase.

English	Traditional	Simplified	Pinyin	Part of Speech	Lesson
A					
after, from now on, later on	以後	以后	*yǐhòu*	t	6
afternoon	下午		*xiàwǔ*	t	6
again	再		*zài*	adv	9
airplane	飛機	飞机	*fēijī*	n	10
airport	（飛）機場	（飞）机场	*(fēi)jīchǎng*	n	10
all right, OK	行		*xíng*	v	6
allow or cause (somebody to do something)	讓	让	*ràng*	v	10
already	已經	已经	*yǐjīng*	adv	8
also, too, as well	還	还	*hái*	adv	3
although	雖然	虽然	*suīrán*	conj	9
altogether	一共		*yígòng*	adv	9
America	美國	美国	*Měiguó*	pn	1
and	和		*hé*	conj	2
ask (a question)	問	问	*wèn*	v	1
at, in, on	在		*zài*	prep	5
B					
Bai Ying'ai	白英愛	白英爱	*Bái Yīng'ài*	pn	2
be	是		*shì*	v	1
be acquainted with, recognize	認識	认识	*rènshi*	v	3

English	Traditional	Simplified	Pinyin	Part of Speech	Lesson
be called, call	叫		*jiào*	v	1
be present, be at (a place)	在		*zài*	v	6
because	因為	因为	*yīnwèi*	conj	3
before	以前		*yǐqián*	t	8
begin, start; beginning	開始	开始	*kāishǐ*	v/n	7
Beijing	北京		*Běijīng*	pn	1
big, old	大		*dà*	adj	3
birthday	生日		*shēngrì*	n	3
black	黑		*hēi*	adj	9
blue	藍	蓝	*lán*	adj	10
book	書	书	*shū*	n	4
both, all	都		*dōu*	adv	2
breakfast	早飯	早饭	*zǎofàn*	n	8
Britain	英國	英国	*Yīngguó*	pn	3
brown, coffee color	咖啡色		*kāfēisè*	n	9
bus	公共汽車	公共汽车	*gōnggòng qìchē*	n	10
busy	忙		*máng*	adj	3
but	但是		*dànshì*	conj	6
but	可是		*kěshì*	conj	3
buy	買	买	*mǎi*	v	9
C					
can, able to	能		*néng*	mv	8
can, know how to	會	会	*huì*	mv	8
can, may	可以		*kěyǐ*	mv	5

English	Traditional	Simplified	Pinyin	Part of Speech	Lesson
cell phone	手機	手机	*shǒujī*	n	10
character	字		*zì*	n	7
chat	聊天（兒）	聊天（儿）	*liáo tiān(r)*	vo	5
cheap, inexpensive	便宜		*piányi*	adj	9
child	孩子		*háizi*	n	2
China	中國	中国	*Zhōngguó*	pn	1
Chinese characters	漢字	汉字	*Hànzì*	n	7
Chinese language	中文		*Zhōngwén*	n	6
city	城市		*chéngshì*	n	10
class, course, lesson	課	课	*kè*	n	6
classmate	同學	同学	*tóngxué*	n	3
classroom	教室		*jiàoshì*	n	8
clothes	衣服		*yīfu*	n	9
coffee	咖啡		*kāfēi*	n	5
cola	可樂	可乐	*kělè*	n	5
college student	大學生	大学生	*dàxuéshēng*	n	2
color	顏色	颜色	*yánsè*	n	9
come	來	来	*lái*	v	5
come back	回來	回来	*huí lai*	vc	6
come in	進來	进来	*jìn lai*	vc	5
computer	電腦	电脑	*diànnǎo*	n	8
concert	音樂會	音乐会	*yīnyuèhuì*	n	8
convenient	方便		*fāngbiàn*	adj	6
cool (appearance, behavior)	酷		*kù*	adj	7
credit card	信用卡		*xìnyòngkǎ*	n	9

English	Traditional	Simplified	Pinyin	Part of Speech	Lesson
D					
dance	跳舞		*tiào wǔ*	vo	4
daughter	女兒	女儿	*nǚ'ér*	n	2
day	天		*tiān*	n	3
diary	日記	日记	*rìjì*	n	8
difficult	難	难	*nán*	adj	7
dining room, cafeteria	餐廳	餐厅	*cāntīng*	n	8
dinner, supper	晚飯	晚饭	*wǎnfàn*	n	3
dish, cuisine	菜	菜	*cài*	n	3
do	做		*zuò*	v	2
doctor, physician	醫生	医生	*yīshēng*	n	2
don't	別	别	*bié*	adv	6
dormitory	宿舍		*sùshè*	n	8
drink	喝		*hē*	v	5
drive a car	開車	开车	*kāi chē*	vo	10
(dynamic particle)	了		*le*	p	5
E					
early	早		*zǎo*	adj	7
easy	容易		*róngyì*	adj	7
eat	吃		*chī*	v	3
eighteen	十八		*shíbā*	nu	3
eldest/oldest brother	大哥		*dàgē*	n	2
eldest/oldest sister	大姐		*dàjiě*	n	2
email/electronic mail	電子郵件	电子邮件	*diànzǐ yóujiàn*	n	10

English	Traditional	Simplified	Pinyin	Part of Speech	Lesson
English language	英文	英文	*Yīngwén*	n	2
enter	進	进	*jìn*	v	5
especially	特別	特别	*tèbié*	adv	10
evening, night	晚上		*wǎnshang*	t	3
every, each	每		*měi*	pr	10
everybody	大家		*dàjiā*	pr	7
exchange, change	換	换	*huàn*	v	9
		F			
family, home	家		*jiā*	n	2
fast, quick; quickly	快		*kuài*	adj/adv	5
father, dad	爸爸		*bàba*	n	2
feel, think	覺得	觉得	*juéde*	v	4
feel embarrassed	不好意思		*bù hǎoyìsi*		10
female	女		*nǚ*	adj	2
final, last	最後	最后	*zuìhòu*		10
fine, good, nice, OK, it's settled	好		*hǎo*	adj	1
first	先		*xiān*	adv	10
foreign country	外國	外国	*wàiguó*	n	4
forget it, never mind	算了		*suàn le*		4
free time	空（兒）	空（儿）	*kòng(r)*	n	6
friend	朋友		*péngyou*	n	3
		G			
Gao Wenzhong	高文中		*Gāo Wénzhōng*	pn	2
Gao Xiaoyin	高小音		*Gāo Xiǎoyīn*	pn	5
get off (a bus, train, etc.)	下車	下车	*xià chē*	vo	10

English	Traditional	Simplified	Pinyin	Part of Speech	Lesson
get up	起床	起床	*qǐ chuáng*	vo	8
give	給	给	*gěi*	v	5
give change	找（錢）	找（钱）	*zhǎo (qián)*	v(o)	9
give or take a test; test	考試	考试	*kǎo shì*	vo/n	6
go	去		*qù*	v	4
go by way of, walk	走		*zǒu*	v	10
go home	回家		*huí jiā*	vo	5
go online, surf the internet	上網	上网	*shàng wǎng*	vo	8
go out	出去		*chūqu*	vc	10
go to, arrive	到		*dào*	v	6
go to a class, start a class, be in class	上課	上课	*shàng kè*	vo	7
goodbye, see you again	再見	再见	*zàijiàn*	v	3
grade in school	年級	年级	*niánjí*	n	6
grammar	語法	语法	*yǔfǎ*	n	7
green	綠	绿	*lǜ*	adj	10
		H			
half, half an hour	半		*bàn*	nu	3
handsome	帥	帅	*shuài*	adj	7
happy	快樂	快乐	*kuàilè*	adj	10
happy, pleased	高興	高兴	*gāoxìng*	adj	5
have, exist	有		*yǒu*	v	2
have a meeting	開會	开会	*kāi huì*	vo	6
have fun, play	玩（兒）	玩（儿）	*wán(r)*	v	5
he, him	他		*tā*	pr	2

English	Traditional	Simplified	Pinyin	Part of Speech	Lesson
Hello!, Hey! (on the phone)	喂		*wéi/wèi*	interj	6
help	幫	帮	*bāng*	v	6
here	這兒	这儿	*zhèr*	pr	9
highway	高速公路		*gāosù gōnglù*	n	10
homework, schoolwork	功課	功课	*gōngkè*	n	7
honorable, expensive	貴	贵	*guì*	adj	1
hope; hope	希望	希望	*xīwàng*	v/n	8
how, how come	怎麼	怎么	*zěnme*	qpr	7
how many, some, a few	幾	几	*jǐ*	nu	2
how many/much, to what extent	多		*duō*	adv	3
how much/many	多少		*duōshao*	qpr	9
however, but	不過	不过	*búguò*	conj	9
hundred	百		*bǎi*	nu	9
		I			
I, me	我		*wǒ*	pr	1
if	如果…的話	如果…的话	*rúguǒ . . . de huà*	conj	9
if	要是		*yàoshi*	conj	6
in addition to, besides	除了…以外		*chúle . . . yǐwài*	conj	8
in that case, then	那		*nà*	conj	4
in the middle of (doing something)	正在		*zhèngzài*	adv	8
interesting	有意思		*yǒu yìsi*	adj	4
(interjectory particle used to soften a question)	呀		*ya*	p	5
introduce	介紹	介绍	*jièshào*	v	5

English	Traditional	Simplified	Pinyin	Part of Speech	Lesson
invite someone (to dinner, coffee, etc.), play the host	請客	请客	*qǐng kè*	vo	4
Is it OK? How is that? How does that sound?	怎麼樣	怎么样	*zěnmeyàng*	qpr	3
it	它		*tā*	pr	9
		J			
job; to work	工作		*gōngzuò*	n/v	2
		K			
know	知道		*zhīdao*	v	8
		L			
late	晚		*wǎn*	adj	7
later	後來	后来	*hòulái*	t	8
laugh at, laugh, smile	笑		*xiào*	v	8
lawyer	律師	律师	*lǜshī*	n	2
length	長短	长短	*chángduǎn*	n	9
letter (correspondence)	信		*xìn*	n	8
Li You	李友		*Lǐ Yǒu*	pn	1
library	圖書館	图书馆	*túshūguǎn*	n	5
like	喜歡	喜欢	*xǐhuan*	v	3
line	線	线	*xiàn*	n	10
listen	聽	听	*tīng*	v	4
little, a bit, some	點（兒）	点（儿）	*diǎn(r)*	m	5
long time	好久		*hǎojiǔ*		4
look for	找		*zhǎo*	v	4
lunch, midday meal	午飯	午饭	*wǔfàn*	n	8

English	Traditional	Simplified	Pinyin	Part of Speech	Lesson
		M			
major (in college), specialty	專業	专业	*zhuānyè*	n	8
make a phone call	打電話	打电话	*dǎ diànhuà*	vo	6
male	男		*nán*	adj	2
many, much	多		*duō*	adj	7
matter, affair, event	事（兒）	事（儿）	*shì(r)*	n	3
meal, (cooked) rice	飯	饭	*fàn*	n	3
(measure word for a pair)	雙	双	*shuāng*	m	9
(measure word for a position in a numerical series, day of the month)	號	号	*hào*	m	3
(measure word for bottled liquid, etc.)	瓶		*píng*	m/n	5
(measure word for bus stops, train stops, etc.)	站		*zhàn*	m	10
(measure word for class periods)	節	节	*jié*	m	6
(measure word for essays, articles, etc.)	篇		*piān*	m	8
(measure word for flat objects such as paper, pictures, etc.)	張	张	*zhāng*	m	7
(measure word for kinds, sorts, types)	種	种	*zhǒng*	m	9
(measure word for letters)	封		*fēng*	m	8
(measure word for long, thin, inflexible objects such as pens, pencils, etc.)	枝		*zhī*	m	7
(measure word for many common everyday objects)	個	个	*gè/ge*	m	2
(measure word for number of family members)	口		*kǒu*	m	2
(measure word for 1/100 of a kuai [equivalent of a cent])	分		*fēn*	m	9
(measure word for 1/10 of a kuai [equivalent of a dime])	毛		*máo*	m	9

English	Traditional	Simplified	Pinyin	Part of Speech	Lesson
(measure word for pants and long, thin objects)	條	条	*tiáo*	m	9
(measure word for people [polite])	位		*wèi*	m	6
(measure word for shirts, dresses, jackets, coats, etc.)	件		*jiàn*	m	9
(measure word for the basic Chinese monetary unit [equivalent of a dollar])	塊	块	*kuài*	m	9
(measure word for things contained in a cup or glass)	杯		*bēi*	m	5
medium, middle	中		*zhōng*	adj	9
meet up/with	見面	见面	*jiàn miàn*	vo	6
Miss, young lady	小姐		*xiǎojiě*	n	1
money	錢	钱	*qián*	n	9
month	月		*yuè*	n	3
morning	上午		*shàngwǔ*	t	6
morning	早上		*zǎoshang*	t	7
mother, mom	媽媽	妈妈	*māma*	n	2
movie	電影	电影	*diànyǐng*	n	4
Mr., husband, teacher	先生		*xiānsheng*	n	1
music	音樂	音乐	*yīnyuè*	n	4
must, have to	得		*děi*	av	6
N					
name	名字		*míngzi*	n	1
need not	不用		*bú yòng*		9
nervous, anxious	緊張	紧张	*jǐnzhāng*	adj	10
new	新		*xīn*	adj	8
new words, vocabulary	生詞	生词	*shēngcí*	n	7

English	Traditional	Simplified	Pinyin	Part of Speech	Lesson
new year	新年		*xīnnián*	n	10
New York	紐約	纽约	*Niǔyuē*	pn	1
next one	下個	下个	*xià ge*		6
noon	中午		*zhōngwǔ*	t	8
not	沒	没	*méi*	adv	2
not, no	不		*bù*	adv	1
not until, only then	才		*cái*	adv	5
now	現在	现在	*xiànzài*	t	3
		O			
o'clock (lit. dot, point, thus "points on the clock")	點	点	*diǎn*	m	3
office	辦公室	办公室	*bàngōngshì*	n	6
often	常常		*chángcháng*	adv	4
older brother	哥哥		*gēge*	n	2
older sister	姐姐		*jiějie*	n	2
once, a bit	一下		*yí xià*	n+m	5
(one's) family name is . . . ; family name	姓		*xìng*	v/n	1
oneself	自己		*zìjǐ*	pr	10
only	只		*zhǐ*	adv	4
or	還是	还是	*háishi*	conj	3
or	或者		*huòzhě*	conj	10
other people, another person	別人	别人	*biérén*	n	4
		P			
pants	褲子	裤子	*kùzi*	n	9
paper	紙	纸	*zhǐ*	n	7

English	Traditional	Simplified	Pinyin	Part of Speech	Lesson
pay money	付錢	付钱	*fù qián*	vo	9
pay with a credit card	刷卡		*shuā kǎ*	vo	9
pen	筆	笔	*bǐ*	n	7
people, person	人		*rén*	n	1
picture, photo	照片		*zhàopiàn*	n	2
play ball	打球		*dǎ qiú*	vo	4
please (polite form of request), to treat or to invite (somebody)	請	请	*qǐng*	v	1
polite	客氣	客气	*kèqi*	adj	6
(possessive or descriptive particle)	的		*de*	p	2
practice	練習	练习	*liànxí*	v	6
precisely, exactly	就		*jiù*	adv	6
(prefix for ordinal numbers)	第		*dì*	prefix	7
prepare	準備	准备	*zhǔnbèi*	v	6
pretty	漂亮	漂亮	*piàoliang*	adj	5
pretty good	不錯	不错	*búcuò*	adj	4
preview	預習	预习	*yùxí*	v	7
previous one	上個	上个	*shàng ge*		7
pronunciation	發音	发音	*fāyīn*	n	8
Q					
quarter (of an hour)	刻		*kè*	m	3
(question particle)	嗎	吗	*ma*	qp	1
(question particle)	呢		*ne*	qp	1
question, problem	問題	问题	*wèntí*	n	6

English	Traditional	Simplified	Pinyin	Part of Speech	Lesson
R					
read aloud	念		*niàn*	v	7
really	真		*zhēn*	adv	7
receive, accept	收		*shōu*	v	9
recently	最近		*zuìjìn*	t	8
red	紅	红	*hóng*	adj	9
review	復習	复习	*fùxí*	v	7
right, correct	對	对	*duì*	adj	4
route, road	路		*lù*	n	10
S					
same, alike	一樣	一样	*yíyàng*	adj	9
say, speak	說	说	*shuō*	v	6
school	學校	学校	*xuéxiào*	n	5
school term, semester, quarter	學期	学期	*xuéqī*	n	8
second oldest sister	二姐		*èrjiě*	n	2
see	見	见	*jiàn*	v	3
see off or out, take (someone somewhere)	送		*sòng*	v	10
send a text message (lit. send a short message)	發短信	发短信	*fā duǎnxìn*	vo	10
(sentence-final particle of exclamation, interrogation, etc.)	啊		*a*	p	6
(sentence-final particle)	吧		*ba*	p	5
September	九月		*jiǔyuè*	p	3
she, her	她		*tā*	pr	2
shirt	襯衫	衬衫	*chènshān*	n	9
shoes	鞋		*xié*	n	9

English	Traditional	Simplified	Pinyin	Part of Speech	Lesson
shop assistant, salesclerk	售貨員	售货员	*shòuhuòyuán*	n	9
simultaneously, at the same time	一邊	一边	*yìbiān*	adv	8
sing (a song)	唱歌（兒）	唱歌（儿）	*chàng gē(r)*	vo	4
sit	坐		*zuò*	v	5
size	大小		*dàxiǎo*	n	9
size	號	号	*hào*	n	9
sleep	睡覺	睡觉	*shuì jiào*	vo	4
slow	慢		*màn*	adj	7
small, little	小		*xiǎo*	adj	4
so	所以		*suǒyǐ*	conj	4
so, this (late, etc.)	這麼	这么	*zhème*	pr	7
some	有的		*yǒude*	pr	4
son	兒子	儿子	*érzi*	n	2
sorry	對不起	对不起	*duìbuqǐ*	v	5
sound recording; record	錄音	录音	*lùyīn*	n/vo	7
spend	花	花	*huā*	v	10
store, shop	商店		*shāngdiàn*	n	9
(structural particle)	得		*de*	p	7
student	學生	学生	*xuésheng*	n	1
study, learn	學	学	*xué*	v	7
study, learn	學習	学习	*xuéxí*	v	7
style	樣子	样子	*yàngzi*	n	9
subway	地鐵	地铁	*dìtiě*	n	10
suitable	合適	合适	*héshì*	adj	9

English	Traditional	Simplified	Pinyin	Part of Speech	Lesson
T					
take a bath/shower	洗澡		*xǐ zǎo*	vo	8
take a taxi	打車	打车	*dǎ chē*	vo	10
talk	說話	说话	*shuō huà*	vo	7
taxi	出租汽車	出租汽车	*chūzū qìchē*	n	10
tea	茶	茶	*chá*	n	5
teach	教		*jiāo*	v	7
teacher	老師	老师	*lǎoshī*	n	1
Teacher Chang	常老師	常老师	*Cháng lǎoshī*	pn	6
television	電視	电视	*diànshì*	n	4
tell	告訴	告诉	*gàosu*	v	8
text of a lesson	課文	课文	*kèwén*	n	7
thank	謝謝	谢谢	*xièxie*	v	3
that	那		*nà*	pr	2
then	然後	然后	*ránhòu*	adv	10
there	那兒	那儿	*nàr*	pr	8
things, objects	東西	东西	*dōngxi*	n	9
this	這	这	*zhè*	pr	2
this year	今年		*jīnnián*	t	3
Thursday	星期四		*xīngqīsì*	n	3
ticket	票		*piào*	n	10
time	時間	时间	*shíjiān*	n	6
time (a point in), moment, time (a duration of)	時候	时候	*shíhou*	n	4
tired	累		*lèi*	adj	8

English	Traditional	Simplified	Pinyin	Part of Speech	Lesson
to, for	給	给	*gěi*	prep	6
today	今天		*jīntiān*	t	3
together	一起	一起	*yìqǐ*	adv	5
tomorrow	明天		*míngtiān*	t	3
too, also	也		*yě*	adv	1
too, extremely	太…了		*tài...le*		3
travel by	坐		*zuò*	v	10
troublesome	麻煩	麻烦	*máfan*	adj	10
try	試	试	*shì*	v	9
twelve	十二		*shí'èr*	nu	3
two, a couple of	兩	两	*liǎng*	nu	2
		U			
understand	懂	懂	*dǒng*	v	7
use	用		*yòng*	v	8
usually	平常		*píngcháng*	adv	7
		V			
very	很		*hěn*	adv	3
very, rather	挺		*tǐng*	adv	9
		W			
wait, wait for	等		*děng*	v	6
Wang Peng	王朋		*Wáng Péng*	pn	1
want	要		*yào*	v	5
want to, would like to	想		*xiǎng*	av	4
watch, look, read	看		*kàn*	v	4
water	水		*shuǐ*	n	5

English	Traditional	Simplified	Pinyin	Part of Speech	Lesson
we, us	我們	我们	*wǒmen*	pr	3
wear, put on	穿		*chuān*	v	9
week	星期		*xīngqī*	n	3
weekend	週末	周末	*zhōumò*	n	4
what	什麼	什么	*shénme*	qpr	1
where	哪裡	哪里	*nǎli*	pr	7
where	哪兒	哪儿	*nǎr*	qpr	5
which	哪		*nǎ/něi*	qpr	6
who, whom	誰	谁	*shéi*	qpr	2
why	為什麼	为什么	*wèishénme*	qpr	3
will, be going to; want to, have a desire to	要		*yào*	mv	6
winter vacation	寒假		*hánjià*	n	10
wish (well)	祝		*zhù*	v	8
with	跟		*gēn*	prep	6
write	寫	写	*xiě*	v	7
Y					
year (of age)	歲	岁	*suì*	n	3
yellow	黃	黄	*huáng*	adj	9
yesterday	昨天		*zuótiān*	t	4
you	你		*nǐ*	pr	1
you (honorific for 你)	您		*nín*	pr	6
younger brother	弟弟		*dìdi*	n	2
younger sister	妹妹		*mèimei*	n	2

Vocabulary by Lesson and Grammar Category

Lesson 1

L1-1

Noun: 小姐，名字，先生
Pronoun: 你，我，什麼
Verb: 請，問，姓，叫
Adjective: 好，貴
Particle: 呢
Proper Noun: 王朋，李友

L1-2

Noun: 老師，學生，人
Verb: 是
Adverb: 不，也
Particle: 嗎
Proper Noun: 中國，北京，美國，紐約

Lesson 2

L2-1

Noun: 照片，爸爸，媽媽，孩子，姐姐，弟弟，大哥，兒子，女兒
Measure Word: 個
Pronoun: 那，這，誰，她，他
Verb: 有
Adjective: 女，男
Adverb: 沒
Particle: 的
Proper Noun: 高文中

L2-2

Noun: 家，哥哥，妹妹，大姐，二姐，工作，律師，英文，大學生，醫生
Measure Word: 口
Numeral: 幾，兩
Verb: 做
Adverb: 都
Conjunction: 和
Proper Noun: 白英愛

Lesson 3

L3-1

Noun:	九月，月，星期，星期四，天，生日，歲，飯，菜
Measure Word:	號，點
Pronoun:	怎麼樣，我們
Numeral:	十二，十八，半
Verb:	吃，謝謝，喜歡，見，再見
Adjective:	大
Adverb:	多
Conjunction:	還是，可是
Time Word:	今年，晚上
Others:	太…了
Proper Noun:	英國

L3-2

Noun:	事（兒），晚飯，同學，朋友
Measure Word:	刻
Pronoun:	為什麼
Verb:	認識
Adjective:	忙
Adverb:	很，還
Conjunction:	因為
Time Word:	現在，今天，明天

Lesson 4

L4-1

Noun:	週末，電視，音樂，書，時候，電影，外國
Pronoun:	有的
Verb:	打球，看，唱歌，跳舞，聽，去，請客
Adjective:	對
Adverb:	常常
Conjunction:	那，所以
Time Word:	昨天

L4-2

Noun:	別人
Verb:	覺得，睡覺，找
Modal Verb:	想
Adjective:	小，不錯，有意思
Adverb:	只
Others:	好久，算了

Lesson 5

L5-1

Noun:	學校，茶，咖啡，可樂，水
Measure Word:	點（兒），瓶，杯
Pronoun:	哪兒
Verb:	進，進來，來，介紹，坐，喝，要，對不起，給
Modal Verb:	可以
Adjective:	高興，漂亮
Adverb:	快
Preposition:	在
Particle:	呀，吧
Others:	一下
Proper Noun:	高小音

L5-2

Noun:	圖書館
Verb:	玩（兒），聊天（兒），回家
Adverb:	一起，才
Particle:	了

Lesson 6

L6-1

Noun:	時間，問題，課，年級，空兒，辦公室
Measure Word:	位，節
Pronoun:	您，哪
Verb:	打電話，在，開會，考試，到，行，等
Modal Verb:	要
Adjective:	方便，客氣
Adverb:	就，別
Preposition:	給
Conjunction:	要是
Time Word:	下午，上午，以後
Others:	喂
Proper Noun:	常老師

L6-2

Noun:	中文
Verb:	幫，準備，練習，說，見面，回來
Modal Verb:	得
Preposition:	跟
Conjunction:	但是
Particle:	啊
Others:	下個

Lesson 7

L7-1

Noun:	字，筆，紙，語法，生詞，漢字
Measure Word:	枝，張
Pronoun:	怎麼，哪裡
Verb:	說話，復習，寫，教，懂，預習，學
Adjective:	慢，容易，多，難
Adverb:	真
Particle:	得
Others:	上個，第

L7-2

Noun: 功課，課文，錄音
Pronoun: 這麼，大家
Verb: 上課，開始，念，學習
Adjective: 早，晚，帥，酷
Adverb: 平常
Time Word: 早上

Lesson 8

L8-1

Noun: 日記，早飯，教室，發音，電腦，餐廳，午飯，宿舍
Measure Word: 篇
Pronoun: 那兒
Verb: 起床，洗澡，上網，告訴，知道
Adjective: 累，新
Adverb: 一邊，正在，已經
Time Word: 中午，以前

L8-2

Noun: 信，學期，專業，音樂會
Measure Word: 封
Verb: 希望，用，笑，祝
Modal Verb: 會，能
Conjunction: 除了…以外
Time Word: 最近，後來

Lesson 9

L9-1

Noun: 商店，東西，售貨員，衣服，襯衫，顏色，褲子，號，長短，錢
Measure Word: 件，條，塊，毛，分
Pronoun: 多少
Numeral: 百
Verb: 買，穿，試，找（錢）
Adjective: 黃，紅，中，便宜，合適
Adverb: 一共
Conjunction: 如果…的話
Others: 不用

L9-2

Noun: 鞋，大小，咖啡色，樣子，信用卡

Measure Word: 雙，種

Pronoun: 它，這兒

Verb: 換，刷卡，收，付錢

Adjective: 一樣，黑

Adverb: 挺，再

Conjunction: 雖然，不過

Lesson 10

L10-1

Noun: 寒假，飛機，票，（飛）機場，公共汽車，地鐵，路，線，出租汽車

Measure Word: 站

Verb: 坐，走，下車，打車，開車，送

Adjective: 綠，藍，麻煩

Adverb: 先，然後

Conjunction: 或者

Others: 最後

L10-2

Noun: 電子郵件，城市，高速公路，手機，新年

Pronoun: 每，自己

Verb: 讓，花，出去，發短信

Adjective: 緊張，快樂

Adverb: 特別

Others: 不好意思

Vocabulary Index (How About You?)

The How About You? vocabulary index is sequenced according to the order of the corresponding images, horizontally from left to right. Exercises that do not include images corresponding to vocabulary items (e.g., in Lesson 1: Dialogue 1) are omitted.

English	Traditional	Simplified	Pinyin	Part of Speech
L1: Dialogue 2				
Mexico	墨西哥		*Mòxīgē*	pn
India	印度		*Yìndù*	pn
Canada	加拿大		*Jiānádà*	pn
Britain	英國	英国	*Yīngguó*	pn
L2: Dialogue 2				
soldier	軍人	军人	*jūnrén*	n
teacher	老師	老师	*lǎoshī*	n
nurse	護士	护士	*hùshi*	n
L3: Dialogue 1				
British food	英國菜	英国菜	*Yīngguó cài*	n
Chinese food	中國菜	中国菜	*Zhōngguó cài*	n
American food	美國菜	美国菜	*Měiguó cài*	n
L4: Dialogue 1				
read books	看書	看书	*kàn shū*	vo
watch movies	看電影	看电影	*kàn diànyǐng*	vo
play ball	打球		*dǎ qiú*	vo
listen to music	聽音樂	听音乐	*tīng yīnyuè*	vo
L4: Dialogue 2				
sleep	睡覺	睡觉	*shuì jiào*	vo

English	Traditional	Simplified	Pinyin	Part of Speech
go shopping	逛街		*guàng jiē*	vo
draw, paint	畫畫兒	画画儿	*huà huàr*	vo
play chess	下棋		*xià qí*	vo
L5: Dialogue				
fruit juice	果汁		*guǒzhī*	n
Coca-Cola	可口可樂	可口可乐	*Kěkǒukělè*	pn
mineral water	礦泉水	矿泉水	*kuàngquánshuǐ*	n
Sprite	雪碧		*Xuěbì*	pn
L5: Narrative				
school	學校	学校	*xuéxiào*	n
library	圖書館	图书馆	*túshūguǎn*	n
home	家		*jiā*	n
L6: Dialogue 1				
home	家		*jiā*	n
office	辦公室	办公室	*bàngōngshì*	n
library	圖書館	图书馆	*túshūguǎn*	n
L6: Dialogue 2				
Japanese language	日語	日语	*Rìyǔ*	pn
Spanish language	西班牙語	西班牙语	*Xībānyáyǔ*	pn
French language	法語	法语	*Fǎyǔ*	pn
L7: Dialogue 2				
Chinese textbook	中文課本	中文课本	*Zhōngwén kèběn*	n
Chinese workbook	中文練習本	中文练习本	*Zhōngwén liànxíběn*	n
Chinese dictionary	中文字典		*Zhōngwén zìdiǎn*	n

English	Traditional	Simplified	Pinyin	Part of Speech
L8: Diary Entry				
classroom	教室		*jiàoshì*	n
dormitory	宿舍		*sùshè*	n
dining room, cafeteria	餐廳	餐厅	*cāntīng*	n
L8: Letter				
business management	工商管理		*gōngshāng guǎnlǐ*	n
chemistry	化學	化学	*huàxué*	n
mathematics	數學	数学	*shùxué*	
L9: Dialogue 1				
sweater	毛衣		*máoyī*	n
coat	外套		*wàitào*	n
suit	西裝	西装	*xīzhuāng*	n
L9: Dialogue 2				
blue	藍色	蓝色	*lánsè*	n
green	綠色	绿色	*lǜsè*	n
pink	粉紅色	粉红色	*fěnhóngsè*	n
L10: Dialogue				
walk	走路		*zǒu lù*	vo
ride a bicycle	騎自行車	骑自行车	*qí zìxíngchē*	vo
take a bus	坐公共汽車	坐公共汽车	*zuò gōnggòng qìchē*	vo
L10: Email				
ride a motorcycle	騎摩托車	骑摩托车	*qí mótuōchē*	vo
drive a car	開車	开车	*kāi chē*	vo
take the subway	坐地鐵	坐地铁	*zuò dìtiě*	vo

Appendix 1: Lesson Texts in Simplified Characters

Lesson 1

Dialogue 1

Exchanging Greetings

At school, Wang Peng and Li You meet each other for the first time.

王朋：你好[a]！
李友：你好！
王朋：请问[b]，你[c]贵姓？
李友：我姓[1]李。你呢[2]？
王朋：我姓王。李小姐[d]，你叫[3]什么名字？
李友：我叫李友。王先生，你叫什么名字？
王朋：我叫王朋[4]。

Dialogue 2

Where Are You From?

Wang Peng and Li You start chatting after bumping into each other on campus.

李友：王先生，你是[5]老师吗[6]？
王朋：我不[7a]是老师，我是学生。李友，你呢？
李友：我也[8]是学生。你是中国人吗？
王朋：是[b]，我是北京人。你是美国人吗？
李友：是，我是纽约人。

Lesson 2

Dialogue 1

Looking at a Family Photo

Wang Peng is in Gao Wenzhong's room and points to a picture on the desk.

王朋：高文中，那是你的[1]照片吗？

They walk toward the picture and stand in front of it.

高文中：是。这是我爸爸，这是我妈妈。
王朋：这[a]个[2]女孩子是谁[3]？
高文中：她是我姐姐。
王朋：这个男孩子是你弟弟吗？
高文中：不是，他是我大哥的儿子[b]。
王朋：你大哥有[4]女儿吗？
高文中：他没有女儿。

Dialogue 2

Discussing Family

Li You and Bai Ying'ai are chatting about their family members and what each of them does.

李友：　白英爱，你家[a]有[5]几口[b]人？

白英爱：我家有六口人，我爸爸、我妈妈、一[c]个哥哥、两[6]个妹妹和[d]我[e]。李友，你家有几口人？

李友：　我家有五口人：爸爸、妈妈、大姐、二姐和我。你爸爸妈妈做什么工作？

白英爱：我爸爸是律师，妈妈是英文老师，哥哥、妹妹都[7]是大学生。

李友：　我妈妈也是老师，我爸爸是医生。

Lesson 3

Dialogue 1

Out for a Birthday Dinner

Gao Wenzhong is talking to Bai Ying'ai about a special day coming up.

高文中：　白英爱，九月十二[1a]号[2]是星期几[2]？

白英爱：　是星期四。

高文中：　那天[b]是我的[3]生日。

白英爱：　是吗？你今年多大[c]？

高文中：　十八岁[d]。

白英爱：　我星期四请你吃饭[4]，怎么样？

高文中：　太好了[e]。谢谢，谢谢[f]。

白英爱：　你喜欢吃中国菜还是[5]美国菜？

高文中：　我是英国人，可是我喜欢吃中国菜。

白英爱：　好，我们吃中国菜。

高文中：　星期四几点？

白英爱：　七点半怎么样？

高文中：　好，星期四晚上见。

白英爱：　再见！

Dialogue 2

Dinner Invitation

Bai Ying'ai asks Wang Peng about his plans for tomorrow.

王朋：　白英爱，现在几点？
白英爱：五点三刻。
王朋：　我六点一刻有事儿。
白英爱：你今天很忙[a]，明天忙不忙[6]？
王朋：　我今天很忙，可是明天不忙。有事儿吗？
白英爱：明天我请你吃晚饭，怎么样？
王朋：　你为什么请我吃饭？
白英爱：因为明天是高文中的生日。
王朋：　是吗？好。还[7]请谁？
白英爱：还请我的同学李友。
王朋：　那太好了，我认识李友，她也是我的朋友。明天几点？
白英爱：明天晚上七点半。
王朋：　好，明天七点半见。

Lesson 4

Dialogue 1

Discussing Hobbies

Gao Wenzhong asks Bai Ying'ai about her weekend plans and wants to invite her to a movie; however . . .

高文中：白英爱，你周末喜欢做什么[1]？
白英爱：我喜欢打球、看电视[a]。你呢？
高文中：我喜欢唱歌、跳舞，还喜欢听音乐。你也喜欢看书，对不对？
白英爱：对，有的时候也喜欢看书。
高文中：你喜欢不喜欢[2]看电影？
白英爱：喜欢。我周末常常看电影。
高文中：那[3]我们今天晚上去看[4]一个外国电影，怎么样？我请客。
白英爱：为什么你请客？
高文中：因为昨天你请我吃饭，所以今天我请你看电影。
白英爱：那你也请王朋、李友，好吗[5]？
高文中：……好。

Dialogue 2

Let's Play Ball

Wang Peng visits Gao Wenzhong and invites him to play ball over the weekend.

王朋：　小高[a]，好久不见[b]，你好吗[c]？
高文中：我很好。你怎么样？
王朋：　我也不错。这个周末你想[6]做什么？想不想去打球？
高文中：打球？我不喜欢打球。
王朋：　那我们去看球，怎么样？
高文中：看球？我觉得看球也没有意思[d]。
王朋：　那你这个周末想做什么？
高文中：我只想吃饭、睡觉[7][e]。
王朋：　算了，我去找别人。

Lesson 5

Dialogue

Visiting a Friend's Place

Wang Peng and Li You visit Gao Wenzhong and meet his sister, Gao Xiaoyin.
(The doorbell rings.)

高文中：　　谁呀？
王朋：　　　是我，王朋，还有李友。
高文中：　　请进，请进，快进来！来，我介绍一下[1]，这是我姐姐，高小音。
李友和王朋：小音，你好。认识你很高兴。
高小音：　　认识你们我也很高兴。
李友：　　　你们家很大[2]，也很漂亮。
高小音：　　是吗？[a]请坐，请坐。
王朋：　　　小音，你在[3]哪儿[b]工作？
高小音：　　我在学校工作。你们想喝点儿[1]什么？喝茶还是喝咖啡？
王朋：　　　我喝茶吧[4]。
李友：　　　我要一瓶可乐，可以吗？
高小音：　　对不起，我们家没有可乐。
李友：　　　那给我一杯水吧。

Narrative

At a Friend's Place

Gao Xiaoyin, Wang Peng, and Li You visited Gao Wenzhong's place.

昨天晚上，王朋和李友去高文中家玩儿。在高文中家，他们认识了[5]高文中的姐姐。她叫高小音，在学校的图书馆工作。她请王朋喝[a]茶，王朋喝了[5]两杯。李友不喝茶，只喝了一杯水。他们一起聊天儿、看电视。王朋和李友晚上十二点才[6]回家。

Lesson 6

Dialogue 1

Calling Your Teacher

李友给[1]常老师打电话……

常老师：喂？

李友：喂，请问，常老师在吗？

常老师：我就是。您[a]是哪位？

李友：老师，您好。我是李友。

常老师：李友，有事儿吗？

李友：老师，今天下午您有时间[b]吗？我想问[c]您几个问题。

常老师：对不起，今天下午我要[2]开会。

李友：明天呢？

常老师：明天上午我有两节[d]课，下午三点要给二年级考试。

李友：您什么时候[e]有空儿？

常老师：明天四点以后[f]才有空儿。

李友：要是[g]您方便，四点半我到您的办公室去，行吗？

常老师：四点半，没问题[h]。我在办公室等你。

李友：谢谢您。

常老师：别[3]客气。

Dialogue 2

Calling a Friend for Help

李友给王朋打电话……

李友：喂，请问，王朋在吗？

王朋：我就是。你是李友吧[a]？

李友：王朋，我下个星期[4]要考中文，你帮我准备一下，跟我练习说中文，好吗？

王朋：好啊，但是你得[5]请我喝咖啡。

李友：喝咖啡，没问题。那我什么时候跟你见面？你今天晚上有空儿吗？

王朋：今天晚上白英爱请我吃饭。

李友：是吗？白英爱请你吃饭？

王朋：对。我回来[6]以后给你打电话。

李友：好，我等你的电话。

Lesson 7

Dialogue 1

How Did You Do on the Exam?

王朋跟李友说话……

王朋：李友，你上个星期考试考得[1]怎么样？

李友：因为你帮我复习，所以考得不错。但是我写中国字写得太[2]慢了！

王朋：是吗？以后我跟你一起练习写字，好不好[a]？

李友：那太好了！我们现在就[3]写，怎么样？

王朋：好，给我一枝笔[4]、一张纸。写什么字？

李友：你教我怎么写“懂”字吧。

王朋：好吧。

李友：你写字写得真[2]好，真快。

王朋：哪里，哪里[b]。你明天有中文课吗？我帮你预习。

李友：明天我们学第七[5]课。第七课的语法很容易，我都懂，可是生词太多，汉字也有一点儿[6]难。

王朋：没问题，我帮你。

Dialogue 2

Preparing for Chinese Class

李友跟白英爱说话……

李友：白英爱，你平常来得很早，今天怎么[7]这么晚？

白英爱：我昨天预习中文，早上[a]四点才[3]睡觉，你也睡得很晚吗？

李友：我昨天十点就[3]睡了。因为王朋帮我练习中文，所以我功课做得很快。

白英爱：有个中国朋友真好。

上中文课……

常老师：大家早[b]，现在我们开始上课。第七课你们都预习了吗？

白英爱和李友：预习了。

常老师：李友，请你念课文。……念得很好。你昨天晚上听录音了吧？

李友：我没听。

白英爱：但是她的朋友昨天晚上帮她学习了。

常老师：你的朋友是中国人吗？

李友：　　　　是。
白英爱：　　　他是一个男的[8]，很帅[c]，很酷，叫王朋。[9]

Lesson 8

Diary Entry

A Typical School Day

李友的一篇日记

十一月三日星期二

今天我很忙，很累。早上七点半起床[1]，洗了澡以后就[2]吃早饭。我一边吃饭，一边[3]听录音。九点到教室去上课[4]。

第一节课是中文，老师教我们发音、生词和语法，也教我们写字，还给了[5]我们一篇新课文[6]，这篇课文很有意思。第二节是电脑[a]课，很难。

中午我和同学们一起到餐厅去吃午饭。我们一边吃，一边练习说中文。下午我到图书馆去上网。四点王朋来找我打球。五点三刻吃晚饭。七点半我去白英爱的宿舍跟她聊天(儿)。到那儿的时候，她正在[7]做功课。我八点半回家。睡觉以前，高文中给我打了一个电话，告诉我明天要考试，我说我已经知道了。

Letter

Writing to a Friend

一封信

这是李友给高小音的一封信。

小音：

你好！好久不见，最近怎么样？

这个学期我很忙，除了专业课以外，还[8]得学中文。我们的中文课很有意思。因为我们的中文老师只会[9]说中文，不会说英文，所以上课的时候我们只说中文，不说英文。开始我觉得很难，后来[a]，王朋常常帮我练习中文，就[10]觉得不难了[b]。

你喜欢听音乐吗？下个星期六，我们学校有一个音乐会，希望你能[9]来。我用中文写信写得很不好，请别笑我。祝

好！

你的朋友

李友

十一月十八日

Lesson 9

Dialogue 1

Shopping for Clothes

李友在商店买东西，售货员问她……

售货员：小姐，您要[1]买什么衣服？

李友：我想买一件[2]衬衫。

售货员：您喜欢什么颜色的[3]，黄的还是红的？

李友：我喜欢穿[a]红的。我还想买一条[2]裤子[b]。

售货员：多[4]大的？大号的、中号的、还是小号的？

李友：中号的。不要太贵的，也不要太便宜[c]的。

售货员：这条裤子怎么样？

李友：颜色很好。如果长短合适的话，我就买。

售货员：您试一下。

Li You checks the size on the label and measures the pants against her legs.

李友：不用试。可以。

售货员：这件衬衫呢？

李友：也不错。一共多少钱？

售货员：衬衫二十一块五，裤子三十二块九毛九，一共是五十四块四毛九分[5]。

李友：好，这是一百块钱。

售货员：找您四十五块五毛一。谢谢。

Dialogue 2

Exchanging Shoes

王朋想换一双鞋，他问售货员……

王朋：对不起，这双鞋太小了。能不能换一双？

售货员：没问题。您看，这双怎么样？

王朋：也不行，这双跟那双一样[6]大。

售货员：那这双黑的呢？

王朋：这双鞋虽然大小合适，可是[7]颜色不好。有没有咖啡色的？

售货员：对不起，这种鞋只有黑的。

王朋：这双鞋样子**挺好的**[a]，**就是它吧**[b]。你们这儿可以刷卡吗？

售货员：对不起，我们不收信用卡。不过，这双的钱跟那双一样，您不用再付钱了。

Lesson 10

Dialogue

Going Home for Winter Vacation

李友跟王朋说话……

王朋：李友，寒假你回家吗？

李友：对，我要回家。

王朋：飞机票你买了吗[1]？

李友：已经买了。是二十一号的。

王朋：飞机是几点的？

李友：晚上八点的。

王朋：你怎么去[a]机场？

李友：我想坐公共汽车或者[2]坐地铁。你知道怎么走[a]吗？

王朋：你先坐一路汽车，坐三站下车，然后换地铁。先坐红线，再[3]换绿线，最后换蓝线。

李友：不行，不行，太麻烦了。我还是[4]打车[b]吧。

王朋：出租汽车太贵，我开车送你去吧。

李友：谢谢你。

王朋：不用客气。

Email

Thanks for the Ride

李友给王朋写电子邮件[a]：

Date: 12月20日
From: 李友
To: 王朋
Subject: 谢谢！

王朋：

谢谢你那天开车送我到机场。不过，让你花那么多时间，真不好意思。我这几天每天都[5]开车出去看老朋友。这个城市的人开车开得特别快。我在高速公路上开车，真有点儿紧张。可是这儿没有公共汽车，也没有地铁，只能自己开车，很不方便。

有空儿的话打我的手机或者给我发短信，我想跟你聊天儿。

新年快要到了[6]，祝你新年快乐！

李友

Appendix 2: Lesson Texts in English

Lesson 1

Dialogue 1

Exchanging Greetings

At school, Wang Peng and Li You meet each other for the first time.

Li You: How do you do?
Wang Peng: What's your family name, please? (lit. Please, may I ask . . . your honorable family name is . . . ?)
Li You: My family name is Li. What's yours?
Wang Peng: My family name is Wang. Miss Li, what's your name?
Li You: My name is Li You. Mr. Wang, what's your name?
Wang Peng: My name is Wang Peng.

Dialogue 2

Where Are You From?

Wang Peng and Li You start chatting after bumping into each other on campus.

Li You: Mr. Wang, are you a teacher?
Wang Peng: I'm not a teacher, I'm a student. How about you, Li You?
Li You: I'm a student, too. Are you Chinese?
Wang Peng: Yes, I'm from Beijing (lit. I'm a Beijinger). Are you American?
Li You: Yes, I'm from New York (lit. I'm a New Yorker).

Lesson 2

Dialogue 1

Looking at a Family Photo

Wang Peng is in Gao Wenzhong's room and points to a picture on the desk.

Wang Peng: Gao Wenzhong, is that picture yours?

They walk toward the picture and stand in front of it.

Gao Wenzhong: Yes. This is my dad. This is my mom.
Wang Peng: Who's this girl?
Gao Wenzhong: She's my older sister.
Wang Peng: Is this boy your younger brother?
Gao Wenzhong: No, he's my eldest brother's son.
Wang Peng: Does your eldest brother have any daughters?
Gao Wenzhong: He doesn't have any daughters.

Dialogue 2

Discussing Family

Li You and Bai Ying'ai are chatting about their family members and what each of them does.

Li You: Bai Ying'ai, how many people are there in your family?
Bai Ying'ai: There are six people in my family: my dad, my mom, an older brother, two younger sisters, and me. Li You, how many people are there in your family?
Li You: There are five people in my family: my dad, my mom, my oldest sister, my second oldest sister, and me. What do your dad and mom do?
Bai Ying'ai: My dad is a lawyer. My mom is an English teacher. My older brother and younger sisters are all college students.
Li You: My mom is also a teacher. My dad is a doctor.

Lesson 3

Dialogue 1

Out for a Birthday Dinner

Gao Wenzhong is talking to Bai Ying'ai about a special day coming up.

Gao Wenzhong: Bai Ying'ai, what day is September 12?
Bai Ying'ai: Thursday.
Gao Wenzhong: That (day) is my birthday.
Bai Ying'ai: Really? How old are you this year?
Gao Wenzhong: Eighteen.
Bai Ying'ai: I'll treat you to a meal on Thursday. How's that?
Gao Wenzhong: That would be great. Thank you very much!
Bai Ying'ai: Do you like Chinese food or American food?
Gao Wenzhong: I'm an Englishman, but I like Chinese food.
Bai Ying'ai: All right. We'll have Chinese food.
Gao Wenzhong: Thursday at what time?
Bai Ying'ai: How about seven-thirty?
Gao Wenzhong: All right. See you Thursday evening.
Bai Ying'ai: See you.

Dialogue 2

Dinner Invitation

Bai Ying'ai asks Wang Peng about his plans for tomorrow.

Wang Peng: Bai Ying'ai, what time is it now?
Bai Ying'ai: A quarter to six.
Wang Peng: I have something to do at a quarter after six.
Bai Ying'ai: You're busy today. Are you busy tomorrow?
Wang Peng: I'm busy today, but I won't be tomorrow. What's up?
Bai Ying'ai: I'd like to invite you to dinner tomorrow. How about it?
Wang Peng: Why are you inviting me to dinner?
Bai Ying'ai: Because tomorrow is Gao Wenzhong's birthday.
Wang Peng: Really? Great. Who else are you inviting?
Bai Ying'ai: I'm also inviting my classmate Li You.
Wang Peng: Awesome. I know Li You. She's my friend, too. What time tomorrow?
Bai Ying'ai: Seven-thirty tomorrow evening.
Wang Peng: OK, I'll see you tomorrow at seven-thirty.

Lesson 4

Dialogue 1

Discussing Hobbies

Gao Wenzhong asks Bai Ying'ai about her weekend plans and wants to invite her to a movie; however . . .

Gao Wenzhong: Bai Ying'ai, what do you like to do on weekends?
Bai Ying'ai: I like to play ball and watch TV. How about you?
Gao Wenzhong: I like to sing, dance, and listen to music. You like to read, right?
Bai Ying'ai: Yes, sometimes I like to read as well.
Gao Wenzhong: Do you like to watch movies?
Bai Ying'ai: Yes, I do. I often watch movies on weekends.
Gao Wenzhong: Then let's go see a foreign movie this evening. OK? My treat.
Bai Ying'ai: Why your treat?
Gao Wenzhong: Because you treated me to dinner yesterday, today I'm treating you to a movie.
Bai Ying'ai: Then invite Wang Peng and Li You as well, OK?
Gao Wenzhong: . . . OK.

Dialogue 2

Let's Play Ball

Wang Peng visits Gao Wenzhong and invites him to play ball over the weekend.

Wang Peng: Gao Wenzhong, long time no see. How are you?
Gao Wenzhong: I'm fine. How about yourself?
Wang Peng: I'm fine, too. What would you like to do this weekend? Would you like to play ball?
Gao Wenzhong: Play ball? I don't like playing ball.
Wang Peng: Then let's watch a ball game. How's that?
Gao Wenzhong: Watch a ball game? I don't think watching a ball game is much fun, either.
Wang Peng: Then what do you want to do this weekend?
Gao Wenzhong: I only want to eat and sleep.
Wang Peng: Never mind. I'll ask somebody else.

Lesson 5

Dialogue

Visiting a Friend's Place

Wang Peng and Li You visit Gao Wenzhong and meet his sister, Gao Xiaoyin.
(The doorbell rings.)

Gao Wenzhong: Who is it?
Wang Peng: It's me, Wang Peng. Li You is here, too.
Gao Wenzhong: Please come in. Let me introduce you to one another. This is my sister, Gao Xiaoyin.
Wang Peng and Li You: How do you do, Xiaoyin! Pleased to meet you.
Gao Xiaoyin: Pleased to meet you, too.
Li You: Your home is very big, and very beautiful, too.
Gao Xiaoyin: Really? Have a seat, please.
Wang Peng: Xiaoyin, where do you work?
Gao Xiaoyin: I work at a school. What would you like to drink? Tea or coffee?
Wang Peng: I'll have tea.
Li You: I'd like a bottle of cola.
Gao Xiaoyin: I'm sorry. We don't have cola.
Li You: Then please give me a glass of water.

Narrative

At a Friend's Place

Gao Xiaoyin, Wang Peng, and Li You visited Gao Wenzhong.

Last night, Wang Peng and Li You went to Gao Wenzhong's home for a visit. At Gao Wenzhong's home they met Gao Wenzhong's older sister. Her name is Gao Xiaoyin. She works at a school library. She offered tea to Wang Peng. Wang Peng had two cups. Li You doesn't drink tea. She only had a glass of water. They chatted and watched TV together. Wang Peng and Li You didn't get home until twelve o'clock.

Lesson 6

Dialogue 1

Calling Your Teacher

Li You is on the phone with her teacher . . .

Teacher Chang: Hello?
Li You: Hello, is Teacher Chang there?
Teacher Chang: This is she. Who is this, please?
Li You: Teacher, how are you? This is Li You.
Teacher Chang: Hi, Li You. What's going on?
Li You: Teacher, are you free this afternoon? I'd like to ask you a few questions.
Teacher Chang: I'm sorry. This afternoon I have to go to a meeting.
Li You: What about tomorrow?
Teacher Chang: Tomorrow morning I have two classes. Tomorrow afternoon at three o'clock I have to give an exam to the second-year class.
Li You: When will you be free?
Teacher Chang: I won't be free until after four o'clock tomorrow.
Li You: If it's convenient for you, I'll go to your office at four-thirty. Is that all right?
Teacher Chang: Four-thirty? No problem. I'll wait for you in my office.
Li You: Thank you.
Teacher Chang: You're welcome.

Dialogue 2

Calling a Friend for Help

Li You and Wang Peng are talking on the phone . . .

Li You: Hello, is Wang Peng there?
Wang Peng: This is he. Is this Li You?
Li You: Hi, Wang Peng. Next week I have a Chinese exam. Could you help me prepare by practicing speaking Chinese with me?
Wang Peng: Sure, but you have to take me out for coffee.
Li You: Take you out for coffee? No problem. So, when can I see you? Are you free this evening?
Wang Peng: Bai Ying'ai is taking me out to dinner this evening.
Li You: Is that so? Bai Ying'ai is taking you out to dinner?
Wang Peng: That's right. I will call you when I get back.
Li You: OK. I'll wait for you to call.

Lesson 7

Dialogue 1

How Did You Do on the Exam?

Wang Peng is talking with Li You . . .

Wang Peng: How did you do on last week's exam?

Li You: Because you helped me review, I did pretty well, but I'm too slow at writing Chinese characters.

Wang Peng: Really? I'll practice writing characters with you from now on. How's that?

Li You: That would be great! Let's do it right now, OK?

Wang Peng: OK. Give me a pen and a piece of paper. What character should we write?

Li You: Why don't you teach me how to write the character "dǒng" (to understand)?

Wang Peng: OK.

Li You: You write characters really well, and very fast, too.

Wang Peng: I'm flattered. Do you have Chinese class tomorrow? I'll help you prepare.

Li You: Tomorrow we'll study Lesson 7. The grammar for Lesson 7 is easy; I understand all of it. But there are too many new words, and the Chinese characters are a bit difficult.

Wang Peng: No problem. I'll help you.

Dialogue 2

Preparing for Chinese Class

Li You is talking with Bai Ying'ai . . .

Li You: Bai Ying'ai, you usually arrive very early. How come you got here so late today?

Bai Ying'ai: Yesterday I was preparing for Chinese. I didn't go to bed till four o'clock in the morning. Did you go to bed very late, too?

Li You: No, yesterday I went to bed at ten. Because Wang Peng helped me practice Chinese, I finished my homework very quickly.

Bai Ying'ai: It's so great to have a Chinese friend.

In Chinese class . . .

Teacher Chang: Good morning, everyone. Let's begin. Have you all prepared for Lesson 7?

Bai Ying'ai and Li You: Yes, we have.

Teacher Chang: Li You, would you please read the text aloud? . . . You read very well. Did you listen to the audio recording last night?

Li You: No, I didn't.

Bai Ying'ai: But her friend helped her study yesterday evening.

Teacher Chang: Is your friend Chinese?

Li You: Yes.

Bai Ying'ai: He's a very cool and handsome guy. His name is Wang Peng.

Lesson 8

Diary Entry

A Typical School Day

An Entry from Li You's Diary

November 3, Tuesday

I was very busy and tired today. I got up at seven-thirty this morning. After taking a shower, I had breakfast. While I was eating, I listened to an audio recording. I went to class at nine o'clock.

We had Chinese for first period. The teacher taught us pronunciation, new vocabulary, and grammar. The teacher also taught us how to write Chinese characters, and gave us a new text. The text was very interesting. Second period was computer science. It was very hard.

At noon I went to the cafeteria with my classmates for lunch. As we ate, we practiced speaking Chinese. In the afternoon I went to the library to use the Internet. At four o'clock, Wang Peng came looking for me to play ball. I had dinner at a quarter to six. At seven-thirty, I went to Bai Ying'ai's dorm for a chat. When I got there, she was doing her homework. I got home at eight-thirty. Before I went to bed, Gao Wenzhong called. He told me there'd be an exam tomorrow. I said I already knew.

Letter

Writing to a Friend

A Letter

This is a letter Li You wrote to Gao Xiaoyin.
Xiaoyin:

How are you? Long time no see. How are things recently?

I've been busy this semester. Besides the classes required for my major, I also need to study Chinese. Our Chinese class is really interesting. Because our Chinese teacher only speaks Chinese and can't speak any English, we only speak Chinese in class; no English. In the beginning, I felt it was very difficult. Wang Peng often helped me practice Chinese, and it doesn't feel so hard anymore.

Do you like listening to music? Next Saturday there'll be a concert at our school. I hope you can come. I don't write well in Chinese. Please don't poke fun at me. Wishing you all the best.

Your friend,
Li You
November 18

Lesson 9

Dialogue 1

Shopping for Clothes

Li You is shopping at a store and the salesperson asks her . . .

Salesperson: Miss, what are you looking to buy?
Li You: I'd like to buy a shirt.
Salesperson: What color would you like? Yellow or red?
Li You: I'd like one in red. I'd also like to buy a pair of pants.
Salesperson: What size? Large, medium, or small?
Li You: Medium. Something not too expensive, but not too cheap, either.
Salesperson: How about these pants?
Li You: The color is nice. If the size is right, I'll take them.
Salesperson: Please try them on.

Li You checks the size on the label, and measures the pants against her legs.

Li You: No need to try them on. They'll do.
Salesperson: And how about this shirt?
Li You: It's not bad either. How much altogether?
Salesperson: Twenty one dollars and fifty cents for the shirt, and thirty-two ninety-nine for the pants. Fifty-four dollars and forty-nine cents altogether.
Li You: OK. Here's one hundred.
Salesperson: Forty-five fifty-one is your change.
Li You: Thank you.

Dialogue 2

Exchanging Shoes

Wang Peng wants to exchange a pair of shoes and he asks the salesperson . . .

Wang Peng: Excuse me, this pair of shoes is too small. Can I exchange them for another pair?
Salesperson: No problem. How about this pair?
Wang Peng: No, they won't do either. This pair is the same size as the other one.
Salesperson: What about this pair in black?
Wang Peng: This pair is the right size, but it's not a good color. Do you have any in brown?
Salesperson: I'm sorry. We only have these shoes in black.
Wang Peng: These shoes look good. I'll take them. Can I use my credit card here?
Salesperson: I'm sorry, we don't take credit cards. But this pair is the same price as the other one. You won't need to pay again.

Lesson 10

Dialogue

Going Home for Winter Vacation

Li You is talking to Wang Peng...

Wang Peng: Are you going home for winter break?
Li You: Yes, I am.
Wang Peng: Have you booked a plane ticket?
Li You: Yes, for the twenty-first.
Wang Peng: When is the plane leaving?
Li You: Eight p.m.
Wang Peng: How are you getting to the airport?
Li You: I'm thinking of taking the bus or the subway. Do you know how to get there?
Wang Peng: You first take Bus No. 1. Get off after three stops. Then take the subway. First take the red line, then change to the green line, and finally change to the blue line.
Li You: Oh no. That's too much trouble. I'd better take a cab.
Wang Peng: It's too expensive to take a cab. I'll take you to the airport.
Li You: Thank you so much.
Wang Peng: Don't mention it.

Email

Thanks for the Ride

Li you writes an email to Wang Peng:

Date: December 20
From: Li You
To: Wang Peng
Subject: Thank you!

Wang Peng:
Thank you for driving me to the airport the other day. But I feel very bad for taking up so much of your time. The past few days I've been driving around to see old friends. People in this city drive very fast. I'm really nervous driving on the highway. But there are no buses or subway here; I have to drive. It's very inconvenient. When you have time, please call me on my cell or send a text message. I'd like to chat with you.

New Year is almost here. Happy New Year!

Li You